Military English

Tactical and Peacekeeping Operations

Intermediate | B1 | STANAG 2

Teacher's Book

Robert Buckmaster

The English Ideas Project

Contents

Welcome to the Course

Military English: Tactical and Peacekeeping Operations is a pre-deployment course for Army personnel who are to be sent on multinational peace support operations, or on training courses in an English language speaking country, or who will be trained by English-speaking instructors.

Your students should, ideally, already have studied up to a pre-intermediate level [Common European Framework A2] before starting the course – that is, they should be ready for an Intermediate/ B1 Level course.

This is not a beginner, elementary or pre-intermediate course in General English. It is a specialised course aimed at preparing soldiers for missions abroad and training in English speaking countries. It is focused on helping the students to operate effectively in critical situations and environments. By the end of the course the students will be able to better understand briefings and orders, and operate well during checkpoint operations, convoys and patrols. The main focus is on these six core areas of military skills, and so the course is focused on infantry soldiering rather than armoured operations, or engineers etc. Resources for soldiers in these specialities might be added later.

The course also deals with General English aspects of working on missions and during training courses, and the work on English grammar in the course seeks to build up a systematic understanding of the key grammar forms by establishing a 'key idea' about the forms in the minds of the students. See below for further discussion on these ideas.

There are three components to the course:

1. Units 1 – 200 in the **Coursebook**.

2. A **Workbook**.

3. Downloadable pictures, maps, PowerPoint Presentations and audio files from the **English Ideas Project** website.

This book tell you how to use these components and integrate them into a coherent course for your students.

The book starts with a Course Overview, and a discussion of Aims and Outcomes. There is also a Course Builder to help you choose which units to do to meet your learners' needs. There are also detailed notes on the methodology of the course. Then there are notes and keys for all the Coursebook units.

You will also need access to a good English-English dictionary, or to the internet to check terms.

Please register your use of the Course at www.englishideas.org, and we will be able to keep you up to date with revisions and extra materials.

Good luck with the course.

Robert Buckmaster

Part 1 How To Use This Course

1. Course Overview

There are three **Phases** to the Course.

Phase One of the course is a series of threads of units. There are General English units, General Military English units and some Specialised Military English units in the Coursebook. In the Workbook, there are Grammar Study Pages, reading tasks on Peacekeeping Operations, Report Writing tasks, Acronym and Abbreviation Study Pages, as well as Consolidation Tasks for certain units. There are also reference materials like the Grammar Reference in the Workbook. You will need to integrate all these elements together into the course.

> **Threads** are very important as they build in automatic revision. For example, there are two units on sport. You do the first and then some time later you do the second. As you do the second unit, the lexis from the first unit will be reactivated. This will help learning. The first Phase of the coursebook is 'threaded' for you. You have to weave in the grammar, and the report writing tasks, and peacekeeping text reading tasks from the Workbook. The second Phase of the coursebook is not threaded and you should decide if you want to thread the units or do the units in their blocks.

Phase Two is organised into blocks of Specialised Military English units and you should decided if you want to do them in sequence or if you want to 'thread' them together like the units in Phase One. There are also some units which focus on General English with a Military Application e.g. terrain descriptions. In the Workbook there are dictation Consolidation Tasks for certain units, as well as blank forms for practice tasks, and checklists to evaluate orders.

Phase Three is best done in sequence; it revises and activates the Specialised Military English of Phase One and Two, and adds Peacekeeping English. Here, the focus is on solving tactical and peacekeeping problems and revising Specialised Military English (e.g. OPs, convoys, checkpoints) with a peacekeeping focus. The students use the language they have learned in Phases One and Two to learn the new language in Phase Three. The main book topics are shown in the diagram below.

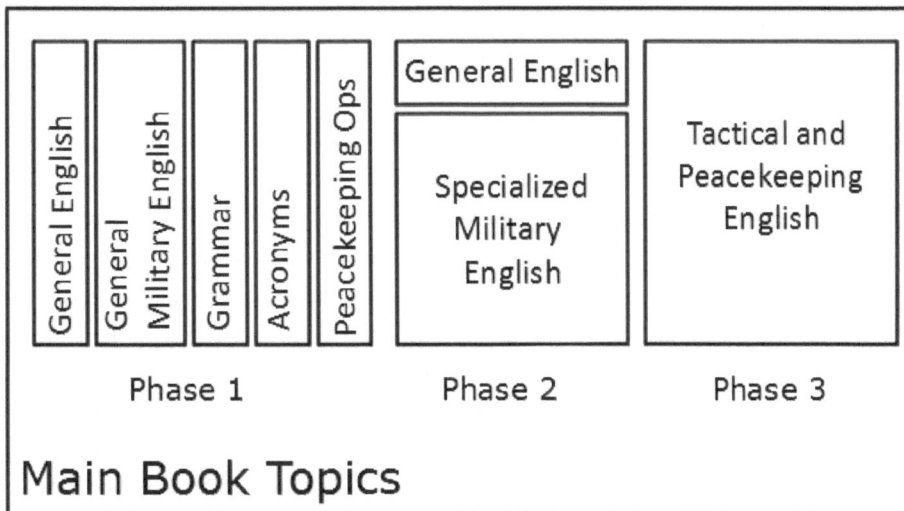

The Balance of Skills

Military English, in the field, is primarily an oral culture. Orders are given orally and soldiers are expected to be able to understand and carry out orders given orally without written support, though they might be able to make notes and ask for clarification. Oral briefings are also very common. Senior officers, and soldiers being trained in an English speaking country, will need to understand and produce written English but on operations, at a tactical level, the most important skills are speaking and listening. In this course, reading and writing are used for learning purposes, while speaking and listening skills are developed for operational purposes. The skills/learning focus is shown in the diagram below:

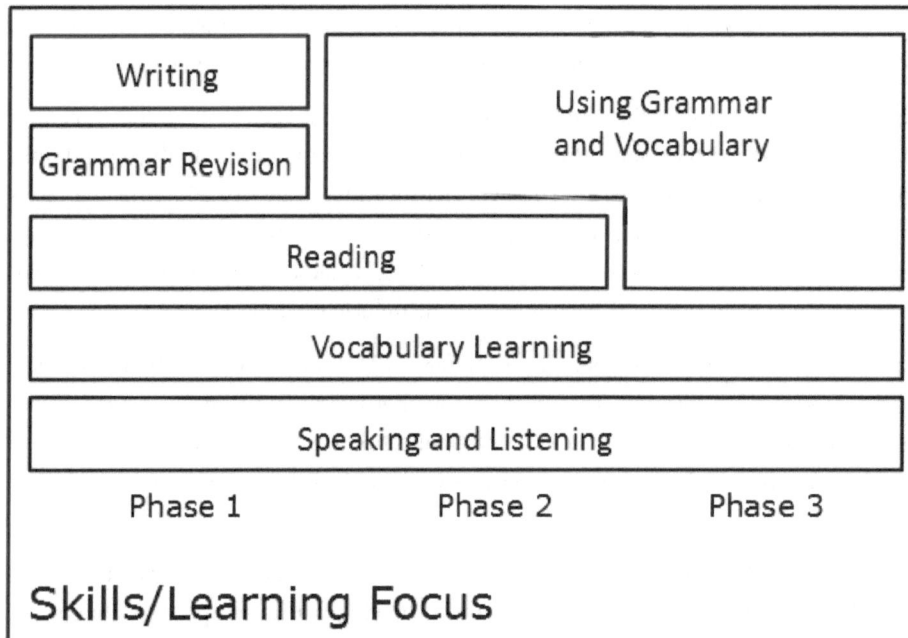

As you can see, Phase 1 has a focus on grammar revision – giving you information about the students' grammatical knowledge and their ability to use the grammar effectively, some writing (in the Workbook), and the main focus in the Coursebook is on vocabulary learning and listening and speaking. Listening and speaking are the key skills which are developed throughout the book. By the end of Phase 1 the students should have a better understanding of grammar and general military English vocabulary and be able to operate interpersonally on missions and training .In Phase 2, there is a switch to using the grammar and vocabulary from Phase 1 to learn the new language in Phase 2. Phase 2 is focused on the core areas of patrolling, convoys, checkpoints and orders and the language necessary for these. Phase 3 is almost entirely devoted to speaking and listening tasks where the students can demonstrate their learning from Phases 1 and 2, and also use this language to learn new Peacekeeping English. The students study tactical English for convoys in Phase 2, for instance, and then use this language to learn about peacekeeping convoys in Phase 3. Phase 3 is thus simultaneously a revision and extension phase. The diagram overleaf shows how the topics are integrated throughout the course, and shows some of the outcomes of the course, and what the students will demonstrate (e.g. their briefing skills, in tests etc.) during the course.

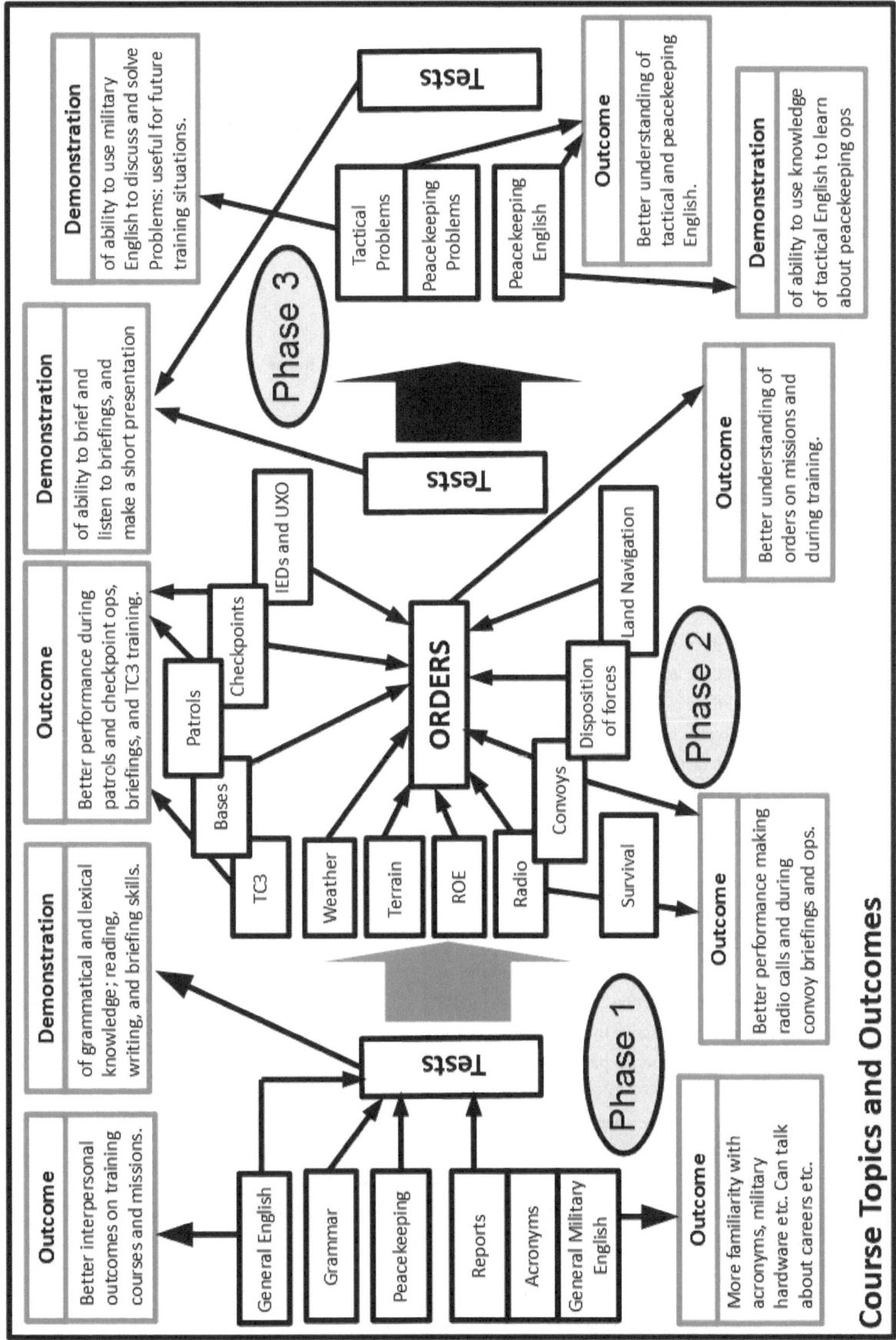

Course Topics and Outcomes

Phase 1

Tests

- General English
- Grammar
- Peacekeeping
- Reports
- Acronyms
- General Military English

Outcome — Better interpersonal outcomes on training courses and missions.

Outcome — More familiarity with acronyms, military hardware etc. Can talk about careers etc.

Demonstration of grammatical and lexical knowledge; reading, writing, and briefing skills.

Phase 2

ORDERS

- TC3
- Bases
- Patrols
- Checkpoints
- IEDs and UXO
- Weather
- Terrain
- ROE
- Radio
- Convoys
- Survival
- Disposition of forces
- Land Navigation

Outcome — Better performance during patrols and checkpoint ops, briefings, and TC3 training.

Outcome — Better performance making radio calls and during convoy briefings and ops.

Outcome — Better understanding of orders on missions and during training.

Demonstration of ability to brief and listen to briefings, and make a short presentation

Tests

Phase 3

Tests

- Tactical Problems
- Peacekeeping Problems
- Peacekeeping English

Outcome — Better understanding of tactical and peacekeeping English.

Demonstration of ability to use military English to discuss and solve Problems: useful for future training situations.

Demonstration of ability to use knowledge of tactical English to learn about peacekeeping ops

Course Aims and Outcomes

This course is designed to teach soldiers (enlisted men, NCOs and junior officers) how to **operate effectively** on multinational tactical and peacekeeping operations. The core tactical and peacekeeping areas are: understanding briefings; understanding orders; patrolling; convoys; and checkpoint operations.

By the end of the course the students should be able to do the following in English.

Interpersonal Skills

- Talk about their families
- Talk about their careers
- Talk about their homes
- Talk about their leisure interests e.g. hobbies, sports, films and music
- Make arrangements to meet etc.
- Ask and answer questions
- Give personal opinions on topics like personal equipment, hobbies, sport etc.

Professional Skills

- Understand and use common acronyms
- Use the NATO/Phonetic Alphabet
- Tell the time
- Talk about the weather and climate
- Talk about their army and unit structure and purpose
- Talk about their training
- Make radio calls including MEDEVAC/CASEVAC
- Understand Tactical Combat Casualty Care
- Understand land navigation
- Describe rural and urban terrain
- Describe people and clothing
- Give a short professional briefing supported by visuals
- Understand ROE
- Describe bases
- Understand and describe convoy operations
- Understand and describe checkpoint operations
- Understand and describe the use of observation posts
- Understand and describe patrol operations
- Understand [and give] orders
- Understand the differences between tactical and peacekeeping missions, patrols, ROE, OPs, checkpoints, and convoys
- Understand and propose solutions to common survival situations
- Understand and propose solutions to common tactical and peacekeeping problems
- Write a short report

The following main military topics are covered:

- Acronyms
- Bases
- Checkpoints
- Convoys
- Force Structure And Formation Purpose
- Forces e.g. Paratroopers, Infantry, Armour Etc.
- Land Navigation: Maps And Terrain
- Military Careers
- Military Hardware e.g. IFV, MBT etc.
- Military Training
- Movement
- Observation Posts
- Orders
- Overwatch
- Patrols
- Peacekeeping Problems
- Personal Equipment
- Radio Communication
- ROE
- Security
- Survival Situations
- Tactical Combat Casualty Care
- Tactical Problems
- Time
- Training
- Using Interpreters
- Weapons
- Weather

Grammar

The main **functional grammar** areas covered are:

- presenting facts
- presenting on-going processes
- looking forwards from now
- looking backwards from now
- describing (terrain, position, people and clothing etc.)
- suggesting/explaining/justifying/reporting
- agreeing/disagreeing and giving opinions
- past narration and evaluating past events
- asking and answering questions
- making comparisons
- discussing hypotheticals
- talking about future plans

The other **main grammar** areas covered are:

- noun and verb phrases
- word order
- articles
- prepositions
- collocations
- text grammar

Level and Difficulty

Level is a difficult concept in English. There are different level systems in the US and UK, and old and new systems. Under the 'old' British level system (Beginner to Advanced), this book is pitched at an Intermediate Level. Under the Common European Framework this is about B1. Under the NATO STANAG 6001 classification the level is STANAG 2. So, students need to be ready for an Intermediate/B1/STANAG 2 course. This does not mean they have to be intermediate already. Some of the units and tasks are at a pre-intermediate level, e.g. talking about your family. Motivated students at a slightly lower level might be able to cope with the materials in the course. You should evaluate the course and decide how it relates, in terms of level of difficulty, to your students' capabilities. Higher level students (e.g. Upper-Intermediate) will also benefit from doing the course if they have only studied General English.

The texts are straightforward authentic-like factual texts written with a number of different grammatical forms. There are no texts written especially to practice the Present Simple, for example. Students at this level should have met most of the grammar forms they need and they will be working to integrate their understanding of the verbs etc. into a coherent system. There are a lot of text-based consolidation tasks to reinforce the grammar.

In the listening tasks there are mostly factual listenings with some opinion. It is essential that students can distinguish between factual presentations and opinions.

In terms of verb forms, more complex forms like the third and mixed conditionals are not found in the coursebook. The most complex forms are second conditionals and some passive forms. While students should understand passive forms they should concentrate on using active forms. The Grammar Reference in the Workbook, though, does include third and mixed conditionals in order to be comprehensive, and there are practice Study Pages on these forms. You may feel that these can be omitted.

The principle learning load of the course is in vocabulary and you should try to build in as much revision practice as possible. You should also carefully consider which units your students should do. Is it enough that they do the first weather unit, for instance, or do they need to do the other units as well? Which terrain units do they need to do? If the students are being sent on training in the UK or USA, for example, they should probably do all the units. If a trainer is coming to train them in Tactical Combat Casualty Care, for example, then they will need to do the medical units in Phase 2. The essential practice in skills is focused on speaking and listening. You should try to give the students as much speaking and listening practice as possible. Don't be afraid of repeating tasks.

Note on British and American English: The texts in this course draw mainly on US Army Field Manuals which are in the public domain and can be exploited for teaching materials without breaching copyright. Other texts have been written in British English. I decided not to standardise the course as a 'British' or 'American English' course but to use both spellings (e.g. *centre/center | manoeuvre /maneuver*) in the texts so that the students will be exposed to both systems. They should ideally decide to use one version (and be consistent) in their own writing. After doing a reading, you could ask the students: '*Is the text written in British or American English?*' and ask them to tell you why. There are also some differences between US and GB military terminology, for example RV (rendezvous; GB) and RP (rally point; US), and coy. (GB) for Company vs co. (US), and the students should be aware of, or on the lookout for, these differences.

2. Your Role

As a teacher you will need to decide how to use the Coursebook and Workbook materials, and decide what support your students need, and what the timing of the tasks during the units will be.

In the **Coursebook** you can decide to **use** the material exactly as written, or you might decide that the tasks need to be **resequenced, supplemented, adapted,** or even **rejected** and **replaced.** You will also need to decide how to **transition** smoothly between the tasks.

You will need to tell the students when to do the Workbook Grammar, Peacekeeping Reading, Report Writing, and Acronym and Abbreviation Study Pages. For example, you might decide to do a unit of the coursebook and then set a Grammar Study Page for homework. The sequence might look like this:

Coursebook	**Unit 1 Introductions and Questions**
Workbook	Study Page: Functional Grammar: Facts
Coursebook	**Unit 2 The NATO/Phonetic Alphabet**
Workbook	Study Page: Acronyms and Abbreviations 1
Coursebook	**Unit 3 Describing Photographs 1**
Workbook	Study Page: Functional Grammar: The Condition Of Something
Coursebook	**Unit 4 Describing Photographs 2**
Workbook	Study Page: Acronyms and Abbreviations 2
Coursebook	**Unit 5 Training**
Workbook	Study Page: Education and Qualifications
Coursebook	**Unit 6 Questions 2**
Workbook	Study Page: Functional Grammar: Active or Passive?
Coursebook	**Unit 7 Ranks**
Workbook	Peacekeeping Fact File 1
Coursebook	**Unit 8 Family**
Workbook	Study Page: Report Writing
Coursebook	**Unit 9 My Role and Responsibilities**
Workbook	Study Page: Functional Grammar: Ongoing Processes
Coursebook	**Unit 10 My Home**
Workbook	Study Page: Acronyms and Abbreviations 3
Workbook	Peacekeeping Fact File 2
Coursebook	**Unit 11 Promotion**
Workbook	Study Page: Functional Grammar: Noun Phrases 1

Or you might want to do two coursebook units and then a workbook element, or save the workbook elements for the weekend, or self-study time in the afternoons. It all depends on the course schedule and intensity, and the needs of your students.

On the next section there is a **Course Builder** to help you decide which of the 200 coursebook units (including tests) and workbook units you should do to meet your students' needs.

Your role also includes decisions about the following issues:

Unit Timing

The units are not written to a standard specification or formula, though there are recurring elements in the units. This is to help with the problem of boredom from predictability. However, this means that some units are shorter than others. Most units will take 40 - 50 minutes. Some units, like briefing units, will take longer depending on how much time you allocate for preparation and how many students you have in the class. How long the materials take the students to do will also depend on the exact level of your students and how much vocabulary they already know. You should also decide what can be missed out or set as homework. Each text, for example, has grammar analysis tasks after it – are you going to do these in class or set them for homework? Or do some in class and others at home? Many units have Consolidation Tasks – are you going to do these in class or set them for homework? With the shorter units you should take the time to do revision tasks. Some revision is built into the course naturally but there is always opportunity for more, and revision is essential for learning.

Adding Randomness

An important part of your role is what I call 'adding randomness'. Life outside the classroom is chaotic and, on active service, dangerous. You should add an element of calculated (on your part) unpredictability (to the students) to the course. After you've done Unit 2 on the NATO phonetic alphabet, you can ask the students at any (suitable) time in the following lessons to spell out words. After Unit 16 you can ask students what the Date Time Group for the lesson is. At the beginning, or before the end of lessons, or between tasks you can ask the students revision questions about language from previous units, as long as you don't spend too much time and interrupt the flow of the lesson. But keep them on their toes and ready for the unexpected question. A little but often, but not constantly, should be your watchword.

Task Timing

How long are you going to allow the students to do each task? You should decide and either tell them in advance how long they have: '*You have five minutes to read the text and answer the questions*'; and/or tell them when the time is nearly up: '*You have one minute left*'.

Checking Answers

How are you going to check answers to tasks like gap-fills? It is not a good idea to ask the students to read out texts without preparation. Just ask them to give the missing word instead.

If you want to give them practice reading a sentence or text aloud make sure that they understand it first, know how to pronounce all the words and have had a chance to practice – reading aloud is a performance, and you should help them to do it well. In a one-to-one situation it is different and you can work with a student doing reading aloud tasks and the preparation/performance blends into one. In a class, you want to avoid loss of face so give the students a chance to practice before asking them to read aloud.

Praise and Feedback

It is important to praise your students but not constantly. Praise genuine success and effort. Think about the best ways to give feedback: orally or in written form? Provide positive and constructive feedback.

Errors

Which errors are you going to correct? Impeding errors make understanding difficult and these are more important than 'slips'. How are you going to correct errors? Orally, or in written feedback? Publicly or privately?

Tests

There are tests at the end of each phase.

Phase 1	Unit 52	Phase 1 Grammar Test
	Unit 53	Phase 1 Reading Test: Exercise Cambrian Patrol
	Unit 54	Phase 1 Writing Test: Peacekeeping Operations Report
	Unit 55	Phase 1 Speaking Test 1: Personnel Biographies
	Unit 56	Phase 1 Speaking Test 1: IFV Briefings

| Phase 2 | Unit 175 | Phase 2 Speaking Test: Adventure Training Briefings |

| Phase 3 | Unit 200 | Phase 3 Test 1: Deployment Briefing: Group Test |
| | | Phase 3 Test 2: A Mini-Presentation on a Military Topic: Individual Test |

3. Course Builder

How to use the **Course Builder**:

1. Look at the course topics under the five different headings: **General English**; **General Military English**; **Specialised Military English**; **Tests** and **Workbook**.

2. Note that some topics have multiple units which make up a course thread.

3. Think about your students' needs: do a Needs Analysis or ask them to list their learning priorities.

4. Decide if you want to do that topic: **yes/no**.

5. If **yes**, decide which units from that topic you want to do.

General English Phase 1			Unit											
Questions	Yes	No	1	6	15									
Describing Photographs	Yes	No	3	4										
Family	Yes	No	8											
My Home	Yes	No	10											
Describing People	Yes	No	12											
Watches	Yes	No	16											
Time and Time Zones	Yes	No	19											
Leisure etc.	Yes	No	20											
Talking about Music	Yes	No	22											
Hypotheticals	Yes	No	24											
Telling the Time	Yes	No	26											
Socialising	Yes	No	28	32										
Films/Movies	Yes	No	35											
Talking about Sport	Yes	No	37	40										
Describing Clothes	Yes	No	43											
Giving Directions	Yes	No	46											
Knives	Yes	No	48											
Animals/ Dangers	Yes	No	51											

General English With a Military Application Phase 2													
Weather and Climate	Yes	No	64	65	66	67	68	69	70				
Terrain: Mountains	Yes	No	71	72	73								
Terrain: Deserts	Yes	No	74	75	76	77							
Temperate Hills/Lowlands	Yes	No	78										
Rivers and Lakes	Yes	No	79										
Tropical Forests	Yes	No	80	81	82								
Estuary and Coast	Yes	No	83	84									
The Urban Environment	Yes	No	85	86	87	88	89	90					
Bridges, Dams etc.	Yes	No	91										
Certainty and Uncertainty	Yes	No	92										
General English Phase 3													
Disasters	Yes	No	190	191	192								
At the Airport	Yes	No	199										
General Military English Phase 1													
The NATO Alphabet	Yes	No	2										
Training	Yes	No	5										
Ranks	Yes	No	7										
Roles and Responsibilities	Yes	No	9										
Promotion	Yes	No	11										
Force Structure	Yes	No	13										
Forces	Yes	No	14	18	25	30	33	36	39	41	42	44	
Formation Purpose	Yes	No	17										
Military Hardware	Yes	No	21	23	45	47	49	50					
Personal Equipment	Yes	No	27	29	31								
Individual Weapons	Yes	No	34										
On the Range	Yes	No	38										

Specialised Military English Phase 2

Radio	Yes	No	57	58	59	60	61	62	62	63			
Land Navigation	Yes	No	93	94	95	96	97	98					
Disposition of Forces	Yes	No	99	100	101	102	103						
Survival	Yes	No	104	105	106	107	108	109	110				
Medical	Yes	No	111	112	113	114	115	116	117	118	119	120	121
Training Exercise	Yes	No	122										
Rules of Engagement	Yes	No	122	123									
Describing Position	Yes	No	124	125									
Bases	Yes	No	127	128	129	130	131	132	133				
Observation Posts	Yes	No	134										
Overwatch	Yes	No	135	136									
Convoys	Yes	No	137	138	139	149	141	142					
IEDS and UXO	Yes	No	143	144									
Checkpoints etc.	Yes	No	145	146	147	148	149	150	151	152			
Patrols	Yes	No	153	154	155	158	159	160					
Movement	Yes	No	156										
Camouflage etc.	Yes	No	157										
Talking about Attacks	Yes	No	161	162	163								
Orders	Yes	No	164	165	166	167	168	169	170	171	172	173	
Debriefing	Yes	No	174										

Specialised Military English Phase 3

Case Study	Yes	No	176										
Tactical Problem	Yes	No	177	178	179	180	181						
Peacekeeping Missions	Yes	No	182										
Peacekeeping ROE	Yes	No	183										
Peacekeeping OPs	Yes	No	184										
Peacekeeping Patrols	Yes	No	185										

Peacekeeping Checkpoints	Yes	No	186										
Peacekeeping Convoys	Yes	No	187										
Using Interpreters	Yes	No	188										
Civil Disturbances	Yes	No	189										
Dealing with the Media	Yes	No	193										
Peacekeeping Problems	Yes	No	194	195	196	107	198						

Tests

Phase 1 Tests	Yes	No	52	53	54	55	56						
Phase 2 Speaking Test	Yes	No	175										
Phase 3 Speaking Tests	Yes	No	200										

Workbook

Grammar Study Pages	Yes	No	1	2	3	4	5	6	7	8	9	10	11
			12	13	14	15	16	17	18	19	20	21	22
			23	24	25	26							
Acronyms and Abbreviations	Yes	No	1	2	3	4	5	6	7	8	9	10	11
			12	13	14	15	16	17	18	19	20	21	22
			23	24	25								
Peacekeeping Readings	Yes	No	1	2	3	4	5	6	7	8	9	10	11
			12										
Report Writing	Yes	No	1	2	3	4	5	6					
Phase 1 Consolidation Tasks	Yes	No	5	7	11	13	17	18	25	30	33	34	36
			37	38	39	40	41	43	47	48	49	50	
Phase 2 Consolidation Tasks	Yes	No	66	68	71	72	74	75	78	79	80	83	87
			89	93	96	97	113	114	115	117	118	119	123
			124	127	129	131	134	136	137	138	143	145	146
			147	150	151	153	154	155	161	163	165	169	

4. Resources Required

This book is designed so it can be used in low and high resource environments.

You should have access to the following:

Essential:

- The Internet: **one-time access** to download resources from the Course website page (on the English Ideas Project website) to a computer, tablet or smartphone [see **Downloadable Electronic Resources** below]. These resources can then be used without an internet connection. A reliable ongoing internet connection is **not** essential. You can share these resources as you wish.

- A computer, tablet or smart phone, and speakers/headphones to play the course audio files.

- Large scale maps [1:50,000, 1:25,000 or 1:10,000] of an urban and a rural area. Many of the units require maps – see the **Maps** note on the next page.

Ideal:

- Walkie-talkies to practice radio communication. It is best to practice radio communication using radios.

- A data projector to project photographs and diagrams etc. from a class computer. If this is not available students can access the materials through the screen of a class computer, or through their tablets or smartphones.

Optional:

- To model checkpoints etc.: Lego bricks, Cuisenaire rods, pencils, matches, coloured ribbons or matches; toy soldiers or game counters; model cars and military vehicles.

- A printer and photocopier to make student copies.

Not necessary, but very nice to have:

- A camera, video camera or phone with a camera to video students making briefings, take extra photographs etc.

Downloadable Electronic Resources

The electronic resources for the course are available for download from the English Ideas Project website: www.englishideas.org/MilitaryEnglish.

There are sets of resources for each phase of the course:

Phase 1	Phase 1 Photographs and Maps
	Phase 1 PowerPoint Presentations (standard and widescreen format)
	Phase 1 Coursebook Audio Files
	Phase 1 Audio Transcripts Wiki (for use on computers, tablets or smartphones)

Phase 2	Phase 2 Photographs and Maps
	Phase 2 PowerPoint Presentations (standard and widescreen format)
	Phase 2 Coursebook and Workbook Consolidation Task Audio Files
	Phase 2 Audio Transcripts Wiki (for use on computers, tablets or smartphones)

Phase 3	Phase 3 Photographs and Maps
	Phase 3 PowerPoint Presentations (standard and widescreen format)
	Phase 3 Coursebook Audio Files
	Phase 3 Audio Transcripts Wiki (for use on computers, tablets or smartphones)

There is also a Teacher Extras Folder of resources.

How To Use The Electronic Resources

You need to decide how you are going to use these resources. There are a number of options.

1. You can download the resources to your computer and project the photographs and maps and presentations on a screen for your students in the classroom, and play the audio files to the students.

2. With a class computer but no projector, you can show the resources on the computer screen and the students gather around the computer to watch; and play the audio files through the computer.

3. With a tablet computer, you can pass the tablet around to the students to review the resources. Play the audio files through the tablet.

4. With a set of tablet computers: each group can use a tablet to view and listen to the resources.

5. With student smartphones: the students can have access to the resources in the classroom and at home. The minimum required is one smart phone per small group of students e.g. 4 – 6 students. Ideally they would each have the resources on their smartphones.

If the students do not have access to the internet, you can download the files and then share through flash drive/memory sticks or through Bluetooth connections.

The **ideal arrangement** is for there to be a classroom computer and projector, and for each student to have the resources on their smartphones.

The **minimum set up** is with one smartphone and some kind of speaker.

The Printable Option

If you do not have computers, tablets or smartphones to view the electronic resources you can print out paper copies of the photographs, maps, presentations and audio transcripts. These can be given to the students or displayed on the classroom walls.

Maps

Maps are **ESSENTIAL** for this course. Many of the units have map reading exercises.

If you do not have your own local military maps you can print out and use the US Geological Survey maps included with the book website materials.

You could also adapt tourist maps to use for the course.

Here's how:

1. Choose a large scale map with a grid on.

2. If there is no grid then you'll have to draw one on.

3. Draw an appropriate grid for the scale of the map.

4. Number the grid.

The **best option** is military maps from your own country.

5. How To Use The Coursebook Units

There are two hundred 'one lesson' units, which gives 200 + hours of learning.

Phase 1: Units 1 - 56

Phase 2: Units 57 - 175

Phase 3: Units 176 - 200

You should use **Phase 1** to check your students' level of English and deal with any problem areas in grammar and vocabulary and skills. You should choose which of these units you need to do. If you students have real problems with any of the grammar, you will need to supplement the course with other grammar materials.

Phase 2, the main body of the course, switches the focus to learning a lot of vocabulary on specialised Military English topics. The focus is on English for tactical operations, so that the student can successfully operate on missions, or during training. You should choose which of these units you need to do.

Phase 3 brings everything together with tactical and peacekeeping problems for the students to solve. The Peacekeeping units are mainly listening, and students have to use the language they learned in Phase 2 to do these units.

Methodology

The course uses an open and transparent methodology: what the students have to do is specified on the page.

These are the design of the elements of the units.

Each unit has a number, title, and a list of the main grammar points of the unit and/or a statement of the purpose of the unit e.g. **Present Simple | Expressing Likes And Dislikes**. Each Task is labelled with a T number e.g. T1, T2, and has the Skill Focus specified e.g. speaking, listening, reading, writing – see the example below.

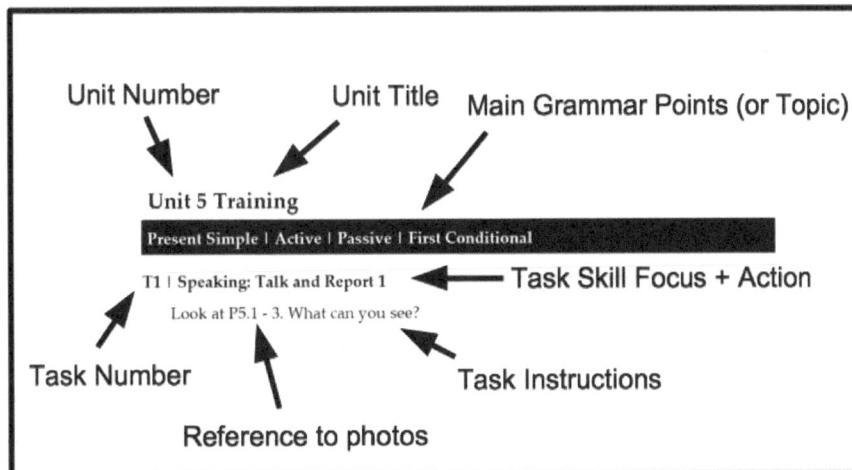

The Task Line might also have the task instructions – as can be seen below.

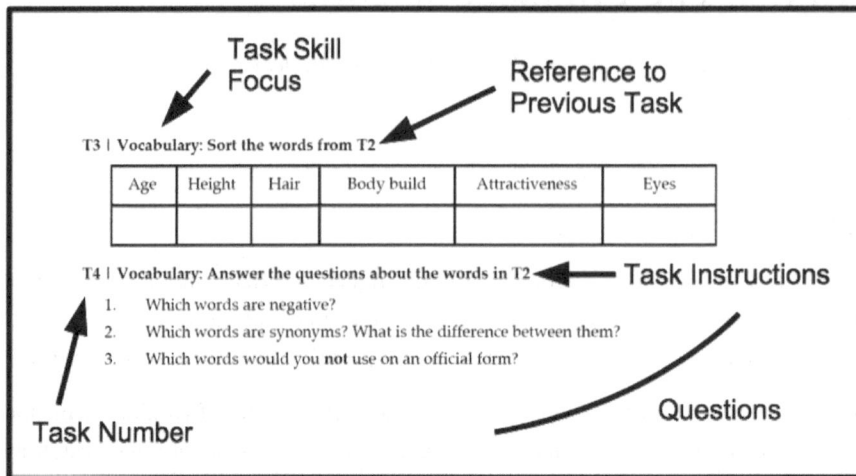

Task Skill Focus				Reference to Previous Task	

T3 | Vocabulary: Sort the words from T2

Age	Height	Hair	Body build	Attractiveness	Eyes

T4 | Vocabulary: Answer the questions about the words in T2 ◀— **Task Instructions**

1. Which words are negative?
2. Which words are synonyms? What is the difference between them?
3. Which words would you **not** use on an official form?

Task Number

Questions

Resources

Photographs are referenced by P numbers e.g. P5.1, where the 5 is the unit number, and .1 is the photo number i.e. the first photo for Unit 5.

Audio Transcripts are referenced with a T number e.g T6.1, where 6 is the unit number, and .1 is the number of the transcript i.e. the first transcript of Unit 6.

Maps are referenced with a M number e.g M70.1, where 70 is the unit number, and .1 is the number of the map i.e. the first map of Unit 70.

Fact Files are referenced by an FF number e.g. FF36.1 Harrier, where 36 is the unit number, and .1 is the number of the FactFile. The Fact Files are found in the Workbook.

Transitions and Foci

You will need to manage the transitions between tasks and focus the students attention on what is important. Do not be tempted to just say: *Page 28. Task 2.* Even just saying: *Now, look at Task 2 on page 28...* is better. You might want the students to close their books and look at the board while you explain/explore/test some language, and then they will open their books again. The students focus, or attention, should <u>not</u> be on the same one thing all the time. There are a number of foci the students could attend to:

the coursebook	the workbook	their notebooks	the teacher
the board	their partner	the floor/ceiling/walls	their inner mind
a listening task	photos/maps	the group	the whole class

Vary the focus and you will create interest and variety. Think: *What should the students be paying attention to? Do they need their books open? What can I usefully write on the board? What should I explain/check before doing a task? What do the students need to be able to do before doing the task? What should they be reminded of? What language do they need?*

Teaching Grammar

As mentioned before, at this level the students should be constructing their personal representation of the grammar system of English. They will have met most of the grammar which they will need and now it is time to systematize it and use it. In the Workbook there are Functional Grammar Study Pages on grammar points, a Reference Grammar and a Quick Functional Grammar. You should use the Study Pages to identify student weaknesses and do remedial work on those points if necessary. The principle approach taken in this grammar is to associate a particular function or key idea with verb forms. So, a student will say to themselves – '*I want to present a fact*'; then they will use the Simple Present, otherwise known as the 'Do Form'. Or a student will say to themselves – '*I want to present a fact in the past*'; then they will use the Simple past, otherwise known as the 'Did Form'. Or a student might think: '*I want to present an on-going (now) process*'; they will use the Present Continuous, or 'be + Do-ing Form': *I'm reading a good book at the moment.* Similarly, the key idea connected with *will* is one of *certainty*, so when the student wants to present their *personal certainty* about something they will use *will*: *I will do it.* | *By the end of the week I will have finished.* | *She will have arrived by now.* In all these cases the speaker is expressing their personal certainty about the following verb ideas. The key is to connect the verb form with a particular function-meaning or key idea.

Apart from this, the students will practise using the grammar by reading texts, doing listening tasks, and in speaking and writing tasks. The Consolidation Tasks and Text Analysis tasks are also designed to focus attention on different areas of grammar, not just verb forms. You should pay special attention to word order and prepositions.

Vocabulary

The main learning load of the course is in vocabulary. There is a lot of vocabulary to learn in the terrain units , for example. You should prioritise which units the student need to study, and build in revision on a progressive timescale. Something new should be revised quickly – the same day in homework, then briefly in the next lesson, then a week or two later, then a month later.

The typical vocabulary lesson has this structure:

Lead-in: a talk and report picture description task. You should ask the students to discuss the pictures in pairs and then elicit a full description of the photo(s) and work with the student(s) to describe the photo fully.

The Target Vocabulary: usually found in a table. There might be photos to help the students in the electronic resources. It is best if these are available on the students' smartphones. You should check the meaning of all these words. The students might already know some of the words and this is great.

You could then ask the students to close their books and test them on the words, or ask them to test their partner. This could be done in various ways: by translation, by definition, by example, by synonym, or by antonym.

A gap-fill: the students should complete the gap-fill to contextualise the target vocabulary. Students could check with their partner before the class check.

Then there might be a listening task which will use some of the target language, or there might be a speaking task with discussion questions which will encourage the students to use the target vocabulary. These tasks are quick-activation tasks and it will be normal for the students to make mistakes with the vocabulary use.

In the sequence of lessons there might be a unit of listening tasks to revise the target vocabulary, and there might be a briefing unit where students should make and listen to briefings which will require use of the target vocabulary. During briefings the students should be active listeners and practise making notes, as if they were on a training course.

You should decide if you are going to start the next lesson with a brief recap of the target vocabulary from the previous lesson.

The pattern is basically to introduce the vocabulary, to contextualise it, and then start using it as soon as possible in listening and speaking tasks.

Skills: Speaking

It is essential that the students are given enough opportunity to practice the language through speaking. There are a number of specific speaking tasks in each unit, and more formal briefing tasks (see **8. Teaching Briefing Skills** below)

In all cases you should monitor the students' language production carefully and provide feedback (both private and public), and correction if necessary.

Pair Work and Group Work

Pair and group work are essential for language learning as the students have the opportunity to practice the language before they speak openly to the whole class. They can also practice reporting what was said/discussed/agreed in the pair and group work. There should always be a feedback stage after pair work or group work – like in the **Talk and Report Tasks** discussed below.

When asking for feedback from pair work it is not necessary to hear from everyone every time but there should be some feedback from the pair work task in open class. Make sure everyone does have the opportunity to talk in the class - both in pairs and in open class.

Talk and Report Tasks

In the units there are many **Talk and Report** tasks. In these tasks the students work in pairs to discuss a picture or question (or topic) and then report to the class what they discussed or decided. They can report on what they agreed ('*We think that....*') or they can report on what each other said ('*Juma said that he thinks.......*).

Picture Description Talk and Report Tasks

It is essential that the students get enough practice describing things and where they are in relation to other things. English uses prepositions to explain the relationships between things. The students will need to understand who is next to who, and who is where, and what is where, both during briefings and on operations, and the most effective way to practice this is through pictures. The students should be encouraged to give as full a description as possible of the photos and make sure their use of prepositions is correct. Many units have one or two picture description tasks – often used as a lead-in to the topic. You could ask the students to talk about the pictures and then ask one or more of them to report to the class and work with them to make their description as full and as accurate as possible. Or you might want them to write down their descriptions and collect them to mark. Either way, do not accept minimal descriptions but extract all the language you can from the photographs.

They should summarise what the photograph shows at the beginning of their description. Then they should focus on the most important object or person in the picture and then start their description from there. They should fully describe that object or person, and then move on to describe the other things or people in the picture, and then, at the end, make general comments about the weather or situation. See **Unit 4** for more on this.

You should help the students build up their speaking skills as this simple example shows:

Teacher: What can you see in the picture?

Student: A soldier.

Teacher: Anything else?

Student: Target.

Teacher: What is he doing?

Student: Shooting.

Teacher: What is he shooting with?

Student: Rifle. A rifle.

Teacher: Where is he shooting?

Student: Target.

Teacher: At a target?

Student: Yes, at a target.

Teacher: OK. Tell me all that in one sentence. Start with 'I can see'.

Student: I can see soldier shooting. A rifle. At a target.

Teacher: Is it a soldier?

Student: Yes, a soldier.

Teacher: Now tell me again. Use 'a soldier'.

Student: I can see a soldier shooting. A rifle. At a target.

Teacher: Good. Now tell me again in one breath.

Student: I can see a soldier shooting a rifle at a target.

You could add a description of what the soldier is wearing, what position he is in (standing or prone), and so on. Do not just accept a minimal description. **Units 3** and **4** do a lot of work on the prepositions and understanding necessary to do picture descriptions effectively.

Skills: Listening

Listening and speaking are the key skills in Military English. Soldiers need to understand what they are told to do in orders and carry out the orders effectively. A general understanding or gist comprehension is <u>not</u> enough in a military situation. It is not enough to understanding that you should '*attack that hill*'. You need to understand exactly who, when and how you are going to attack, and to understand what the enemy might do in response, and understand what is happening (and planned to happen) on both your flanks and to your rear. You need to understand your role in the attack and the role of everyone else in the unit. You need **complete comprehension** of an order – otherwise people will die. There is also no opportunity for negotiation of meaning in a tactical situation, though there will be opportunities for clarification, which is why your students should practice asking and answering questions.

To help students do this you need to approach listenings in a particular way. The listening tasks in Phase 1 and 2 are 'learning listenings' – to be exploited as learning tasks rather than test tasks. The listenings in Phase 3 are revision listenings with a peacekeeping twist and you can use these more as 'test listenings'.

What is a 'test listening'?

Any listening task you do where you set questions and then ask the students to listen to answer the questions is a test. You are testing whether they can understand enough to answer those particular questions about a particular section of the listening text. It is not (except indirectly) a learning task.

If you do all your listenings as test listenings, then you are not helping your students.

You have a number of options with listenings.

1. Ask the students to listen and answer the questions or make notes (according to the task) as you play the whole text. This is a test listening.

2. Ask the students to listen and answer the questions, or make notes (according to the task), as you listen to the text in sections. After each section stop and check comprehension and listen again if required and focus on the problem areas. You might want to transcribe problem sections on to the board so they can read and listen at the same time. This is a learning task way of doing the listening. This might take some considerable time. You might also what to ask the students to predict what will come in the next part of the listening.

3. Or you could ask the students to listen and answer the questions or make notes (according to the task) as you play the whole text the first time they listen (test), and then play the listening again section by section as in 2 above. This is a test – teach approach which you might want to follow-up with another listening test.

There are also **Transcript Tasks** in some units where the students either fill in the gaps in the text and then listen to check, or listen and fill in the gaps as they listen (like a test).

The **Phase 2 Consolidation Tasks** are all dictation exercises to reinforce the learning of the language from those units.

A main course aim is to build up the students' lexical and grammatical knowledge and understanding of spoken speech so that they can understand long stretches of speech.

There is one more kind of listening task in the Coursebook: **Listen to a Reading of the Text** tasks. In these tasks the students can listen and read the text which they have earlier read and understood. This is essential as they will hear the words being pronounced in context. They should then decide which words they need to practice saying. This could be done in class or at home.

Skills: Reading

The texts in the Coursebook are used to contextualise the language. There are some texts with comprehension questions (a form of test) but you should deal with understanding of the whole text. It is not enough just to an-swer the comprehension questions and then move on. Check any other unknown words or phrases after the questions have been answered. Then choose at least one verb phrase, noun phrase and prepositional phrase from the text to explore with the students. You could ask them to explain the forms and then discuss how and why there are used. This can act as a bridge into the Text Analysis Tasks which follow the texts.

Text Analysis Tasks

After the students have read the unit texts for understanding, they can then analyse the texts in detail [as outlined for the students in the **Study Guide** in the **Workbook**]. These tasks are called **Language Analysis: Analyse the Text** tasks. You can do these tasks in class or set them for homework. The students can focus on one grammar point e.g. verbs or noun phrases, or analyse a number of text points. You should help the students choose what to focus on. In the Teacher's Notes below there are notes called '**Suggested Language Focus**' for these texts. These will give you some ideas of what you might want to focus on with these texts. Of course you can focus on other things as well. With the word order notes you might want to take the sentence highlighted in the notes and write it on the board with the word order mixed up and ask the students to unmix the words. This could provide an extra classroom task if you need it. Or you might want to do a quick test of the dependent prepositions after doing the reading. There will be further word order tasks in the **Consolidation Tasks** for these units.

Consolidation Tasks

Certain units have **Consolidation Tasks** based on the unit's reading texts. These tasks can be found in the Workbook. See the Workbook section for details about these.

Skills: Writing

Written tasks (from the Coursebook and Workbook) should be set, a deadline given, and then collected for marking. How are you going to correct the writing? Are you going to underline the errors? Or use a error marking code? Or write a comment? What other feedback are you going to give? Should the students rewrite the task?

You should consider these areas:

- **Text organisation** and **structure**: Is the text logically organised from the introduction to the conclusion? Are the sentences in the paragraphs logically organised? Are cohesive devices used appropriately?

- **Grammar range** and **accuracy**: Is a range of grammar forms used? Is the grammar accurate? Are the verbs correct? Are the noun phrases clear? Are the prepositions used correctly? Do the errors impede communication?

- **Vocabulary range** and **accuracy**: Is the correct vocabulary used? Is the spelling accurate? Do the errors impede communication?

Homework Options

Many units have tasks which you can set for homework [e.g. **Text Analysis, Text Listening Tasks, Writing Tasks,** and **Consolidation Tasks**], but you could do them in class if you have time.

The **Teacher's Notes** for each Phase of the Course which follow below provide the Keys for Tasks in each Unit, certain reminders, and there are discussions of options and suggestions of extra tasks you might want to consider when appropriate.

6. How to use the Workbook

The Workbook contains:

➢ **A Study Guide**: A Guide to getting the most learning out of a reading text. You might want to work through this Guide with the students at the beginning of the Course.

➢ **A Self-Assessment Grid**: A Grid for the students to do at the beginning and the end of the Course. This Grid will give you useful information about the students' learning needs, so you should ask the students to do this and then look at the results. This will help you to complete the **Course Builder**.

➢ **Functional Grammar Study Pages**: These 30 Grammar Study Pages are designed to help the students integrate their grammar knowledge into an effective functional understanding of English grammar. It includes units on verbs, noun phrase and preposition grammar. These pages can be done as homework or in class during Phase 1. They will give you useful information about your students' command of key functional grammar points and you should then decide if you need to supplement these pages with more exercises from other sources. The units are arranged in a suggested order but you may want to change the order. IMPORTANT: Make sure you do **Study Page 13** (page 30), and **Study Page 26** (page 45) in the Workbook before you do **Unit 24** in Phase 1 of the Coursebook. The Keys for these tasks are in **Part 5** of this book.

➢ **Acronyms and Abbreviations Study Pages**: These 25 Study Pages present a core set of acronyms and abbreviations to be done during Phase 1. Note the speaking task at the bottom of each of these pages. Students can check their answers in the **Reference: Acronyms and Abbreviations List** section of the Workbook.

➢ **Peacekeeping Fact File Reading Tasks**: These are twelve texts about UN Peacekeeping operations around the world to be done during Phase 1. There are ten questions to answer for each reading text. The key is provided. You should set these reading texts at intervals during Phase 1. The Phase 1 Test 3 at the end of Phase 1 (Unit 54 in the Coursebook) is to write a report based on these readings. These texts build up the students' familiarity with some terrain and climate vocabulary, which will be studied in more detail in Phase 2, and also confidence with certain peacekeeping terminology about UN missions. The Keys for these tasks are in Part 5 of this book.

➢ **Report Writing**: There are two introductory units on report writing which you could do in class or set for homework during Phase 1. A Key is provided for these. These two units are followed by four writing tasks. The students should read the information given and write a report based on that information. There is also a Reference page of useful language for reports. Phase 1, as already mentioned, has a reporting writing task as part of the end of phase tests (Unit 54). The Keys for these tasks are in Part 5 of this book.

➢ **Fact Files**: These Fact Files are used for certain tasks in some units in Phase 1.

➢ **Consolidation Tasks Phase 1**: Units with texts in Phase 1 have Consolidation Tasks in this part of the Workbook. The sequence of tasks is the same in each unit.

- A Punctuation Task
- An Article (a/an/the) Gap-fill Task

- A Verb Gap-fill Task
- A Preposition Gap-fill Task
- One (or sometimes two) Word Order Tasks

Students should choose which of the tasks they think are most useful for themselves. They could do one task or two or all five or six tasks. They should check their answers with the original texts in the Coursebook. These tasks ensure that the students reread the texts and really think about the grammar and vocabulary of the texts.

➢ **Consolidation Tasks Phase 2**: Many (but not all) Units in Phase 2 have these Consolidation Tasks. In each case it is a dictation task where the students should listen to five sentences and write down what they hear. These sentences revise key language from the Units and give the students more listening practise with a variety of accents. This is important as we are working towards the students being able to understand the language when used orally. The students should have these recordings downloaded to their smartphones, tablets, computers, or audio players. The Keys are given in the Audio Transcripts Wiki for Phase 2 so that the students can check the dictations. The students can attempt to listen to the whole sentence and then write it down, or they can listen-pause-write-listen-pause write.

➢ **Blank Forms**: These forms are to be used when planning patrols, making radio calls etc.

➢ **Evaluation of Orders**: These are to be used when evaluating orders etc.

➢ **Revision: I SPELL Challenge**: This list of city names can be used to practice the NATO/Phonetic Alphabet throughout the Course.

➢ **Reference: Table of Ranks**: Students should compete this table with the ranks from their army.

➢ **Reference: Acronyms and Abbreviations List**: this list can be used as reference and to check the **Acronyms and Abbreviations Study Pages.**

➢ **Reference: Radio PROWORDS**: A reference list of PROWORDS with an explanation of each.

➢ **Reference: Language for Briefings and Talk and Report**: Useful language to use during Talk and Report tasks etc. You should draw your students' attention to these pages and encourage them to sue them as reminders during the course.

➢ **Reference: Grammar**: These Grammar Reference pages explain the main points of the grammatical system from a functional perspective. You should familiarise yourself with the terminology used as some of it will be new to you and the students.

➢ The **Quick Functional Grammar** pages are to help the students quickly decide which verb forms to use.

➢ The **Topic Vocabulary** pages are blank pages for the students to record useful vocabulary and phrases (and even grammar) about key topics. They could do this while studying a topic but it is probably best left to when the topic is finished, and this process will act as revision. These pages will then be personal reference pages of the most important words etc. on each topic. Your students should complete these pages during **Phase 3** of the Course.

➢ The **Mini-Dictionary** is a selected glossary of key terms.

➢ The final section is a set of **Key Tactical Verbs** which the students should be familiar with, and be able to translate into their own language. I suggest that you look at these section at the beginning of **Phase 2**.

7. Teaching Briefing Skills

The students will need to make briefings during the course.

There are four kinds of briefings.

1. Group Briefings

The students work as a team and prepare a briefing using the prepared slides. One of the students from the group briefs the class. The others will be the preparation team helping the briefer to prepare. The whole group has the responsibility for the quality of the briefing.

2. One-Slide and Two Slide Briefings

The students work alone and prepare a briefing using the prepared slides and speaking notes. Each student has one or two slides to present on their own.

3. Simulation Briefings

The students work in a group and present their solution to a scenario. This may include demonstrating radio calls. PowerPoint slides are not necessary for these briefing.

4. Tactical and Peacekeeping Problem Briefings

The students work as a group and solve problems and then present their solutions to the class. PowerPoint slides are not necessary for these briefing, though they can be used and are provided as Briefing Slides.

Options for Briefings

What technology you have will determine how the students can present.

There are a number of options:

- Use a computer/tablet and projector and present the slides on a screen
- Use smartphones: everyone views the briefing slides on their smartphone while the briefer talks.
- The speaker puts the information from the prepared slides onto large sheets of paper or the black/whiteboard and uses these instead of the slides.
- Use a print out the PDF file of the briefing slides from the Electronic Resources.

It is important to note that the students do not need to prepare the presentation slides for the presentations. They should use the already prepared materials. They should introduce themselves, present the slides(s) and ask for questions. Each briefing, even if it is 1 slide should be a full briefing,.

Feedback

The students should get two kinds of feedback on their briefings.

1. The other students should give the briefers **public positive feedback** on the **good aspects** of the briefing, and explain what they did not understand.

2. You, as the teacher, should give the briefers **private feedback** based on the form on the next page.

Briefing Feedback

Provide feedback on the following areas:

Briefer Confidence: Was the briefer confident?

Eye-contact: Did the briefer make eye contact with the audience?

Did the briefer scan the whole audience using the lighthouse technique?

Body Language: What was the briefer's body language like? Confident? Defensive? Aggressive?

Audience engagement/focus: Was the audience engaged/paying attention/interested/bored?

Briefing Structure: Was the briefing well-structured?

Was the information well-sequenced?

Were transitions signalled?

Were the key points emphasised?

Use of Briefing Visuals: Did the briefer make effective use of the visuals?

Voice: Was the briefer's voice loud and clear enough to be heard and understood throughout the room?

Or was the briefer's voice too quiet/loud?

Pronunciation: Think about: word individual sounds | word stress | chunking | pausing | intonation

Language used: Think about range and accuracy in: verb forms | noun phrases | word order | appropriate terminology

Errors made: What language errors were made?

Which of these errors impeded communication?

Which were just slips?

Improvements to be made: What are the main areas to focus on?

Decide on the key improvements to be made, and tell the student.

Mix good feedback with constructive feedback: good point /weak point

The students have a copy of this form in the Coursebook.

Part 2: Phase 1 Notes and Keys

Unit 1

About the Unit

This is an introduction Unit for you to introduce yourself to the students and for them to find out about each other. It is the first of three units focused on questions (the second is **Unit 6**, and the third is **Unit 15**), and you should gather information on how well the students cope with the range of questions. You should use this information in planning any remedial grammar work on questions your students need.

Task 1

Tell the students to complete the sentences in the frame. Monitor as they do so and help. Then tell the class about yourself. Tell students to introduce themselves.

Task 2

Elicit the questions you should ask to get the information in T1 from the students. Write these questions on the board:

> 1. What is your name?
>
> 2. What do you do?
>
> 3. Where do you work?

Use these three sentences and the Language Reminder box to focus on word order in questions.

Task 3

Tell students to silently read the 10 example questions and decide: past or now?

Key

Past: 2. Were you at the party? 3. Where did you go to school? 5. When did you join the army? 8. Where were you born?

Now: 1. Are you happy? 4. What do you do? 6. Do you have any children? 7. Do you like ice-cream? 9. Where do you live? 10. How old are you?

Discuss the grammar with the students.

Task 4

Tell the students to listen to the questions and underline the most stressed words and listen to the intonation (it rises). Optional: do a choral drill of the questions. Then ask them to practice the questions with their partners.

Task 5

Study and discuss the example.

Key	
State:	1. Where do you live? 3. What's your job?
Process:	2. What are you doing? 4. Where are you going? 5. What were you doing last night?

Optional: drill the questions.

Task 6

This tasks introduces more questions through a focus on word order. Tell the students to work alone or in pairs to reorder the questions. Monitor and help. Elicit the correct answers to the board. Drill the questions.

Key		
	1.	Are you married or single?
	2.	Do you do any sports?
	3.	What do you hope to do in the future?
	4.	What do you like doing in your free time?
	5.	Why did you join the army?
	6.	Do you have any children?
	7.	What did you do on your last birthday?

Task 7

Tell students to stand up and mingle and ask questions from T3, T5 and T6. Then ask them to report to class what they found out from their partners. This is a final practice of all they have done in the Unit.

Options and Decisions: When asking for feedback from pair work, it is not necessary to hear from everyone every time but there should be some feedback from the pair work task in open class. Make sure everyone does have the opportunity to talk in the class - both in pairs and in open class.

Unit 2

About the Unit

This unit is a straightforward series of practice activities for the NATO phonetic alphabet. Your students should have some familiarity with the alphabet already.

Task 1 to 10

Run through the tasks in order. Take as long as you have in the unit to give a good practice of the alphabet.

Options and Decisions: In the **Workbook** there is a list of world capital cities in **Spelling Challenge: World Cities**. You can use this for **T8** if your students cannot think of ideas.

Periodically throughout the rest of the course you can practice the alphabet by repeating **T8**. Your students need to be completely confident about using the alphabet by the end of Phase 1. Or you might want to randomly ask students to spell a word during lessons, between tasks.

Unit 3

About the Unit

This is the first of two units on describing photographs (the second is **Unit 4**). This language is important in briefings ('The man on the left is a high value target...'), and when in an OP, or on overwatch, or working as or with a sniper etc.

Task 1

Tell the students to study the diagram in the book or ask the students to close their books and then you draw the diagrams on the board - explaining each phrase as you do so.

Task 2

Project picture P3.1 from your computer onto a screen or tell students to look at P3.1 on their smart phones or tablets. They should check the text in T2 describing the photograph. Monitor and help. Check as a class.

Key	The picture shows a river running through a town. In the foreground there is a grey surface of some kind. On the left [right] there is a blue sculpture – of a map, two buildings and a cyclist. In the centre there is a grassy embankment and a single tree. In the background there are some buildings, a bridge over the river and a tower. On the right [left] you can see cars parked in front of a three-storey building.

Task 3

Key	The picture shows houses in the mountains. [1] **In the foreground** of the picture there is a garden with washing hanging on the line. [2] **In the bottom right-hand corner** there is a white two-storey house with a balcony and a red roof. [3] **On the right** is a wooded hill. [4] **In the centre** of the picture there are some trees and another white house with a grey roof; and some more house roofs. [5] **In the background** there are tree covered mountains. [6] **On the left** there is a grassy slope and some trees. [7] **In the bottom left-hand corner** there is a ditch, an earth embankment and a wire fence. The sky is blue with some white clouds.

Task 4

In this task the students should write short descriptions of P3.3. and 3.4. Monitor and help. Students could correct their partner's texts or you could ask them to pin their texts on the classroom walls; everyone then could go around and read/correct the texts. Or you could collect the texts and check them later.

Task 5

Tell students to work in pairs. They should look at P3.5. One student should describe the picture but make mistakes. The other student should listen and correct the mistakes. Then they should change roles for P3.6.

Options and Decisions: Collect your own pictures for more practice.

Don't forget: Spelling Challenge: World Cities to practice the NATO Alphabet

---

Unit 4

About the Unit

This is the second unit about describing position in photographs and in real life scenes. The first was the 'external view' of **Unit 3**. This unit practices talking about things in relationship to each other. This is more complex than **Unit 3**. There is an optional Presentation about picture descriptions for you to give at the end of this unit.

Task 1

It is best to introduce these concepts in diagrams on a board or paper. Build up the viewer perspective of the first diagram in stages, starting with X. Then go on to deal with A and B, and Z and Y. Then use yourself, or a volunteer student to show the subject perspective of the second diagram.

Task 2

Tell students to look at P4.1 on their smart phones or tablets, or you could project the picture from your computer. They should check the text in T2 describing the photograph. Monitor and help. Check as a class.

Key	There are no mistakes.

Task 3

Now direct the students attention to P4.2. They should complete the text with words from the table. Monitor and help. Check as a class.

Key The photo shows a winter scene in a forest. There is a group of people gathered around an open fire in front of some trees. The ground is covered in snow. In the [1] **centre** of the group there is a blonde woman in a black jacket, blue jeans and a multi-coloured hat. To her [2] **right** there is a tall girl in a black coat and blue hat with a fur pompom. To her [3] **left** there is a group of three people. There is a woman in [4] **front** in a red jacket and black hat holding a sausage in the fire. [5] **Behind** her is a woman in a grey coat and grey hat. [6] **Behind** her is a a woman with long brown hair, in a beige coat, hat and scarf. [7] **Behind** them you can see a grey car parked on the road. To the [8] **left** of the fire are two more people. In the [9] **foreground/front**, a man in a black coat and orange hat is squatting down by the fire. To his [10] **left** is a girl in a purple coat and multi-coloured trousers, with a red scarf and grey hat.

Task 4

In this task the students should write short descriptions of P4.3. and 4.4. Monitor and help. students could correct their partner's texts or you could ask them to pin their texts on the classroom walls; everyone then could go around and read/correct the texts. or you could collect the texts and check them later.

Task 5

Tell students to work in pairs. They should look at P4.5. One student should describe the picture but make mistakes. The other student should listen and correct the mistakes. Then they should change roles for P4.6.

Presentation on Picture descriptions

There is an optional, though highly recommended, presentation explaining how to think about picture descriptions. These picture descriptions are a key way of revising and practising language throughout the course. Work through the presentation. The examples and information from the slides are also found in the photo resources: P4.7 to P4.17.

Options and Decisions: Collect and show your own pictures for more practice, or ask the students to bring in challenging or interesting photos to describe – they could show the photos on their mobile phones and challenge each other to give a good description.

Don't forget: Spelling Challenge: World Cities to practice the NATO Alphabet

---

Unit 5

About the Unit

This unit focuses on the topic of basic training - soldiers are interested in each other's training, and the grammar focus is on the active and passive. There is a strong focus on the 'passive' in the course, starting from Study Page: Functional Grammar: The Condition Of Something.

Task 1

This is the first 'Talk and Report' task in the book. These tasks ask the students to talk about something e.g. answer some questions or describe pictures and then to report back to class what they discussed. These tasks are mostly at the beginning of the units and act as warmers. Students should do these tasks quite quickly. The talking in pairs with their partner should be seen as practice for the reporting in open class. There is a **Talk and Report Language Page** in the Workbook.

Tell the students to work in pairs and look at P5.1 and P5.2. They should work together to prepare a description of each photograph. Monitor and help. Elicit a description of each picture.

Task 2

Tell the students to discuss the three questions in pairs and then ask three students to answer the questions. See if everyone agrees. If a student uses interesting/useful vocabulary in their answers, highlight it on the board.

Task 3

Tell the students to read the text (silently) on the next page and answer the three questions in T3.

Check the answers as a class.

Key	1.	10 weeks

> 2. Phase 1
> Drill & Ceremony training; the seven "Army Core Values"; unarmed combat training map reading; land navigation; obstacle courses; TC3 training; Nuclear Biological and Chemical Defense; introduced to their standard-issue weapon; landmines; FTX Hammer; APFT.
>
> Phase 2
> Basic Rifle Marksmanship and combat training; obstacle course tasks, Tactical Foot Marches, Field Training Exercises, and continual physical training and drill; FTX Anvil; marksmanship tests.
>
> Phase 3
> Weapons Training; 10 km and 15 km Tactical Foot Marches, Field Training Exercises and MOUT (Military Operations in Urban Terrain); FTX Forge

Check any other unknown words or phrases afterwards. Choose at least one verb phrase, noun phrase and prepositional phrase from the text to explore with the students.

Repeat this process for Task 4 and Task 5

Task 4

> **Key**
> 1. At infantry school a soldier learns how to maintain and use small arms, anti-armour and indirect fire weapons systems; to operate and maintain vehicles; conduct land reconnaissance; learns about minefield safety; learns how to operate communications equipment operation; and how to prepare fighting positions and construct barriers.

Check any other unknown words or phrases afterwards. Choose at least one verb phrase, noun phrase and prepositional phrase from the text to explore with the students.

Task 5

> **Key**   1. 3 weeks + 4 weeks + ? + 62 weeks [This tests their ability to deal with incomplete information]

Check any other unknown words or phrases afterwards. Choose at least one verb phrase, noun phrase and prepositional phrase from the text to explore with the students.

Task 6

This task - **Language Analysis: Analyse the Text -** is an optional task which you could do in class if you have time or set as homework. There is a Student's Guide on Using Texts in the Workbook. However, you might want to draw the students' attention to certain parts of the text in class after they have read it and you have checked any problem vocabulary or grammar. Ask the students to close their books. Then quiz them: '*Number 1: What's the preposition?depend___?'* Students answer orally, or write down the answers; they can work alone, or in pairs. Or you could choose a sentence from the text (or a long phrase) and write it on the board with the words mixed up. The students then have to unmix the words. Word order is very important in English. They can read the text again to check their answer.

Suggested Language Focus		
Verb Phrases	learns about X	
	learns how to do X	
	If you pass the selection process you can join the Special Forces Qualification Course (SFQC), which has five phases and can last up to 62 weeks.	
	If you complete this course you qualify as a Special Forces soldier. Then you will have Live Environment Training (LET), which is Immersion Training in foreign countries, and this varies in length.	
Noun Phrases	the final week of training	their standard-issue weapon
	a special four week preparation course at Ft Bragg	
Prepositions	tests them on	how to
	go through	train for
	with their weapons	lasts for
	finishes with	concentrate on
	depends on	begins in
	learn about	
Collocations	physical fitness	unarmed combat
	team thinking	graduation ceremony
	obstacle courses	conduct land reconnaissance
	Tactical Foot Marches	military occupational speciality
	Field Training Exercises	fighting positions

Task 7

The reading texts in T3 – 5 are recorded. Students should listen to these recordings and decide which words they need to learn how to say properly. This could be done as homework if the students have the audio files downloaded to their phones/tablets.

Task 8

Tell the students to write (up to) three similar texts about the training in their army. If they only know about basic training then they should write about that. They can ask their partner to check it before doing T8. Later, you can collect the writing to mark.

Task 9

Tell the students to prepare a briefing for you about their training based on their texts from T8. This is an unstructured task for you to evaluate how good they are at making short presentations. You can ask them to work in pairs or small groups to prepare the briefing. Later briefing tasks in the course will be more detailed and structured.

Task 10

This is the first unit with Consolidation Tasks. Each unit with a text has these tasks. These are a set of tasks based on the texts. They can be found in the **Consolidation Tasks** section of the **Workbook**. These tasks focus on punctuation, articles, verbs, prepositions, collocations and word order. You can ask the students to do particular tasks or give them the choice of which tasks to do. They might want to do all of them. They can use the text in the book to check the gap-fills and reordering tasks. If you have time you can also do some of these tasks in class.

Don't forget: Spelling Challenge: World Cities to practice the NATO Alphabet

---

Unit 6

About the Unit

This is the second unit focused on questions. This unit considers future and Present Perfect before now questions, as well as revising questions from **Unit 1**. Again, this unit is designed to give you information about your particular students' knowledge of these question forms. See how well they do in this unit and then devise remedial teaching as necessary.

Task 1

Start by asking the students to write down questions they remember from **Unit 1**. They can peer check. Monitor and help.

Task 2

Tell the students to look at the questions and decide if they are about the past, present or future.

Key		
Past	What did you do last night?	Where were you born?
Now	Where do you live?	Are you happy?
	Do you have any plans for the weekend?	What are you doing?
Future	Will you be at the party on Friday?	
	Are you going anywhere in the summer?	

Check as a class and discuss any problems. Students ask and answer the questions and then report what they found out from their partner. Make sure they use the correct grammar when reporting.

Task 3

This task focuses on the difference between specific past (Simple Past), before now past (Present Perfect) and Before Now/Up to Now (Present Perfect).

Key	
Specific Past	What did you do last weekend? Did you see the CO yesterday?
Before Now Past	Have you been to Paris?
Before Now/Up to Now	How long have you lived here?

Check as a class and discuss any problems.

Students ask and answer the questions and then report what they found out from their partner. Make sure they use the correct grammar when reporting.

Task 4

Tell the students to reorder the words in the sentences to make questions. Monitor and help. The first one can be done as an example as it is the same question as T3 Example 3.

Key		
	1.	How long have you lived here?
	2.	Have you been abroad a lot?
	3.	Do you have a hobby?
	4.	How long have you been in the army?
	5.	Will you be seeing John later?
	6.	Are you having a party for your birthday?
	7.	When are you going shopping next?
	8.	Will you be able to go to the meeting?

Task 5

Listen to check T4. Students underline the words most stressed in the sentences. The intonation rises.

Task 6

Tell students to mingle to ask the questions in T4. Then ask them to report to class what they found out. This is a final practice of all they have done in the unit.

Don't forget: Spelling Challenge: World Cities to practice the NATO Alphabet

About the Unit

This unit is about ranks and passive verb forms. There is a lot of work to do in this unit and how quickly your students work through the material will depend on their familiarity with the passive. You will have to decide which tasks to set for homework or omit. In the Workbook there is a Table of Ranks on page 212.

Task 1

Tell students to find out the answer to the two questions. Elicit the question they should ask:

1. What rank are you?

2. When did you join the army?

3. When were you commissioned?

All students should stand up to mingle and ask and answer the questions.

Task 2

Tell the students to underline the verb forms. The focus is on the passive.

1. He <u>was accepted</u> into the army in 2005.

2. He <u>was shipped</u> out (sent) to Iraq with his unit in 2007.

3. He <u>was promoted</u> to corporal in 2008.

4. He <u>was made</u> a platoon sergeant in 2009.

5. He <u>was awarded</u> a battlefield commission to second lieutenant in 2010.

Check the vocabulary and concept of the passive. Use the **Language Reminder** box and the **Grammar Reference** in the Workbook.

Agree on a translation of sentences 1 – 5 with the class if this is possible.

Task 3

Tell students to read through Text 1 on the next page and add ranks to the table below the texts. They can check with their partner before a class check.

Task 4

Repeat the procedure for T3 with Text 2. Check the whole table.

Key

9. Second Lieutenant	18. General
8. Sergeant Major	17. Lieutenant General
7. First Sergeant	16. Major General
6. Master Sergeant	15. Brigadier General
5. Staff Sergeant	14. Colonel
4. Sergeant	13. Lieutenant Colonel
3. Corporal	12. Major
2. Private First Class	11. Captain
1. Private	10. First Lieutenant

Check any other unknown words or phrases in the text afterwards.

Task 5

Set the Text Analysis tasks in class or for homework.

Suggested Language Focus		
Word Order	He was promoted to first lieutenant while serving at Fort Hood with the First Cavalry Division.	
Prepositions	accepted by	as a second lieutenant
	shipped out as	while serving
	on 20 February 1943	at Fort Hood
	shipped out as	with the First Cavalry Division
	promoted to	took over C Company
	in B Company	of the 2nd Battalion
	following the battle of Cisterna	served at West Point
	in February 1944	On his promotion to Lieutenant Colonel
	at Regimental Headquarters	in the first Gulf War.
	in 1975	after 30 years service

Task 6

Tell the students to listen to the texts to decide which words they need to practice saying. This can be done as homework.

Task 7

Students discuss with their partner and report to you (and the class) about the differences in ranks between their army and the US army. Tell them to create a table of equivalent ranks for their army if there are major differences.

Task 8

Tell students to write out 10 sentences to practice the phrases in the examples. This could be set as homework.

Task 9

Check the words and phrases in the table and then ask students to discuss the roles and responsibilities for some ranks in their army. You could leave the choice of ranks up to them or you could assign ranks for them to discuss. Tell them to report back to the class on their discussion.

Task 10

Tell the students to write about two ranks. They should complete the frame in the first box for the first text. The second text is a freer exercise. Do a peer check or collect the texts to check.

Task 11

Assign or offer the choice of **Consolidation Tasks in Workbook** to students.

Don't forget: Spelling Challenge: World Cities to practice the NATO Alphabet

---

Unit 8

About the Unit

This unit is about family so soldiers can talk about their families if they want to when socialising on missions.

Task 1

Before you check the meaning of the words in T1 you could show the students a picture of your family and introduce them.

Task 2

Tell the students to read the text about the soldier's family. Tell them to note down what they learn about the soldier; e.g. He is an orphan; he is married. Then they can draw a family tree for the soldier. Check with P8.1.

Task 3

Focus the students' attention on the verbs used in the text. Are they active or passive? Past or present? Why are they used?

Task 4

Tell the students they will listen to another soldier talking about his family. Again ask them to make notes about the soldier and then draw a family tree. They can check with T8.2.

Task 5 and Task 6 are linked.

Tell students to prepare a short talk about their family. They can work in groups or as a class and tell each other about their families, and as they listen they should make notes and/or draw a family tree so they can answer the questions in T6.

Unit 9

About the Unit

This unit revises some of the language from **Unit 7** but personalises it.

Task 1

Tell the students to write down 5 things they are responsible for, then tell their partners and then report on what their partner said.

Task 2, **Task 3** and **Task 4** are linked tasks focused on developing the students listening (and speaking) skills.

In **Task 2** ask the students to listen and make notes about the speakers' ranks and responsibilities. Listen a second time if necessary. Check as a class. See the Transcript Wiki for the key.

In **Task 3** the students should choose one speaker and write down exactly what he said in the first two sentences. Listen as many times as necessary. Check with the transcripts T9.1 – T9.5.

Once they have their version of the transcript they should listen again – **Task 4** - and mark the pauses and which words are stressed most. This is raising awareness of chunking in English.

Task 5

Tell students to prepare a talk on their role and responsibilities using the frame in the Language Reminder. They should follow the procedure outlined below the Language Reminder so that they practice with their partner before telling the class about their role and responsibilities. If you have a very large class ask them to practice in pairs and then work in small groups for the second telling.

Unit 10

About the Unit

This unit focuses on the language of homes which will be useful if soldiers want to talk about their homes, or when on house clearing operations in urban warfare.

Task 1

Tell the students to look at P10.1 and see if they can name the items marked. They can check with P10.2.

Task 2

Discuss the differences between the meaning of the words in T2. You can ask the students what kind of home they live in, or ask them to ask their partner and report to the class.

Task 3 and Task 4 are linked.

The students should be familiar with at least some of the words in the table in Task 3. Tell the students to read through the list and mark the words they do know. Get them to check with their partner before discussing unknown words as a class. Once you have checked the new words, ask the students (either alone or in pairs) to sort the words into the categories in Task 4. Check as a class.

Key						
Rooms	**Furniture and fittings**	**Building material**	**Household goods and equipment**	**Description**	**Amenities**	**Parts of building**
kitchen	chair	brick	coffee-	pre-fabricated	running	garage
bathroom	drawers	tiles	maker	faces south	water	balcony
hall	cupboard	asbestos	washing	timber-	toilet/WC/	terrace
en-suite bath-	bookcase	metal	machine	framed	lavatory	garden
room	shelves	thatch	music	spacious	central	roof
bedroom	rug		centre/hi-fi	light and airy	heating	ceiling
study	wardrobe		computer	cramped	swimming	window
utility room	coat rack		microwave	roomy	pool	shed
dining room	carpet		oven	open plan		storage space
guest bedroom	radiator		pots and	wooden		basement / cel-
living room	table		pans			lar
	sofa/settee		TV			stairs
	armchair		dishwasher			greenhouse
	sofa bed					floor
	shower					attic
	bath					
	mirror					
	bed					
	stool					

Tasks 5 – 6 are linked. If students live in a house they should do Task 5. If they live in a flat/apartment/barracks they should do Task 6.

They should read through the text and delete the unnecessary words and add words in the gap until the text is true for them. Then, using the text they should tell the group or class about their home. If they are weaker students they can read the text. If they are stronger students, they should tell without reading, having practised first.

Teacher's Note: storey (GB spelling); story (US spelling)

Task 7

Tell students to imagine their dream home and make an informal presentation about it using 'would'. Tell them to make notes about what they are going to say, then to practice their presentation with a partner. This will give them the opportunity to use vocabulary from the unit which they might not have used in T5/6. Monitor and help.

Task 8

Consolidation Tasks in Workbook.

Don't forget: Spelling Challenge: World Cities to practice the NATO Alphabet

---

Unit 11

About the Unit

This unit develops the language and grammar done in **Unit 7**. The focus is on language to describe a career in the army.

Task 1

Tell the students to study the example sentences. They should focus on the words in bold and decide if they are verbs, nouns, preposition + (adjective) + noun. Check as a class, then ask the students to decide if the sentences are active or passive.

Key	
	1. He <u>was</u> **promoted** to the rank of sergeant. Verb; passive
	2. He <u>was</u> **demoted** from sergeant to corporal. Verb; passive
	3. He <u>was</u> **reduced** in rank to lieutenant. Verb; passive
	4. The court martial **demoted** him to private. Verb; active
	5. He <u>was</u> **busted down** to private. Verb; passive (informal)
	6. He **reverted** <u>to being</u> a two star general after commanding CENTCOM as a four star general. Verb; active
	7. He <u>applied</u> for a **transfer** to the artillery. Noun; active
	8. He <u>was</u> **transferred** to Minden army base in Germany to serve with the British Army of the Rhine. Verb; passive
	9. I <u>was</u> **posted** to Aden in 1978. Verb; passive
	10. I <u>have been</u> **posted** to Gibraltar – I leave next month. Verb; passive
	11. My **posting** <u>lasted</u> 3 years. Noun; active
	12. It<u>'s</u> a hardship **posting** – you get extra pay. Noun; active
	13. He **spent** six months **on secondment** with another regiment before returning to his regular unit. Prep. + noun; active
	14. He <u>was</u> **seconded** to the infantry to serve as FAC. Verb; passive
	15. He <u>was</u> sent to the Embassy in Amman for six months **on detached duty** from the Task Force. Prep. + adjective + noun; passive
	16. He <u>has been</u> **assigned** to teach a course at the Military Academy. Verb; passive
	17. My best **assignment** <u>was leading</u> jungle warfare training in Borneo. Noun; active
	18. He <u>is</u> on assignment in Sri Lanka. Prep. + noun; active

Task 2

Tell the students to read the text and answer the 3 questions.

Key		
	1.	It is not clear how many times he was promoted in the navy. In the army he was promoted six times according to the text.
	2.	He was demoted once.
	3.	Yes, he served in the navy and army twice.

Check any other unknown words or phrases afterwards. Choose at least one verb phrase, noun phrase and prepositional phrase from the text to explore with the students.

Task 3

Set the Text Analysis tasks in class or for homework.

Suggested Language Focus	
Word Order	Joe Ronnie Hooper served in the United States Navy from December 1956 to 1959, reaching the rank of Petty Officer 3rd Class. He then enlisted in the United States Army as a Private First Class in May 1960.
Noun Phrases	an Article 15 non-judicial punishment
Prepositions	as a Private First Class assigned as Platoon Sergeant to the 508th Infantry in Panama assigned to at Fort Benning commissioned as enlisted in promoted to re-enlisted in June 1968 retired in February 1974 as a First Lieutenant served as served in volunteered for

Task 4

Tell the students they will listen to another soldier talking about his career. They should complete the table as they listen. Listen again if necessary. Class check/Check with the transcript T11.1.

Key	Rank	Where based	Duties
	2nd Lieutenant	Catterick	Leading and training 30 riflemen
	Lieutenant	Catterick	More responsibility; morning training
	Captain	Catterick	Company 2nd in command; planning training for 120 men; deputising for CO; company maintenance and logistics; company operations cell; input into company commander's plans
	Senior captain	Catterick	Not stated.

Task 5

Use the transcript as a source of language for T6.

Task 6

Tell the students to prepare notes on their career to date and then to tell their partners. Their partner should make notes. Students should report to the class about their partner's career.

Task 7

Consolidation Tasks in Workbook.

Don't forget: Spelling Challenge: World Cities to practice the NATO Alphabet

---

Unit 12

About the Unit

This unit focuses on describing people using the Present Simple. As an optional extension task you could ask the students to describe people they saw in the past.

Task 1

Tell the students to look at P12.1 and compare the two men in the picture.

Task 2, 3 and **4** are linked. The students should be familiar with at least some of the words in **Task 2** . Tell the students to read through the words in the table in **Task 2** and mark the ones they know. Then discuss the meanings of new words. Discuss the difference between a well-built man and well-built woman. Tell them to categorise the words by sorting them into the table in **Task 3**. Tell them to copy the table into their notebooks. Monitor and help. Check as a class.

Key					
Age	**Height**	**Hair**	**Body build**	**Attractiveness**	**Eyes**
old	tall	dark brown	well-built	good-looking	green
20-something	short	blonde	average weight	beautiful	blue
middle-aged	average height	brown	slim	attractive	brown
pre-teen		long	strong-looking	handsome	
mid-thirties		curly	overweight	ugly	
teenager		light brown	thickset	sexy	
late fifties		wavy	fat	hot	
child		straight	thin	pretty	
adult					

Then in **Task 4** discuss the words with regards to the three question.

Task 5

Tell the students to consider the words in the table and decide which are generally only used for men e.g. beard, stubble, moustache.

Task 6

Do the first sentence as an example on the board. **Key:** 1. He <u>is</u> very handsome.

Then ask the students to decide on the correct verb in the remaining example sentences.

Key		
	1. He <u>is</u> very handsome.	11. He **has** a scar on his face.
	2. She **is** very beautiful.	12. She **is** overweight.
	3. He **is** bald. [compare with: He has a bald head]	13. She **is** blonde.
		14. She **has** blonde hair.
	4. He **has** a moustache.	15. He **is** middle-aged.
	5. He **has** a beard.	16. He **is** in his mid-thirties.
	6. She **is** slim.	17. She **is** twenty-something.
	7. He **has** a receding hairline.	18. He **is** twenty-ish.
	8. He **has** a tattoo on his arm.	19. He **is** well built.
	9. He **is** tattooed.	20. He **is** strong-looking.
	10. He **is** scarred.	

Task 7

Tell students to write a number of questions to ask about someone using the words in T2 and T5, then to practice asking and answering the questions with a partner.

Task 8

In this task ask students to make notes for a description of a person in the class or a famous person. Each student should take it in turns to tell the group/class their description. The other students should listen and figure out whom is being described.

> **Don't forget:** Spelling Challenge: World Cities to practice the NATO Alphabet

Unit 13

About the Unit

This unit focuses on force structure and a comparison between the US and British armies and your students' army. Your students should be able to describe their army's force structure at the end of the unit.

Teacher Briefing

The table on the next pages shows the unit/formations for American and British (and Commonwealth) armies, their map symbol, a description, number of personnel and the typical commander. The complexity is in the details and differences between individual militaries, so this is not a definitive guide.

Platoons can be organised in different ways. The smallest recognised formation is the squad, which might be divided into two fire teams. The US infantry platoon is organised into three infantry squads, a weapons squad and a platoon HQ [FM 3-21.8 The Infantry Rifle Platoon and Squad].

The US infantry fire team has four soldiers: A team leader (TL) (sergeant), a grenadier, an automatic rifleman (machine gunner), and a rifleman. The automatic rifleman can lay down a base of fire; the grenadier can deliver high explosives indirect fires on point and area targets; the rifleman provides accurate fire on point and area targets. The TL leads by example. The fire teams make up the squads. There are two fire teams and a squad leader in a squad. The squad leader is a (staff) sergeant. He controls the whole squad through the two team leaders. The squad can provide a base of fire (one team) while the other manoeuvrers (fire and movement). The infantry weapons squad provides heavier firepower for the entire platoon. It has two medium machine gun teams, two medium close combat missile teams and a weapons squad team leader. The weapons squad can be divided up between the squads as required.

In some armies the squads can be combined into sections if necessary. A platoon leader might decide to organise the men in his platoon by sections or by squads for a particular mission or manoeuvrer. So, he might give orders to section leaders, who will then give orders to squad leaders, who will then brief his fire team soldiers. Or the platoon leader might give orders directly to squad leaders, who will then give orders to their fire team members.

Unit/Formation	Map Symbol	Description	Number of Personnel	Typical Commander
Army Group	XXXXX	Several Armies	120,000 to 500,000	(US) General of the Army (UK/Commonwealth) Field Marshal
Army	XXXX	5 to 10 Divisions	100,000	(US) General (UK/Commonwealth) General
Corps	XXX	Several Divisions	30,000 to 60,000	(US) Lieutenant General (UK/Commonwealth) Lieutenant General
Division (div)	XX	Several Brigades/ Regiments	10,000 to 20,000	(US) Major General (UK/Commonwealth) Major General
Brigade (bde)	X	Several battalions or regiments	2,000 to 5,000	(US) Colonel/Brigadier General (UK/Commonwealth) Brigadier
Regiment (regt/rgt/reg) /Group	III	3 to 7 battalions	500 to 2,000	Colonel
Battalion (bn)	II	2 to 6 companies	300 to 1,000	Lt. Colonel
Company (co/coy)	I	Several Platoons	60 to 250	(US) Captain (UK/Commonwealth) Major
Platoon (plt)	• • •	Several Squads	25 - 40	(US) Second Lieutenant (UK/Commonwealth) Lieutenant/Captain
Section (sec)	• •	2 to 3 Fire Teams	7 - 13	(US) Sergeant/Staff Sergeant (UK/Commonwealth) Corporal/Sergeant
Squad (sqd)	•	1 to 2 Fire Teams	5 - 10	(US) Corporal or Sergeant (UK/Commonwealth) Lance Corporal
Fire Team/crew	Ø		3 - 5	

Note: There are variations on abbreviations e.g. regiment can be abbreviated in different ways. The abbreviations list in the Workbook is <u>not</u> comprehensive as such a list would need to be a separate book in itself.

Task 1

Tell the students to discuss the questions in pairs, agree on answers. Check as a class. Does everyone agree?

Task 2

Tell students to read the text and find out the size of US army formations. Note that the numbers are approximate and vary between units.

Key	Squad: 8 - 12 soldiers
	Platoon: 2 - 4 squads: 16 to 55 soldiers
	Company: 3 to 5 platoons: 60 to 250 soldiers
	Battalion: 2 - 6 companies: 300 – 1000 soldiers
	Brigade Combat Team: 2 – 7 combat battalions: 3 – 5,000 soldiers
	Division: 3 brigades: 10-15,000 soldiers
	Army corps: 2 – 5 divisions: 20-50,000 soldiers
	Army: 2 + corps: 40,000 + soldiers

Check any other unknown words or phrases afterwards. Choose at least one verb phrase, noun phrase and prepositional phrase from the text to explore with the students.

Task 3 Set the Text Analysis tasks in class or for homework.

Suggested Language Focus		
Word Order	In the US Army there are a number of different formations. A squad is typically commanded by a corporal, sergeant or staff sergeant. The smallest is the squad, which consists of 8 to 12 soldiers.	
Prepositions	led by commanded by consists of depend on composed of	with 300 to 1,000 soldiers with a command sergeant major as principle NCO comprised of combine to make
Collocations	brigade combat team infantry brigade combat team combat battalions brigade support battalion engineer battalion	infantry battalions field artillery battalion major tactical operations army corps

Task 4

Tell the students they will listen to a short talk about US army force structure. They should make notes. Check as a class. Check with the Transcript in the Workbook if necessary.

Key	Information about squad being two fire teams; 4 soldiers in a fire team; two teams more flexible. Can do battle drill alpha – one team provides suppressing fire while other team assaults on the flanks.

Task 5

Tell students to think about differences between the US Army and their army in pairs. Use the Language Reminder box. Check as a class. Does everyone agree?

Task 6

Tell the students to reread the text in T2 and find the text patterns (a – e). This is in preparation for the writing task in T9.

Task 7

In this task you can tell your students to read a text about the British army. You could omit this task if you do not have time or set it for homework.

Task 8

Tell the students to listen to the text to decide which words they need to practice saying. This can be done as homework.

Task 9

Set the writing task as homework or do in class if you have time. They should use the texts from the unit as models.

Task 10

Consolidation Tasks in Workbook.

Don't forget: Spelling Challenge: World Cities to practice the NATO Alphabet

Unit 14

About the Unit

This unit looks at the terminology to describe parties to a conflict, with a range of grammar forms; actives, passive, modals and conditionals. You might want to focus on the modals and conditionals in the text if your students have problems with them.

Task 1

Tell students to look at P14.1 and discuss what kind of person it is. They should consider what he is wearing and carrying. Elicit ideas from a couple of students and discuss as a class. Is he a soldier? A civilian? An insurgent? Ask students to justify their opinions: 'He is not a soldier because.....'

Task 2

Tell students to look through the words in the table and mark the ones they do know. Then they discuss the ones they do <u>not</u> know with their partner. Have a class check on the unknown words – see if students can help each other but do <u>not</u> explain the unknown words yourself as they will find out the meanings in Task 3.

Task 3

Tell the students to read the text in T3 and figure out the unknown words from the text. The text explains all the words from T2. Ask the students to re-read the text and answer the questions below the text as if they were government or rebel forces.

Task 4

As a class agree, with reference to the text in T3, a translation of all the words in T2.

Check any other unknown words or phrases afterwards. Choose at least one verb phrase, noun phrase and prepositional phrase from the text to explore with the students.

Task 5

Set the Text Analysis tasks in class or for homework.

Suggested Language Focus		
Verb Phrases	the government has collapsed If you do not support the government they will be **freedom fighters**, who you might also call **rebels, guerrillas, partisans** or **insurgents** but <u>not</u> **terrorists**.	
Noun Phrases	a multi-sided civil war	
Prepositions	opposed to organised by fight against	defend themselves against on your side involved in a conflict
Collocations	civilian targets monitoring ceasefires	war-torn regions aid distribution

Task 6

Tell the students to listen to the text to decide which words they need to practice saying. This can be done as homework.

Task 7

Tell the students that they are going to listen to someone talking about a conflict. They should listen and make notes about the facts and the speaker's opinion. Use T14.1 to check.

It is very important that students can distinguish when a speaker is telling them facts and when he is giving his opinion. This is the first of a number of fact and opinion listening tasks.

Key	
Fact:	Basic facts about WW2: started 1939; finished 1945; number of casualties: 50 to 85 million; Belligerents: Allies vs Axis Powers
Opinion:	'I think the First World War is more important'; it made Britain weaker and led directly to WW2. WW1, WW2 and the Cold War all one long war.

Task 8

Tell students to prepare a short talk about a conflict. This could be done as homework. Students give their talks to the class or in smaller groups. You could also set this task as a writing task if you think that is better.

Don't forget: Spelling Challenge: World Cities to practice the NATO Alphabet

Unit 15

About the Unit

This is the third unit focusing on questions, and focuses on Wh-Questions, Do/Did Questions and What If Questions

Task 1

Tell students to work in pairs and discuss P15.1. When they have discussed the picture, ask the class these questions: What can they see? Who are the people? Where are the people? What are the people in the picture doing? Then elicit these questions to the board and look at the word order and verbs.

Task 2

Tells students to reorder the words to make questions.

Key	
	1. What time do we leave?
	2. When do we get back?
	3. How many people are going on the patrol?
	4. What if we are ambushed?
	5. What if we get casualties?
	6. What kit do we need to take?
	7. What radio frequency are we going to use?
	8. Where are we going?
	9. What is your call sign?
	10. What do we do if we get separated?
	11. What is the name of this operation?

12. Will we have air cover?

13. How much ammunition should we take?

14. How much food and water should we take?

15. How many radio checks are there?

16. What is the target map reference?

17. How long is the mission?

18. What is the mission objective?

19. What type of mission is it?

20. Do we have good intel?

Task 3

Tell the students to look at the questions in T2 and answer the questions about them.

Key	Facts Now	Where are we going?
		What is your call sign?
		What is the name of this operation?
		How many radio checks are there?
		What is the target map reference?
		How long is the mission?
		What is the mission objective?
		What type of mission is it?
		Do we have good intel?
	The Future	What time do we leave?
		When do we get back?
		How many people are going on the patrol?
		What kit do we need to take?
		What radio frequency are we going to use?
		Will we have air cover?
		How much ammunition should we take?
		How much food and water should we take?
	The Past	-
	Hypotheticals	What if we are ambushed?
		What if we get casualties?
		What do we do if we get separated?

Task 4

Follow the instructions. If you have more than 12 students split the class into groups. Write out the situations below on pieces of paper and distribute them to the students.

The situations are:

1. I am driving down a road.
2. I am in a shop.
3. I am surfing the internet
4. I am walking down the street.
5. I am getting dressed.
6. I am eating.
7. I am preparing for an exercise.
8. I am looking at a map.
9. I am cleaning my gear.
10. I am reading a book.
11. I am studying.
12. I am writing.

The students should ask quick-fire questions like, for Situation 1:

Where are you driving?   What is the weather like?
Which road is it?   Is the road busy?
What are you driving?   Why are you driving?
Who is with you?

Unit 16

About the Unit

This unit focuses on time and time zones. **Unit 19** is about actually telling the time using the 24 hour clock.

Task 1

Ask a student what time of day it is. Then tell the students to copy the timeline and moon and sun table into their notebooks and label it with the words in the table. Monitor and help if really necessary. Ask students to check with their partner but do not check as a class. The following listening task acts as a check.

You could copy the timeline on the board and elicit ideas. This is a provisional answer.

Task 2

Tell students they will listen to a talk about time words and they should listen and check their timeline. They should also listen for the differences between the three kinds of twilight. Check as a class – update the timeline on the board. You could check with P16.1 at this stage or leave this until Task 3.

Task 3

Tell the students to do both tasks in Transcript Tasks 1 on p. 61. They should listen to the first part and mark the pauses and words with most stress. Then they should do the gapfil (2) and listen to check. Check with the transcript if necessary. Check with P16.1 if you haven't already done so in Task 2.

Task 4

Tell the students to discuss the questions about time zones and report their ideas.

Task 5

Tell the students to listen to the talk about time zones and make notes about the cities mentioned. The cities are marked on the map on page 30. This is an unstructured listening task as students need practice in making notes. Elicit what they heard from the students. Listen again if required.

Task 6

Ask the students to complete the two gap-fills in Transcript Tasks 2. They can work in pairs or check with their partner. Listen to check. Check with the transcript if necessary.

Task 7

Tell students to work in pairs and study the information about Date Time Group and then calculate the DTG for today.

Task 8

If necessary explain the concept of summer time/daylight savings time and ask students to think of ideas for and against. This is a relatively unstructured discussion task.

> **Don't forget:** Spelling Challenge: World Cities to practice the NATO Alphabet

Unit 17

About the Unit

This unit focuses on Brigade Combat Teams and formation purpose. The grammar focus is on active and passive verb forms,.

Task 1

Tell the students to discuss the question and then report on their ideas.

Task 2

Ask the students to read the text on p. 55 to see if their ideas from T1 were correct. Check as a class.

Task 3

Tell students to re-read the text and answer the questions.

Key		
	1.	Infantry, Stryker, Armored
	2.	Students should infer this answer from the text: Infantry – mobile; Stryker – intermediate force; armored – heavy force.
	3.	Recon: to find the enemy; artillery – more precise and rapid response to threats.
	4.	HQ: so that it is a self-contained deployable unit
	5.	Support and fire units as part of the formation.
	6.	Highly mobile, easily deployable and versatile

Check any other unknown words or phrases afterwards. Choose at least one verb phrase, noun phrase and prepositional phrase from the text to explore with the students.

Task 4

Set the Text Analysis tasks in class or for homework.

Suggested Language Focus		
Prepositions	consists of commanded by capable of below divisional level designed for consists of	without delay conduct high tempo offensive operations against operate in multiple combat situations transported by
Collocations	combat arms branch infantry brigade combat team Brigade Combat Team air assault a distribution company field maintenance company medical company field artillery battalion engineer battalion brigade support battalion combined arms (tanks and IFVs) battalions infantry fighting vehicles	armoured BCT organic reconnaissance capabilities rapid response high tempo offensive operations multiple combat situations mixed terrain defense conventional and unconventional forces mobile security missions stability operations joint team missions combat arms branch

Task 5

Tell the students to listen to the text to decide which words they need to practice saying. This can be done as homework.

Task 6

Tell students to discuss the question and report.

Task 7

This writing task can be done in class, alone or in pairs, or set for homework.

Task 8 Consolidation Tasks in Workbook.

About the Unit

This unit focuses on the differences between motorized infantry mechanised infantry and armoured infantry. The grammar focus is on active and passive verb forms, modals (can) and allow to do.

Task 1

Tells students to look at P18.1 in pairs and describe what they can see. Ask one student to describe the picture to the class.

Task 2

In this second Talk and Report tasks students should discuss the differences between the three terms. Elicit definitions from the students and see if everyone agrees. Do not comment on the correctness of their opinions.

Task 3

Tell students to read the text on the next page to see if their definitions agree with the text. Class check: were the students correct?

Task 4

Tell the students to re-read the text and answer the four questions.

Key	
	1. WW2
	2. Protection and firepower
	3. IFVs – more protection and firepower
	4. crew, fuel and ammunition, mechanics, recovery crew and vehicles

Check any other unknown words or phrases afterwards. Choose at least one verb phrase, noun phrase and prepositional phrase from the text to explore with the students.

Task 5

Set the Text Analysis tasks in class or for homework.

Suggested Language Focus		
Prepositions	limited by	engage the enemy with their individual weapons
	attempt to	
	respond to	fighting on foot
	protection from hostile fire	as part of
	provide the troops with	during movement
	equipped with	confronted by
	engage in rapid tactical movement	manoeuvre for advantage
	uses APCs for	

Collocations	motor transport	armoured infantry
	mechanised forces	armour protection
	amoured formations	combat supplies
	soft-skinned	engage the enemy
	hostile fire	individual weapons
	Motorized infantry	combined arms operations
	rough ground	close terrain
	suppressive fire support	anti-armour defence
	Mechanised infantry	light infantry
	tactical movement	anti-armour capability

Task 6

Tell the students to listen to the text to decide which words they need to practice saying. This can be done as homework.

Task 7

Tell students they will listen to a talk. Tell them to make notes under two headings: facts and opinions. After the listening – check as a class. Then check with T18.1

Key

Fact: Fully tracked; crew of three; carry 8 infantrymen; 30 mm autocannon; 5.56 MG4 machine gun; 2000 rounds; Spike anti-tank guided missiles; 6 shot 76 mm grenade launcher; 70 km/h; 600 km range; provide suppressive fire support; anti-armour capabilities.

Opinion. Puma is best IFV in world; might withstand a hit from a tank with maximum armour protection; I love the Puma.

Task 8

Consolidation Tasks in Workbook.

Extra Task: You could ask the students to brief you on the IFVs which their army uses and to give their opinion about it.

Don't forget: Spelling Challenge: World Cities to practice the NATO Alphabet.

About the Unit

This unit follows on from **Unit 16** and looks at how to tell the time and how to say numbers.

Task 1

Ask students to practise the numbers in the table in pairs. Monitor. Do a class check. Drill the numbers if necessary.

Task 2 and **Task 3**

Repeat the procedure for T1 for these sets of numbers.

Task 4

Ask the students to write down 10 random numbers and dictate them to their partner. Monitor them as they do this and drill any numbers which cause problems.

Task 5

Repeat the procedure from T1 for this set of numbers.

Task 6

Ask the students to write down 10 more random numbers and dictate them to their partner. Monitor them as they do this and drill any numbers which cause problems.

Task 7

Repeat the procedure from T1 -3 for this set of numbers.

Task 8

Ask the students to write down 10 random decimal numbers and dictate them to their partner. Monitor them as they do this and drill any numbers which cause problems.

Task 9

Ask a student what time it is. Using the examples in Task 9 explain the use of the 24 hour clock.

Task 10

Repeat the procedure from T1 for these times.

Task 11

Ask the students to write down 10 times and dictate them to their partner. Monitor them as they do this and drill any times which cause problems. Do an open class practice as well.

Task 12

Books closed. Ask several students: What time do you get up? Elicit the question to the board. Tell the students to write down five more *What time..?* questions, then to ask and answer and then report back to the class. Collate the answers: Who gets up the earliest etc.?

About the Unit

This is a general English unit of free time activities and expressing likes and dislikes. In social interaction on missions your soldiers might like to talk about what they like doing in their free time.

Task 1

Tell the students to look at the two pictures and to discuss them in their pairs. Ask them to describe what they can see in detail. Elicit a description of the each picture from two students.

Task 2

In this second Talk and Report task tell the students to look at the Language Reminder box and then find out from their partner what they love doing in their free time. Elicit what question they should ask before they start. Then ask them to report about their partner.

Task 3

Tell the students to go through the words in the table and tick the ones they know. Then do a quick class check of the new words/phrases. Tell them that each word or phrases goes with a particular verb. Tell them to decide which verb and to complete the table. Class check.

Key			
I go	**I play**	**I do**	**I**
fishing	chess	voluntary work	travel a lot
swimming	football	woodwork	watch TV
shooting	computer games	drawing	make things from wood.
out with my friends	cards	nothing	repair cars
clubbing	board games		paint pictures
out drinking	the piano		collect stamps and coins
walking	with my children		read novels
climbing			sing in a choir
birdwatching			listen to music
to the gym			cook
to the movies			write stories
to concerts			spend time with my friends
			help my children with their homework

Task 4

Ask the students: what is the opposite of love? Hate. Tell them to look at the table in T4. Ask them to think of things they love/hate etc. doing and to complete the table. Monitor and help.

Task 5

Ask the students to compare their table with their partner's and then report to the class on their findings.

Task 6

Close books. Write the first sentence from T6 on the board. Ask the students which word is stronger – love or adore? Adore.

Tell the students to study the other sentences and decide which word in bold is stronger. Class check.

Key		
	1.	adore
	2.	loathe
	3.	detest
	4.	crazy

Students should then write true sentences about themselves. Monitor and help. Then students should tell the class their sentences. Correct major pronunciation errors. What do the students have in common?

Task 7

Task 6 was about vocabulary, this task is about grammar. Ask the students to study the examples. Discuss with the class. Then they should write similar examples which are true for them. Monitor and help. Ask a number of students to tell the class one or more of their sentences. Correct major pronunciation errors. What do the students have in common?

Don't forget:

1. Spelling Challenge: World Cities to practice the NATO Alphabet.

2. Test the students on telling the time using the 24 hour clock, and using numbers, and DTG.

Unit 21

About the Unit

This unit focus on some technical language used to describe different kinds of weapons platforms.

Task 1

Tell the students to look at the picture and to discuss it in their pairs. Ask them to describe what they can see in detail. Elicit a description of the picture from a student.

Task 2

Ask the students to work in pairs and list their army's equipment in the categories in the table. Class check.

Task 3

Ask the students to look at the words in the table and tick the ones they know. They can then check the new words in the pictures.

Task 4

Ask the students to look at the table in T4. Check all the words in the first column. The ask the students to decide which of the vehicles in P21.2 – P21.6 go in the second column.

Key	
take-off weight	A10-A, Apache helicopter
top speed	All
operational range	All
flight crew	A10-A, Apache helicopter
service ceiling	A10-A, Apache helicopter
projectile	All except for Bedorb
cruising speed	A10-A, Apache helicopter
diesel engine	Bedfor, Palladin, Warrior
6-speed manual transmission.	Bedford
ferry range	A10-A, Apache helicopter

Task 5

Key	1. Leopard 2	4. Blackhawk
	2. M109A7	5. Bedford
	3. Puma IFV	

Check any other unknown words or phrases afterwards. Choose at least one verb phrase, noun phrase and prepositional phrase from the text to explore with the students.

Task 6: as instructions in Coursebook.

Unit 22

About the Unit

This unit focusses on music to enable the student to talk about their likes and dislikes.

Task 1

Ask students to discuss the questions in pairs and then report.

Task 2

Ask students to look through the genres of music and mark the ones they like/dislike. Elicit a few opinions about music e.g. My favourite kind of music is _____. I really dislike _____. You can refer students back to the language used in **Unit 20 T4**.

Task 3 and Task 4 are linked. Tell students to look through the words in the table in T3 and mark the ones they know. Do a class check of new words. Then ask the students to complete the sentences in Task 4 with words from T3.

Key		
	1.	Brahms is my favourite **composer.**
	2.	The Beatles were the most famous pop **group** in the sixties.
	3.	Ringo Starr was the **drummer** for The Beatles.
	4.	I hear they have gone into the **recording** studio to record a new **album** of songs.
	5.	**Bands** often use **session** musicians when recording in the studio.
	6.	Sir Georg Solti **conducted** many famous **orchestras.**
	7.	Can you play a musical **instrument**?
	8.	I hate songs where you can't hear the lyrics.
	9.	I prefer going to see a band play **live** in **concert** than listen to recorded **CDs.**
	10.	Paul Simon was a **singer-songwriter** and wrote and sang many popular songs.

Task 5

Ask students to check in pairs the adjectives in the table in Task 5. Do class check of unknown words. Discuss if the words are positive or negative.

Key	**Positive**	peaceful	catchy
	beautiful	relaxing	exciting
	haunting	wonderful	
	Negative	annoying	repetitive
	depressing	irritating	awful
	gives me a headache	boring	unoriginal

Task 6

Ask them to read the review. Is it positive or negative? [Positive] Why?

Task 7

Tell the students to ask and answer the questions and then report on what their partner said.

Optional Task: You might want to collate the answers from the class in some way e.g. a table of the board, or ask groups to make posters.

Don't forget:

1. Spelling Challenge: World Cities to practice the NATO Alphabet.

2. Test the students on telling the time using the 24 hour clock, and using numbers, and DTG.

About the Unit

This unit follows on from **Unit 21** and uses the same texts.

Task 1

Ask the students to find out from each other what they remember about the hardware in **Unit 21**.

Task 2

Key				
	1.	Blackhawk	10.	M109
	2.	Bedford	11.	Leopard 2/M109
	3.	Blackhawk	12.	Bedford/Blackhawk
	4.	M109	13.	Blackhawk
	5.	Leopard	14.	Blackhawk/M109?
	6.	Blackhawk	15.	Bedford: unarmoured
	7.	Blackhawk/M109	16.	Leopard 2
	8.	Blackhawk/Bedford	17.	Bedford: unarmed
	9.	Blackhawk	18.	A matter of opinion.

Task 3

This task uses the Fact Files in the Workbook. Elicit from the students questions they can ask to get information about one of the weapons platforms. Write the questions on the board.

e.g.

1. How long/wide/high is the Challenger?
2. What are the dimensions of the Challenger?
3. How fast is the Challenger?
4. How heavy is it?
5. How many crew does it have?
6. What is its armament?
7. What armour does it have?
8. What is its range?

Put students into pairs and they ask and answer about the four vehicles. One student asks about the Challenger, the other about the Abrams etc.

Follow-up Task. Ask the students to work in groups compare the Challenger and Abrams, and the Warrior and Bradley and decide which is the best tank and IFV.

Task 4 T

Tell the students to write a text based on one of the Fact Files listed. They should use the texts in **Unit 21** as models. This could be done for homework.

Don't forget:
1. Spelling Challenge: World Cities to practice the NATO Alphabet.
2. Test the students on telling the time using the 24 hour clock, and using numbers, and DTG.

The **Language Revision Tasks** in the Box is the first of occasional revision task boxes which appear throughout the book. These are all self-check exercises.

Unit 24

About the Unit

This unit is slightly different as it is a **grammar structure practice unit focussed on practising conditional clauses** using 'would'. It follows directly on from **Study Page: Functional Grammar: Expressing Distant Certainty** in the Workbook. Make sure you set that Study Page for homework or look at it in class <u>before</u> you do this unit.

Task 1

Put the students into groups or they can work as individuals, or work as a class. Appoint one student per class or group as question master.

Ask the students to read through the procedure outlined in Task 1. Clarify any points necessary. Then follow the procedure.

Task Cards

Situation 1

You are a lieutenant. Your senior NCO has hit a private.

What would you do?

Situation 2

You are a lieutenant. One of your privates has hit a Corporal.

What would you do?

Situation 3

You are a corporal. Two of your privates have had a fight.

What would you do?

Situation 4

You are a corporal. One of your privates has been caught stealing from the other men.

What would you do?

Situation 5

You are a lieutenant. One of your privates was AWOL for 2 days. He has just retuned to base.

What would you do?

Situation 6

You are a lieutenant. Your senior NCO reports to you that one of your privates is heavily in debt because of gambling.

What would you do?

Situation 7

You are a captain. You notice that one of your lieutenants has not gained the respect of his men.

What would you do?

Situation 8

You are a corporal leading a night patrol. One of your men twists his ankle.

What would you do?

Situation 9

You are lieutenant patrolling through tropical rain forest towards your objective when you are ambushed by a much larger force.

What would you do?

Situation 10

You are a corporal in an OP observing an enemy held town from a mountain ridge. You are discovered by two teenage boys and an old man herding goats.

What would you do?

Situation 11

You are a staff sergeant training local friendly forces in another country. You think one of your trainees is behaving suspiciously. He seems to be readying himself to shoot someone, possibly you and your colleagues.

What would you do?

Situation 12

You are lieutenant on deployment in another country. You suspect one of the medical orderlies in your detachment is dealing drugs to the locals.

What would you do?

Situation 13

You are lieutenant being inserted into a semi-desert area with your platoon on a 10-day mission to observe enemy forces moving along a main road. You land at the LZ but realise that the terrain is absolutely flat with no cover. There seem to be isolated houses in the area with dogs barking.

What would you do?

Situation 14

You are lieutenant on a route march in a semi desert area in full battle order (rucksacks, personal weapons, ammunition etc.). You have 5 kms left of the march to go. You notice one of your soldiers seems to be suffering – he is staggering, cannot walk in a straight line and seems to be having difficulty focusing.

What would you do?

Situation 15

You are the company CO. Your unit is on 24 hours notice to deploy to a mountainous region. Your first sergeant reports that most of your men have not been issued with proper sleeping bags.

What would you do?

Situation 16

You are the company CO. You have just returned from a 10 day large scale field exercise. Your men are tired, hungry and dirty. As your reach the base after a forced march you receive an immediate notice to deploy in 24 hours.

What would you do?

Situation 17

You are lieutenant and you have just been inserted by helicopter at the LZ. The helicopters have left to return to base and you realise that you are at the wrong LZ. You are 25 kms from the right LZ, which is over a 1500 m high mountain ridge. What would you do?

Situation 18

You are lieutenant patrolling along a jungle track. There is a river approximately 20 m to your left, running parallel to the track. On each side of the path there is dense but not impenetrable undergrowth. Your point man signals that the enemy is moving down the track towards you in unknown strength.

What would you do?

Situation 19

You are a lieutenant on a peacekeeping mission and you think that your translator is not translating what you say accurately and not translating everything you say.

What would you do?

Situation 20

You are a sergeant and you realise a corporal is having an affair with a private's wife.

What would you do?

Task 2

Give feedback on language errors and the positive aspects of the students' performance.

Don't forget:

1. Spelling Challenge: World Cities to practice the NATO Alphabet.

2. Test the students on telling the time using the 24 hour clock, and using numbers, and DTG.

Unit 25

About the Unit

This unit focuses on the history and use of tanks. The main grammar focus is on past tenses.

Task 1

Tell the students to look at P24.1 and to describe in detail what they can see. Ask one student to describe the picture to the class.

Task 2 and **Task 3** are linked.

Before the reading in (**Task 3**) ask students to try to answer the questions. Don't worry if they cannot answer them. Do not tell them the correct answers. Then tell the students to read the text in **Task 3** and find the answer to the questions.

<table>
<tr><td>Key</td><td>

1. When were tanks first developed? WW1; 1915
2. Who first developed tanks? The British and French.
3. When were they first used successfully? At the Battle of Soissons and Battle of Amiens
4. How are modern MBTs used? In co-operation with infantry and ground attack aircraft; to engage tanks and fortifications, and soft targets such as light vehicles and infantry.
5. What are the characteristics of MBTs? Main armament 90 to 120 mm, weight of the vehicle: 45-70 tons, and max. speed of 65 km/h; an operational range of up to 500 km; sophisticated fire-control systems; armour: steel, composite ceramic and alloys, explosive reactive armour, or slat armour, and electronic countermeasures against missile attack.

</td></tr>
</table>

Task 4 Tell the students to read the text again and answer the questions.

<table>
<tr><td>Key</td><td>

1. Which generals are mentioned in the text? General Guderian; General Rommel; General Montgomery; General Patton
2. Which countries did they fight for? Germany, Germany, Britain, America respectively.
3. Which tanks fought in the Battle of Kursk? Russian T34 and JS2 tanks beat the German Tiger and Panther tanks.
4. Who won the battle? The Soviet Union / Russia
5. What was General Patton's greatest achievement? Disengaging 6 divisions from front line combat during the middle of winter, then turning north to relieve Bastogne during the Battle of the Bulge in 1944.

</td></tr>
</table>

Check any other unknown words or phrases afterwards. Choose at least one verb phrase, noun phrase and prepositional phrase from the text to explore with the students.

Task 5

Set the Text Analysis tasks in class or for homework.

Suggested Language Focus		
Word Order	The largest tank battle of the war was the Battle of Kursk.	
Prepositions	developed in	during July and August 1943
	protected by	during the middle of winter
	armed with	working in co-operation with infantry
	defeated by	a compromise between
	under General Rommel	used to
	During the Second World War	designed to
	on the Eastern Front	
	an engagement between German and Soviet forces	

Collocations	penetrate defensive lines	ground attack aircraft
	barbed wire	armour protection
	went into action	soft targets
	trench line system	fire-control systems
	infantry support	explosive reactive armour
	came into their own	electronic countermeasures
	armoured units	operational range

Task 6

Tell the students to listen to the text to decide which words they need to practice saying. This can be done as homework.

Task 7

Tell students they will listen to a talk. Tell them to make notes under two headings: facts and opinions. After the listening – check as a class. Then check with T24.1

Key	Fact: facts and figures about Panthers and T34s: see transcript.
	Opinions: 'It is difficult to decide which is the better tank. But the real question is not which is the best tank. The real question is what is the most important tank? I think the answer to this is clear. The Soviet T34 was the most important tank in World War 2.'

Task 8

Tell students to discuss the questions in pairs and then report to the class.

Task 9

Consolidation Tasks in Workbook.

Unit 26

About the Unit

This unit focuses on the topic of watches. Watches are key personal military equipment. This unit teaches key vocabulary about watches and looks at comparisons and question formation.

Task 1

Tell students to discuss the two questions in pairs. Then discuss their ideas as a class.

Task 2

Ask the students to look at P16.1 and see if they know the parts of a watch. They can check with P16.2. Model/drill the pronunciation of the words as required.

Task 3

This task is a pre-reading prediction task. You could ask the students to consider the questions alone, or in pairs, or in groups. Ask for some ideas in open class. Don't comment on the ideas but you could ask the students to give reasons for their ideas for the second question.

Task 4

Tell students to read the text and see if they agree or disagree with the writer. When they have read the text check the answers to the questions in T3 and see if the students agree with the writer's ideas for the requirements of a military watch.

Check any other unknown words or phrases afterwards. Choose at least one verb phrase, noun phrase and prepositional phrase from the text to explore with the students.

Task 5

Set the Text Analysis tasks in class or for homework.

Suggested Language Focus		
Noun Phrases	an essential piece of kit	
Prepositions	on your wrist	in the dark
	type of	painted with
	rely on	around your neck
	for smart occasions	on top of
	wind up	on night operations
	as long as	runs on batteries
	requirements for	
Collocations	smart occasions	rotating bezel
	show the time	luminous markings
	air pressure	night operations
	electronic compass	elapsed time

Task 6

Tell students to copy the table in T6 into their notebooks (with bigger spaces to write). Tell they they will listen to a man describing four watches. Students should look at P16.3 and identify the watches and complete the table with notes.

Key	Watch 1	Watch 2	Watch 3	Watch 4
Description	Blue Monster blue face with a rotating diving bezel	stainless steel case, blue dial and bezel	Swiss dress watch; a gold case with a white dial	a retro pilot style watch
Features	200m; luminous dial; automatic; rotating bezel; day/date; stainless steel case	chronograph with stopwatch features; Eco-Drive	Quartz; second hand dial; Roman numerals	Luminous dial; date; 24 hour clock; 100 m water resistance
When does he wear it?	Every day	Doesn't say	On special occasions	For a change when he doesn't want to wear his Blue monster
Opinion	Toughest, everyday watch	Good-looking and heavy	Oldest watch; very small and light	Likes the 24 hour clock markings

Task 7

Listen again and tell students to write down the phrase the speaker uses to compare the watches. Check with the T16.1.

Key	It's not as good a timekeeper as a	It's a good looking watch but it's heavy
	This is my toughest watch	It's the oldest of these four watches
	bigger and heavier	not as good as

Task 8

Tell students to complete the questions. Monitor and help. Check as a class.

Key		
	2.	Is it waterproof?
	3.	How many functions does it have?
	4.	Is it quartz or automatic?
	5.	How accurate/reliable is it?

Task 9

Put the students into pairs or small groups and ask them to ask and answer the questions in T9 and T8. Ask some students to report back on their discussion.

Task 10 Consolidation Tasks in Workbook.

Don't forget:
1. Spelling Challenge: World Cities to practice the NATO Alphabet.
2. Test the students on telling the time using the 24 hour clock, and using numbers, and DTG.

About the Unit

This unit focuses on personal equipment e.g. body armour, belts, webbing etc., and there is the first one-slide briefing tasks where students present what is important when buying various items.

Task 1

Tell students to list what equipment they take with them on active duty. Monitor and then elicit a selection of the words to the board and check everyone knows their meaning.

Task 2

Tell students to look at P26.1 and identify what the soldiers are wearing. Check with the words on the board from Task 1. Then ask them to look at P26.2 and P26.3 to check they know all the words.

Task 3

Tell the students to read the text about the British Army Virtus body armour system and find out what are the advantages of the new armour e.g. the helmet is lighter etc. The students should look at P26.4 to P26.7 as they read to help them understand the text. Check new and important vocabulary.

Task 4

Set the Text Analysis tasks in class or for homework.

Suggested Language Focus		
Word Order	The new Virtus system uses the latest materials.	
Prepositions	consists of	linked to
	in a prone position	easier to carry
	in the same way	scaled up or down
	to the side of the head	carry loads with or without armour
Collocations	the latest materials.	night vision goggles
	significantly lighter	body armour
	slimmer profile	heavy loads
	a Scalable Tactical Vest	full body armour system
	blunt impact protection	quick-release mechanism
	a prone position	type of threat

Task 5

Tell the students to listen to the text to decide which words they need to practice saying. This can be done as homework.

Task 6

Tell students to discuss the question in pairs and then report to the class. Does everyone agree? What are their reasons for their opinions?

Task 7

Tell students to discuss the question in pairs and then report to the class.

Don't forget:

1. Spelling Challenge: World Cities to practice the NATO Alphabet.

2. Test the students on telling the time using the 24 hour clock, and using numbers, and DTG.

Do the **Language Revision Tasks** or set it for homework.

Unit 28

About the Unit

This unit considers a range of language used to make arrangements to meet.

Task 1

Tell students to describe P27.1 in detail in pairs and then ask one student to describe it to the class.

Task 2

Quickly run through the questions about days to see how good they are with days of the week and some of the more subtle meanings e.g. this weekend vs next weekend. Either do it as a class or in pairs with a class check. There is also some work on these ideas on Study Page 10. Functional Grammar in the Workbook.

Task 3

Ask students to read through the dialogue and check the meaning of the words in bold. You could also ask some comprehension check questions like: *When are they meeting? Can they meet tomorrow? Why not?*

Task 4

Tell students to complete the dialogue with words from T3 in the correct form.

Key	
Andrew:	Are you [1] **free** this evening John? Do you fancy going out for a drink?
John:	Sorry Andrew. I'd love to – that's just what I need - but I've got to finish a report for tomorrow and I can't [2] **postpone** it any more. What about tomorrow?
Andrew:	No, I'm afraid I'm busy tomorrow night. I've already [3] **arranged** to go to the Pearson's for dinner.

John:	That's a pity. I'll have finished my report. What about Saturday night?
Andrew:	Well I'm [4] **supposed** to be going out with Jake and Claire. But they haven't [5] **confirmed** it yet.
John:	Maybe I could tag along. I get on with them.
Andrew:	All right then. That's [6] **settled**. Saturday – about seven
John:	Great, I'm looking forward to it already.

Check as a class. Ask simple comprehension questions to check understanding of the dialogue.

Task 5

Tell the students they will listen to a conversation. Tell them to write down the names of the people and what they decide to do. Class check:

Key	Rob, Sarah and Sue. Possibly go to the cinema at 7 on Saturday.

Task 6

Tell the students they will listen to a conversation. Tell them to write down the names of the people and what they decide to do. Class check:

Key	Peter and John, fishing and shooting.

Task 7

Tell students to read through the transcript and check they understand everything. Then students listen again and mark the pauses and which words are most stressed. Students practice the dialogue in pairs. Monitor and correct pronunciation.

Task 8

Tell students to work in pairs and write a short dialogue making an arrangement to meet. Monitor and help. They should practice in pairs and then perform it to the class.

Don't forget:

1. Spelling Challenge: World Cities to practice the NATO Alphabet.

2. Test the students on telling the time using the 24 hour clock, and using numbers, and DTG.

About the Unit

This unit continues the focus on personal equipment from **Unit 27**.

Task 1

Tell the students to look at P29.1 and describe what they can see. Ask one student to report to class and develop their description.

Task 2

Ask students to talk in pairs about what they can remember about the Virtus body armour system from **Unit 27**. Elicit from class what the students remember.

Task 3

Focus the students' attention on the Language Reminder and then ask them to work in pairs to talk about their favourite piece of kit. Keep this quite short as they will be talking at more length about kit later.

Task 4

Tell students they are going to listen to a soldier talking about kit. Ask them to make notes and see if they agree with the speaker. After the listening they can check their notes with their partner. Ask them if they want to listen a second time before checking as a class. Do they agree? Use the Transcript T29.1 as a key.

Task 5 and **Task 6** are linked.

Task 5

Tell the students to work in pairs and look at P26.8 to P26.27 and discuss what is important to consider when buying these things. The pictures are annotated with words to give them some ideas for the important features for each item. Focus their attention on the Language Reminder. Monitor and help as necessary.

This task is part of preparation for Task 6 so there is no need for class feedback on their ideas. If time is short give each pair four or five of the pictures to talk about.

Task 6

When they have discussed the pictures in Task 5 allocate one item from the twenty in the **Unit 29 Briefing Slides** to each student. There are twenty items. If you have more than 20 students then pair some students up.

On the **Unit 29 Briefing Slides** each item is presented on one slide. Each student (or pair) should prepare a briefing on that slide. They should script what they are going to say using the words/phrases from the Language Reminder and then practise it. Then they should present their item to the class. Make sure the students introduce themselves properly and ask for questions. Give the students feedback on their performance based on the Presentation Feedback Sheet.

About the Unit

This unit focuses on the language associated with paratroopers, with a focus on past tenses.

Task 1

Tell the students to look at P28.1 – P28.4 and describe what they can see. Elicit descriptions from a number of students.

Task 2 and **Task 3** are linked.

Task 2 is a prediction exercise. See how much the students know before they read the text. It doesn't matter if they do not know the answers to the questions. Ask them to read the text to find out the answers. Class Check.

Key	1.	Before WW2
	2.	(and 4) Operation Weserübung – Yes; Operation Colossus -?; Operation Overlord – Yes; Operation Market Garden – No – not relieved in time.

Task 4

Tell students to read the text again to answer three more questions. Class check

Key	1.	Surprise
	2.	Not landing together; being shot on the descent; not being relieved in time.
		What do you think? Students' ideas here: e.g. bad weather; lack of surprise;

Check any other unknown words or phrases afterwards. Choose at least one verb phrase, noun phrase and prepositional phrase from the text to explore with the students.

Task 5

Set the Text Analysis tasks in class or for homework.

Suggested Language Focus	
Word Order	Paratroopers generally use circular parachutes opened by a static line attached to the plane. Paratroopers have to carry all their food and equipment and weapons.

Prepositions	into action	parachuted into Italy
	behind enemy lines	in Operation Colossus
	protect areas against airborne assault	blow up
	near Tripoli in Libya	opened by
	at the Military School	limited in how long
	during the invasion of Denmark	landing on target
	on April 9	on or near the objective
	used in the invasion of	landed in the target area
	took place on February 10	
Collocations	behind enemy lines	airborne operations
	seize strategic objectives	successful drops
	a tactical advantage	ground troops
	the element of surprise	relieve the cut-off paratroopers
	airborne assault	special forces units
	parachute units	an effective fighting force
	the invasion of Denmark	target area
	high casualties	ground fire

Task 6

Tell the students to listen to the text to decide which words they need to practice saying. This can be done as homework.

Task 7

Tell students they will listen to a talk. Tell them to make notes under two headings: facts and opinions. After the listening – check as a class. Then check with T28.1

Key	Fact: The text is basically all fact
	Opinions: The only opinion is that Operation Mercury is an interesting WW2 battle.

Task 8

Ask students to discuss the questions in pairs before report to class.

Task 9

Consolidation Tasks in Workbook.

Unit 31

About the Unit

This is the third unit on kit (the first two were **Unit 27** and **Unit 29**) but this is focused on equipment used for hobbies. The main grammar focus is on 'use to do something' and noun phrases.

Task 1

Tell students to look at P29.1 and see if they know the words for the things marked A – H. They can check with P29.2.

Task 2

Tell students they are going to listen to a man talk about his hobby. They should listen and answer the questions.

Key	
	1. A big shoulder bag is bad for your back.
	2. Someone can steal something out of it.
	3. One camera and two lenses.
	4. a spare battery; cleaning gear -lens pen and lens tissue; a pen and notebook; spare fast 16 GB memory cards

Task 3

Tell students to listen again and make notes to answer the two questions.

Key	
	1. Small mirrorless camera; 18-55 mm zoom lens and 55-200 mm telephoto zoom lens
	2. Street photography and nature photography; a spare battery – power camera; cleaning gear (lens pen and lens tissue): to clean lenses; a pen and notebook: to take notes; spare fast 16 GB memory cards: takes a lot of pictures.

Task 4

Tell the students to complete the transcript and listen to check. Finally they can look at Transcript T29.1

Task 5 and **Task 6** are linked. Use the examples and Language Reminder in **Task 5** to look at adjective order; then in **Task 6** students reorder the phrases.

Key	
	1. an excellent high-capacity lithium battery
	2. poor quality plastic toys
	3. an unreliable sports car.
	4. a beautiful Swiss wristwatch.
	5. a green waterproof jacket

Task 7 and **Task 8** are linked. Study the examples in **Task 7** and then ask students to reorder the sentences in **Task 8**.

Key	
	1. There's room for all your gear here.
	2. I have my laptop ready to make notes.
	3. I need the information to help me with my research
	4. the I use shots targets to the check binoculars my on.
	5. I always take a magnesium fire starter with me so I can always start a fire

Task 9

In this task students should talk about things they need to do a hobby. Then ask the students to report about their partner's hobby and what they need for it.

> **Don't forget:**
> 1. Spelling Challenge: World Cities to practice the NATO Alphabet.
> 2. Test the students on telling the time using the 24 hour clock, and using numbers, and DTG.

Unit 32

About the Unit

This unit focusses on different ways to talk about the future and make plans and arrangements. The grammar focus is on *Will | Would | Going To | Present Continuous | Past Continuous*. Your students should have met *going to* and the *Present Continuous* before and will be familiar with the use of *will* for making decisions. They will be less familiar with *would* and the use of the *past continuous* here.

Task 1

Tell the students to describe the photos in pairs and then ask five students to describe one photo to the class.

Task 2

Ask the students to study the example sentences and decide which are about plans.

Key		
	1.	I went shopping yesterday. Past event.
	2.	I'm going camping with my kinds in the summer. Plan.
	3.	I'm thinking of going to the cinema at the weekend. Do you fancy coming? Idea.
	4.	I was thinking about buying a new car. Idea.
	5.	I'm taking next week off. Plan.
	6.	I would like to have a holiday soon. Wish.
	7.	I'm enjoying my day off so far: I got up late; had a great breakfast and now I'm playing with the kids. Past events and current activity.
	8.	We're planning on going on safari to Namibia in summer. Plan.
	9.	Next week I hope to have time to finish repairing the roof. Hope.
	10.	I'm playing tennis with John tonight at 7. Arrangement, which is a kind of plan.

Task 3 to **Task 6** are grammar study tasks with example sentences. Study/discuss the examples with your students in **Tasks 3 – 5** before looking at the decision-making process in **Task 6**.

Task 7

This is a mingling task. Students should follow the instructions. Monitor and give feedback. Stop the task before it goes on too long. Ask the students to report back on their arrangements.

Unit 33

About the Unit

This unit focuses on the role of combat engineers. Grammar: Mainly Present Simple and do-ing clauses.

Task 1

Tell the students to look at P33.1 and describe what they can see. Ask them to describe the people and what they are doing.

Task 2

Ask the students to discuss the two questions in pairs and then elicit some answers. This is a pre-reading task so do not tell the students if they are right or wrong.

Task 3

Students read the text to answer the questions in Task 2. Class check of the answers. Were they correct? Elicit what they were correct about. This will give you some idea of how much they understand about the text.

Task 4: Ask students to read the text again and answer the questions.

Key		
	1.	What is the difference between combat engineer, sapper and pioneer? None.
	2.	What is a wet gap crossing? A river crossing.
	3.	What do engineers do with fighting positions? Build and destroy.
	4.	How do engineers help the air forces? Building airstrips.
	5.	What kinds of things do engineers do after combat operations have finished? De-mining. Provide humanitarian support in areas like water production, electrical supply and infrastructure reconstruction, building hospitals etc.
	6.	Why should engineers be able to construct wire obstacles? Force protection.
	7.	What is an ESV? Engineer Squad Vehicle

Check any other unknown words or phrases afterwards. Choose at least one verb phrase, noun phrase and prepositional phrase from the text to explore with the students.

Task 5

Set the Text Analysis tasks in class or for homework.

Suggested Language Focus		
Prepositions	across the battlefield	from knots & lashings to building construction techniques
	routes through minefields	
	Behind the front lines	clearance of explosive devices
	in areas like water production	proficient in

Collocations		
	combat engineers	electrical supply
	basic combat training	infrastructure reconstruction
	specialised training	basic demolitions
	wet gap crossing operations,	basic explosive hazards
	building roads	constructing wire obstacles
	the front lines	fixed bridge building
	transport routes	basic urban operations
	construct camps and bases	operating heavy equipment
	temporary airstrips	basic field engineering
	clear mines	force protection
	conduct bomb disposal	protective structures
	post-conflict reconstruction phase	defensive obstacles
	humanitarian support	entrenching tools
	water production	bridging equipment
	destroying fighting positions and fortifications	
	clearing terrain obstacles and routes through minefields	

Task 6

Tell the students to listen to the text to decide which words they need to practice saying. This can be done as homework.

Task 7

Tell students they will listen to a talk. Tell them to make notes under two headings: Training and Skills. After the listening – check as a class. Then check with T33.1

Key	
Training	9 weeks BCT; 6 weeks AIT
Skills	Using engineer tools and vehicle operations; mine and countermine operations; basic combat construction; demolitions; fixed bridging and river crossing operations; constructing fighting positions; building bridges; preparing obstacles and defensive positions; place and detonate explosives; clear routes; destroy enemy fortifications; spot mines; use mine detectors.

Task 8

Consolidation Tasks in Workbook.

Don't forget:
1. Spelling Challenge: World Cities to practice the NATO Alphabet.
2. Test the students on telling the time using the 24 hour clock, and using numbers, and DTG.

About the Unit

This unit is about personal weapons. Grammar: Present Simple and Present Perfect.

Task 1

Tell students to look at P32.1 and P32.2 and write down the parts of a pistol and rifle. Check with P32.3 and P32.4. Also look at P32.5

Note: Cover up T3 before doing T2.

Task 2

Ask students if they know which personal weapons the British, US and Swiss army use.

Task 3

Students read the text to find out if they were correct. Class check.

Check any other unknown words or phrases afterwards. Choose at least one verb phrase, noun phrase and prepositional phrase from the text to explore with the students.

Task 4

Set the Text Analysis tasks in class or for homework.

Suggested Language Focus		
Word Order	The SA80 A2 L85 IW has been the standard issue service rifle of the British Armed Forces since 1987	
Noun Phrases	an air-cooled, gas-operated, magazine-fed carbine a 30 round magazine a barrel length of 370 mm standard iron sights standard issue service rifle of the **British Armed Forces** the standard 5.56 mm NATO round full 30 round magazine the standard magazine capacity a grenade launcher standard dioptric sights	
Prepositions	chambered for of about 500 m behind the trigger up to 400 m fitted with a grenade launcher	chambered in without the magazine set on muzzle velocity of 911 m/s effective range of 600 m

Collocations	telescoping stock	service rifle
	standard iron sights	standard magazine capacity
	cyclic rate of fire	Picatinny rail
	a grenade launcher	

Task 5

Tell the students to listen to the text to decide which words they need to practice saying. This can be done as homework.

Task 6

Focus on the words in the box and elicit the meanings. Then ask the students to complete the text. Ask them to check with their partner before the class check. They should use the text in T3 to help them.

Key	The American M4 carbine is [1] **lighter** than the British SL85 IW at 3.4 kg [2] **compared** to 5 kg. They [3] **both** use a standard 30 round magazine in the NATO 5.56 calibre. The M4 has a slightly [4] **lower** muzzle velocity (880 m/s) than the SL85 IW (940 m/s) but a 100 m [5] **longer** effective range even though the M4 barrel is much [6] **shorter** (370 mm) than the SL85 IW (518 mm) . The M4's rate of fire is [7] **higher** (700–950 round/min) than the SL85 IW (610 to 775 rounds per minute). The bullpup design of the SL85 IW makes it [8] **shorter** (780 mm) than the M4 with the stock extended (840 mm).

Task 7

Ask the students to work in groups and prepare a briefing for you on the personal weapons their army uses.. One students in the group will give the briefing. Prepare feedback notes for the group.

Task 8

Ask the students to write texts about one or more of the weapons or write texts comparing two or more of the weapons and their army's individual weapons, using the Fact Files. Collect the writing, mark and return the next unit. This could be done as homework or in class depending on the time available.

Task 9

Ask the students to work alone and prepare a briefing based on the Fact Files. This is a repeat of Task 8 but using spoken language rather than written, and a repeat of Task 7 but for different weapons. If you have a large class put the students into groups for the presentations. This could be done as a revision task after Task 8 in a sub-sequent lesson.

Task 10

Consolidation Tasks in Workbook.

Extra Task: Use P34.6 and P34.7 for extra writing practice about weapons.

About the Unit

This unit focuses on types of film, describing the plot and giving your opinion about the film. Grammar: Present Simple/Past Active/Passive. It is a long unit so you might want to split it or omit some sections, depending on how important the topic is for your students.

Task 1

Ask students to discuss the questions in pairs and then report on what their partner said.

Task 2

Check the types of film in table and then ask students to match the types of film with the synopses below.

Key		
	A: science fiction (Aliens 2)	E: Children's/cartoon (The Jungle Book)
	B: war (Black Hawk Down)	E: fantasy (Lord of the Rings)
	C: thriller/action (Die Hard)	G: horror (The Evil Dead)
	D: gangster (The Godfather 1)	H: western (The Searchers)

Task 3

Ask the grammar question: **Key:** present tenses are used in the synopses to make the story more immediate.

Check any other unknown words or phrases afterwards. Choose at least one verb phrase, noun phrase and prepositional phrase from the text to explore with the students.

Task 4

Ask the students to read the review and check they know the words in bold, then answer the questions.

Key	
	1. Mario Puzo
	2. Al Pacino; Robert De Niro; Robert Duvall; Diane Keaton
	3. Gangster film (deduced, as second part of gangster film mentioned in T2)
	4. Six Oscars

Task 5

Check the meaning of the words in the table. Ask the students to decide if they are positive or negative.

Key	Positive		
		gripping	fantastic
		entertaining	enjoyable
		a moving performance	funny
		beautiful	powerful
		exciting	

Negative	terrible	unbelievable
	awful	a waste of time and money
	violent	appalling
	laughable	the worst performance ever
	incomprehensible	nonsensical
	a let down	badly/well written
	disappointing	rubbish
	boring	plot hole

Task 6

Ask the students to complete the sentences with words from **Task 5.**

Key	
	1. It was very <u>badly</u> written. The plot was full of <u>holes</u>. I didn't understand it - it was completely <u>incomprehensible</u>.
	2. I had great expectations for the film but it was very <u>disappointing/boring/ badly written</u> and a complete waste of <u>time</u> and <u>money</u>. I felt really let <u>down</u>.
	3. It was really <u>violent</u> – hundreds of people were killed by the hero. Even though a lot of the stunts were completely <u>unbelievable</u> I loved it – it was <u>fantastic</u>.
	4. She gave a really <u>moving</u> performance. It was such a <u>beautiful</u> and romantic story. I cried at the end.
	5. I laughed all the way through the film. It was really <u>enjoyable/funny</u> and <u>funny/enjoyable</u>. I really recommend you go and see it.
	6. I didn't know what was going to happen next. It was really exciting and <u>gripping</u>. I was really surprised at the ending.

Task 7

Tell the students to write a review of their favourite film using the frame given and words from the unit. Collect the writing to mark and return with comments/corrections next unit. More advanced students could also be asked to write about the worst film they have ever seen.

Task 8

Ask students to make brief notes and then tell the class (or group) about the worst film they have ever seen. This could be set as a homework task.

Task 9

Consolidation Tasks in Workbook.

Don't forget:

1. Spelling Challenge: World Cities to practice the NATO Alphabet.

2. Test the students on telling the time using the 24 hour clock, and using numbers, and DTG.

About the Unit

This unit focuses on army air power and co-ordination with a Forward Air Controller (FAC); Grammar: Present Simple, Modals

Task 1

Ask the students to look at P36.1 and P36.2 and describe what they can see and talk about the connection between the two pictures.

Task 2

Ask the students to answer the questions by reading the text. Check they understand the questions before reading.

Key		
	1.	How can air power be used to support army operations? Transport troops, insert special ops forces behind enemy lines, CASEVAC, for reconnaissance and for close air support (CAS)
	2.	What are "assets"? Planes
	3.	What kind of aircraft can be used? Helicopters, ground attack aircraft, High-altitude bombers
	4.	What is a FAC? Forward Air Controllers
	5.	What three things does a FAC have to do? The FAC directs air power to attack enemy targets, tries to avoid friendly fire incidents and makes sure that non-combatants are not targeted.
	6.	What are the components of a US Army Division? e.g. three brigade combat teams (BCTs), a combat aviation brigade (CAB), a division artillery brigade, and a sustainment brigade,
	7.	How many helicopters are there in a US Army full spectrum combat aviation brigade? $(3 \times 8) + (3 \times 7) + (3 \times 10) + (4 + 4) + (3 \times 4) + (5 \times 3) = 118$

Check any other unknown words or phrases afterwards. Choose at least one verb phrase, noun phrase and prepositional phrase from the text to explore with the students.

Task 3

Set the Text Analysis tasks in class or for homework.

Suggested Language Focus	
Word Order	CAS is action by aircraft against targets in close proximity to friendly forces on the front line

Prepositions	close proximity to friendly forces	takes care of divisional support and logistics
	on the front line	a variety of missions
	used for	in an Attack Reconnaissance Battalion
	different kinds of	in an Attack Reconnaissance Squadron
	transport troops to and from the battlefield	in a Command Aviation Company
	for reconnaissance	in a Heavy Helicopter Company
	for close air support	in an Air Ambulance Medical Company
	call in air strikes	for reconnaissance
	organised into	
Collocations	air power	on the front line
	army missions	Forward Edge of the Battle Area
	transport troops	enemy targets
	special ops forces	friendly fire incidents
	behind enemy lines	full spectrum combat aviation brigade
	special army units	Attack helicopters
	air force assets	Attack Reconnaissance Battalion
	army aviation	Reconnaissance helicopters
	fixed wing aircraft	Attack Reconnaissance Squadron
	ground attack aircraft	Medium-lift helicopters
	High-altitude bombers	Command Aviation Company
	GPS guided weapons	Heavy-lift helicopters
	close proximity to friendly forces	Heavy Helicopter Company

Task 4

Tell the students to listen to the text to decide which words they need to practice saying. This can be done as homework.

Task 5

Tell students they will listen to a talk about an aircraft. Tell them to make notes about the 4 bullet points. After the listening – check as a class. Then check with T36.1

Key	
Name of aircraft:	A10 Thunderbolt II
Weapons carried:	30 mm rotary cannon; AGM-65 Maverick missiles, cluster bombs and hydra rocket pods; 2 sidewinder missiles
Special features:	Short take off and landing; easy to maintain
Performance:	700 kph; 9000 m ceiling; 900 km range.

Task **6** and **7** are linked. In **Task 6** tell the students to write a text based on one of the Fact Files listed. Then they should give a briefing based on one of the Fact Files. This could be done in groups or as a class, or set for individual homework.

Task 8: Consolidation Tasks in Workbook.

Don't forget:

1. Spelling Challenge: World Cities to practice the NATO Alphabet.

2. Test the students on telling the time using the 24 hour clock, and using numbers, and DTG.

Unit 37

About the Unit

This is the first unit on sport (the second is **Unit 40**). The focus here is vocabulary to do with sport. Grammar: Present Simple.

Task 1

Tell the students to look at P37.1 and describe what they can see.

Task 2

Ask students to discuss the questions in pairs and then report.

Task 3 – 5 follow the same pattern. Check the vocabulary in the tables and then ask students to complete the texts with the words given.

T3 Key   There are many different ways of [1] **classifying** sports. There are [2] **team** sports using a ball like football (or soccer), rugby, American football, field hockey. These are played on [3] **pitches** (football and rugby) or on fields (hockey and American football) and have goals at either end. The teams try to [4] **score** goals by putting the ball into the back of the net of the opposing goal (football and hockey), or score a touchdown (American football) or a try (rugby), and then converting a kick over the goal posts for further points (rugby), or [5] **kicking** the ball over the posts for a field goal. Other team sports with a ball also involve a [6] **bat** – like cricket and baseball. Cricket is played by two teams of 11 players on an oval pitch. Two [7] **batsmen** at a time go out to bat against the other team and try to score runs. A bowler bowls at one batsman, who tries to hit the ball away from the wicket. Each batsman has to safely run from one wicket to another to score one run. Baseball is played on a diamond with one [8] **batter** facing the opposing team and trying to make a home run around the four bases. Other ball sports are played on [9] **courts** with nets (like tennis, badminton and volleyball) or with baskets (basketball) or in a walled court (like squash). Tennis, badminton and squash (played with [10] **racquets)** and can be an [11] **individual** sport or played with a partner in [12] **doubles**. Volleyball and basketball are team sports.

T4 Key	Track and field sports (athletics) include running various [1] **distances** around a stadium track (like the 100 m sprint and 400 m races), or longer distance [2] **road** races like the 26 mile marathon. In the field [3] **enclosed** by the track there are places for [4] **events** like the shot put, javelin, pole vault, long and high jump. A triathlon involves running, swimming and cycling; a pentathlon has [5] **competitions** in shooting, swimming, fencing, equestrianism, and cross country running. The decathlon takes place [6] **over** two days and [7] **combines** ten track and field events. Day 1 [8] **consists** of the 100 m sprint; long jump; shot put; high jump and 400 m race. Day 2 includes the 110 m hurdles, discus throw, pole vault, javelin throw and 1500 m race.

T5 Key	Water sports include swimming, water polo, rowing, canoeing and kayaking and sailing. There are [1] **strength** sports like weight [2] **lifting** and [3] **endurance** sports like cycle road races like the Tour de France and ultra running competitions. Some sports use [4] **powered** machines, like in motor racing – motorcars (like Formula 1 and NASCAR) and motorcycles – and in yachting – like the America's Cup. [5] **Indoor** sports include swimming, gymnastics and ice-hockey and squash and badminton already mentioned before. Football can also be played inside in its five-a-side [6] **variant**. Most [7] **martial** arts competitions are held inside, like boxing, wrestling, karate, kung-fu, aikido, fencing, judo for example, though archery and pistol and rifle [8] **shooting** events can be done outside.

Task 6

Tell the students to listen to the texts to decide which words they need to practice saying. This can be done as homework.

Task 7

Ask students to discuss the questions in pairs and then report.

Task 8

Consolidation Tasks in Workbook.

Unit 38

About the Unit

This unit is about firing ranges and range safety. Grammar: Present Simple and Modal Verbs

Task 1

Tell the students to look at P36.1 and P36.2 and describe what they can see.

Task 2

Ask students to discuss the questions in pairs and then report. Correct their language but unless you are 100% sure about something do not challenge their answers.

Task 3

Tell the students to order the range rules into a logical order. The first one is done for them.

Key	**General range safety rules – Suggested Order**

Always wear eye and ear protection.

Never eat, drink or smoke on the firing line.

Obey the range officer at all times.

Know how the firearm operates.

Be sure the firearm and ammunition are compatible.

Only use one calibre of ammunition when shooting at one time. If you are using different firearms with different calibres, use one at a time and pack that firearm and ammunition away before using the next one.

Always keep firearms pointed in a safe direction i.e. away from people and at the target backstop or bullet trap down range.

Only shooters are permitted on the firing line.

Always keep your gun unloaded until you are in a position on the firing line and and the range has been cleared for live firing: the range is declared "hot."

When the range is "hot" all shooters must check with others to ensure there is no one down range.

Always keep your finger off the trigger and outside the trigger guard, until ready to fire or until you hear the command "commence firing".

Be sure of the target and what is beyond it before you start shooting.

All shooters are responsible for their rounds staying within the confines of the range.

Only shoot at the target in line with your position on the firing line.

Shooters may only move safe guns to and from the firing line when the range is "hot."

Immediately stop shooting when anyone calls "cease firing."

Cold range: you must check with others to ensure firearms are unloaded, actions open and firearms laid down on the shooting bench (they are "benched") before going down range. No one is permitted to handle firearms or stand at the firing line while there is a cold range for any reason.

You should wash your hands and face after shooting.

Check any other unknown words or phrases afterwards. Choose at least one verb phrase, noun phrase and prepositional phrase from the text to explore with the students.

Task 4

Check the students understand and can explain the terms in the table.

Task 5

Ask students to discuss the questions in pairs and then report.

Task 6

Check the words in the table and then ask the students to complete the text with these words.

After learning how to disassemble, clean, and [1] **reassemble** your weapon, as well as safe handling and [2] **malfunction** procedures you will learn and practice the four [3] **fundamentals** of Army marksmanship. The steady position teaches you how to correctly [4] **grip** and handle your weapon during different firing and non-firing [5] **stances**. The aiming fundamental includes correct [6] **sight** alignment and proper eye focus: you should focus on the front sight with the target blurry, and take into account factors like distance and the wind (shown by flags on the range). You must know and practice proper breath [7] **control** to hold your breath for a natural pause. When you fire a weapon you gently [8] **squeeze** the trigger rather than pulling it. The US Army Marksmanship Qualification Course has 40 [9] **pop-up** targets set up from 50 meters to 300 meters that you must [10] **engage** in the order they show. There are 20 targets prone [11] **supported**, 10 targets prone unsupported, and 10 targets kneeling. At some points multiple targets will show at the same time and you have to engage both targets before they drop. You have forty [12] **rounds** for the forty targets. Hitting 23 to 29 of the targets will earn you the the marksmanship [13] **qualification**. If you hit 30 to 35, you will qualify for the sharpshooter badge but to get an [14] **expert** badge, you must hit 36 to 40 of the targets.

Check to see of their army requirements are similar. Check any other unknown words or phrases afterwards. Choose at least one verb phrase, noun phrase and prepositional phrase from the text to explore with the students.

Task 7

Ask the students to work in groups and draw up a firearms training plan. Students should present their plan to the class.

Task 8

Consolidation Tasks in Workbook.

Don't forget:

1. Spelling Challenge: World Cities to practice the NATO Alphabet.

2. Test the students on telling the time using the 24 hour clock, and using numbers, and DTG.

Unit 39

About the Unit

This unit focuses on intelligence; Present Simple, Modal Verbs, Past Tenses and Active and Passive

Task 1

Tell the students to look at P39.1 – P39.4 and describe what they can see.

Task 2

Ask the students to discuss the questions in pairs and then report. Don't comment on their ideas as they will read the text to check in T3.

Task 3

Ask the students to read the text and see if their answers to the T2 questions were correct.

Task 4

Ask the students to read the text again and answer the questions underneath it.

Key		
	1.	They collect information and analyse it.
	2.	No.
	3.	Human intelligence
	4.	Image intelligence
	5.	Signal intelligence
	6.	Intelligence, surveillance, reconnaissance
	7.	Intelligence
	8.	Enemy, friendly and neutral actors' courses of action
	9.	To assess how useful it is.
	10.	Strategic: whole country capabilities etc; Operational: for the force commander on ops; Tactical: for patrols

Check any other unknown words or phrases afterwards. Choose at least one verb phrase, noun phrase and prepositional phrase from the text to explore with the students.**Task 5**

Set the Text Analysis tasks in class or for homework.

Suggested Language Focus		
Prepositions	from a range of sources	of the opposition
	analysis of photographs	changes in enemy capabilities
	analysis of information	associated with
	from spies	courses of action
	from voice and data transmissions	reliability of raw intelligence
	reports from the front line	an assessment of
	information from	briefing patrols on the current situation
	advice to commanders	debrief patrols after operations

Collocations	military intelligence officers	intelligence operations
	situational awareness	enemy capabilities
	intelligence systems	assess risks
	a range of sources	neutralize intelligence threats
	reconnaissance flights	courses of action
	reconnaissance patrols	raw intelligence
	Imagery Intelligence	Strategic intelligence
	Human intelligence	Operational intelligence
	Signals intelligence	Tactical intelligence
	intelligence "product"	force commander
	All-Source Intelligence specialist	political assessment
	Counter-intelligence	

Task 6

Tell the students to listen to the text to decide which words they need to practice saying. This can be done as homework.

Task 7

Tell students they will listen to a talk. Tell them to make notes under two headings: facts and opinions. After the listening – check as a class.

Key	
Fact:	Very important role to play; don't have a good reputation; never be 100% certainty; self-discipline; confident; intelligent; physically and mentally fit to perform under pressure; make quick decisions.
Opinion:	In my opinion, the main requirement is saying what you don't know when you don't know.

Task 8

Ask students to complete the extract from the transcript with verbs, then listen to check. They can check with the transcript T39.1.

Task 9

Ask the students to work in groups and imagine they are a company sized force on the front lines in a mountainous area of their country during a war with an enemy country. Ask them to discuss the question: What intelligence do you need before you launch your next attack? Then they should brief the class on their requirements. What do they want to know?

Task 10

Consolidation Tasks in Workbook.

About the Unit

This is the second unit on sport and looks at winter and extreme sports, sporting organisations and competitions. The grammar focus is Present Simple, Active and Passive and Modal Verbs

Task 1

Ask students to discuss the questions in pairs and then report.

Tasks 2 – 4 follow the same pattern. Check the vocabulary in the tables and then ask students to complete the texts with the words given.

T2 Key	Winter sports include skiing (cross-country and downhill), ski-jumping, ice skating, snowboarding and the bobsled and luge. The winter [1] **Biathlon** combines cross-country skiing and [2] **rifle** shooting. Most winter sports are held outside and [3] **depend** on snow and [4] **cold** temperatures, except for ice-hockey and skating, which are held in ice arenas.

T3 Key	Extreme sports have a high level of [1] **inherent** danger and includes such sports as wakeboarding, waterskiing, gliding, rallying, motocross, surfing, windsurfing, kiteboarding, parachuting, skateboarding, mountain biking, as well as non-vehicle extreme sports like [2] **rock** climbing, canyoning, ice climbing, and parkour.
	Doping [3] **scandals** where athletes try to [4] **cheat** by taking performance enhancing [5] **drugs** regularly hit certain sports like cycling and athletics. The sports governing bodies try to [6] **catch** cheats by taking regular blood and urine [7] **samples** from athletes in training and during competitions.

T4 Key	Most organised sports have clubs and federations, who make the [1] **rules** for the sports and [2] **hold** competitions. Competitions can be local, regional, [3] **national** and international (like the European championships) as well as global – like the Olympics, Athletics World Championships and football World Cup. Clubs or individuals or teams take [4] **part** in the championships and there are usually [5] **stages** to the competition. There might be many heats for runners leading up to a [6] **final** for the fastest, or rounds of competition leading to quarter-finals, semi-finals and finally the final, as in football. Matches and competitions are controlled by [7] **referees** and linesmen (e.g. football), umpires (cricket), umpires and referees (tennis) and [8] **judges** (athletics). Teams and sportsmen and women compete to [9] **beat** the other team, player or athlete and [10] **win** the match, game, medal, trophy or competition. Professional teams and individual athletes have managers, coaches and [11] **physiotherapists** to help them train and perform better. Some athletes and teams turn in an [12] **outstanding** performance and win, while others are disappointing and [13] **lose** or are defeated. The winners have the satisfaction of [14] **winning** while

the losers have the satisfaction of [15] **playing** the game.

Task 5

Tell the students to listen to the texts to decide which words they need to practice saying. This can be done as homework.

Task 6

Tell the students to write about a sport and to include the information listed. This could be set for homework. Collect the writing and give feedback on it.

Task 7

Ask students to quiz each other about a sport they do and then report.

Task 8

Consolidation Tasks in Workbook.

> **Don't forget:**
>
> 1. Spelling Challenge: World Cities to practice the NATO Alphabet.
>
> 2. Test the students on telling the time using the 24 hour clock, and using numbers, and DTG.

Unit 41

About the Unit

This unit focuses on different aspects of civil affairs. The main focus is on peacekeeping civil affairs but the listening takes a slightly different view.

Before doing **Task 1** you could exploit the quotation. What other key roles are there? What is a 'toolkit'?

Task 1

Tell the students to look at P40.1 – P40.2 and describe what they can see.

Task 2

Ask the students to answer the questions. Elicit some of their ideas. As this is a pre-reading task do not comment on the quality of their answers.

Task 3

Tell the students to read the text to answer the questions in Task 2. Class check the answers.

Check any other unknown words or phrases afterwards. Choose at least one verb phrase, noun phrase and pre-positional phrase from the text to explore with the students.

Task 4

Set the Text Analysis tasks in class or for homework.

Suggested Language Focus		
Noun Phrases	the core functions of multidimensional UN peacekeeping operations	
	the protection of civilians	
Prepositions	for the first time	a range of activities
	for civil affairs	aimed at
	in UN peacekeeping	in the peace process
	at the local level	facilitating dialogue between interest groups
	of state authority	working with civil society
	liaise with	in close coordination with other partners
	on behalf of	build on
	coordinate with	In each of the roles they perform
	on the ground	contributing to
Collocations	Policy Directive	civic conditions
	Civil Affairs	gather information
	operation context	a range of activities
	local level	facilitating dialogue
	conflict management	direct outreach
	state authority	state authority
	local communities	administrative functions
	monitor the situation	close coordination
	conduct analysis	

Task 5

Tell the students to listen to the text to decide which words they need to practice saying. This can be done as homework.

Task 6

Tell the students to complete the collocations from the text without looking at the text. They can check with the text.

Task 7

Tell students they will listen to a talk. Tell them to make notes under two headings: facts and opinions. After the listening – check as a class. Then check with T41.1.

Key	Fact: 3 sections of goals: pre-engagement; during ops; post-war. 1. Provide commanders with information about civilians in the AO 2. Minimise civilian casualties 3. Securing the peace through peacekeeping, hearts and minds, reconstruction and re-education programmes Opinion: No opinion; all presented as fact.

Task 8

Consolidation Tasks in Workbook.

Don't forget:

1. Spelling Challenge: World Cities to practice the NATO Alphabet.

2. Test the students on telling the time using the 24 hour clock, and using numbers, and DTG.

Unit 42

About the Unit

This is the first of two units on Special Forces. The second unit is **Unit 44**. The grammar focus is on past tenses and passive verb forms.

Task 1

Tell the students to look at P42.1 – P42.4 and describe what they can see.

Task 2

Check the words in the table and then tell students to complete the paragraph.

Key	Special Forces and Special Operations Forces are units trained to perform [1] **unconventional** missions like airborne operations, counter-**[2] insurgency**, [3] **counter**-terrorism, [4] **covert** operations, [5] **hostage** rescue, intelligence operations, and sabotage and [6] **demolition**, support of air-force operations.

Task 3

Tell the students to read the text to answer the questions. You could ask them to try to answer the questions first before reading the text.

Key		
	1.	Who first asked for Special Forces? Winston Churchill.
	2.	What was the first unit formed? Commandos/Special Service Brigade
	3.	How many soldiers were in each Commando? 450 men in 75 man troops/ 15 man sections each
	4.	Where were the Commandos trained? In Scotland
	5.	Are the Commando's Special Forces? No, they are are considered to be special-purpose infantry units

Task 4

Tell the students to read the text to answer the questions. Again, you could ask them to try to answer the questions first before reading the text.

Key		
	1.	Whose idea was it to form the Special Air Service? David Stirling's
	2.	Where did they first operate? In North Africa.
	3.	Was the unit successful? Not at first. The first operation was a disaster.
	4.	What were the Chindits? Long range penetration groups operating from bases deep behind Japanese lines in Burma.
	5.	Where did the Americans get the idea for Special Forces? From the British Commandos and Chindits
	6.	Who controls US Special Forces? United States Army Special Operations Command.

Check any other unknown words or phrases afterwards. Choose at least one verb phrase, noun phrase and prepositional phrase from the text to explore with the students.

Task 5

Set the Text Analysis tasks in class or for homework.

Suggested Language Focus		
Prepositions	date from 1940 took place on 23 June 1940 in the mountains of Scotland learn about in World War 2	by men behind German and Italian lines suggest to modelled on took part in
Collocations	Special Forces Commando raid physically fit live fire exercises land navigation unarmed combat small boat operations	river crossings special-purpose infantry units theatre commander better results long range penetration groups jungle warfare expertise similar operations

Task 6

Tell the students to listen to the texts to decide which words they need to practice saying. This can be done as homework.

Task 7

Tell students they will listen to a talk. Tell them to make notes under two headings: facts and opinions. After the listening – check as a class. Then check with T42.1.

Before the listening you could suggest that they listen for unit names and the numbers of personnel in the unit formations; other key facts are the missions undertaken by the different units.

Key Fact:	US Navy SEALS; 9 teams x 300 men; 8 platoons and support staff in a team. Small unit mil operations. DEVGRU: counter-terrorism Marine Raider Regiment: 3 battalions; each battalion: 3 companies; each company: 4 x 14 marine special ops teams. US Army: Rangers and Green Berets. 75th Ranger Regiment; light infantry; direct action raids; 4 battalions; 3600 personnel Green Berets: 5 primary missions; seven Special Forces groups; 4 battalions each; three companies in each battalion. Each company 6 ODAs (12 men in each).
Opinion:	Interesting but complex area; lot of confusion; most famous – SEALs and Delta Force

Task 8

Ask students to discuss the questions in pairs and then report.

Task 9

Consolidation Tasks in Workbook.

Don't forget:
1. Spelling Challenge: World Cities to practice the NATO Alphabet. 2. Test the students on telling the time using the 24 hour clock, and using numbers, and DTG.

Unit 43

About the Unit

This unit focuses on describing clothes, and what people carry e.g. suitcases etc..

This unit looks at a lot of vocabulary but your students should be familiar with some of it and there are a lot of photographs to support the students.

Task 1

Tell the students to look at P43.1 and describe what they can see.

Task 2

Ask the students to look at the words in the table and mark which ones they do not know and then to check with the pictures indicated. Clear up any questions about these words, and check the pronunciation.

Task 3

Ask students to discuss the differences between the words in the table and clear up any problems.

Task 4

Check the meaning of the words and the pronunciation. Use the pictures to help.

Task 5

Ask the students to discuss the questions in pairs and report to the class.

Task 6

Check the meaning of the words and the pronunciation. Use the pictures to help. Ask for ideas for the question below the table.

Task 7

Check the meaning of the words and the pronunciation. Use the pictures to help.

Task 8

Check the meaning of the words and the pronunciation. Use the pictures to help. Discuss the questions below the table.

Task 9

Check the meaning of the words and the pronunciation. Use the pictures to help.

Discuss the questions below the table.

Task 10

Check the meaning of the words and the pronunciation. Use the pictures to help. Then discuss the differences between the words.

Task 11

Check the meaning of the words and the pronunciation. Use the pictures to help.

Discuss the questions below the table.

Task 12

This task is about clothing which might not have been dealt with above. The students are provided with a frame to help them.

Task 13

This is a practice task. There are a number of photos (43.42 – P43.58). Assign a photograph to a student and ask them to describe what they are wearing (from this unit) but also what they look like, which is revision of a **Unit 12**.

You could change this into a speaking task, or add a speaking task after the writing task, by asking to students to mingle and go around with the photograph on their phone and introduce the person(s) in the picture to people as a member of their family. They should not only describe the person in the photograph but also talk about their relationship to that person, and that person's hobbies and interests.

Or you might want to display the descriptions and ask the students to go around, read the texts and identify which person is being described from the set of photos.

Don't forget:

1. Spelling Challenge: World Cities to practice the NATO Alphabet.

2. Test the students on telling the time using the 24 hour clock, and using numbers, and DTG.

Unit 44

About the Unit

This is the second unit on Special Forces. The grammar focus is on **present** and **past tenses** and **passive verb forms**, with the addition of some work on **prepositions.**

Task 1

Tell the students to look at P44.1 and P44.2 and describe what they can see.

Task 2

Ask the students to work together and then report what they can remember about Special Forces from **Unit 42**.

Task 3

Check the words in the table and then tell students to complete the paragraph.

Key	Special operations are defined as "Special operations are military activities [1] **conducted** by specially designated, organized, trained, and equipped forces, [2] **manned** with selected personnel, using [3] **unconventional** tactics, techniques, and modes of employment. These activities may be [4] **conduc-ted** across the full range of military operations, independently or with [5] **conventional** forces, to help achieve the desired end-state. Politico-military considerations may require [6] **clandestine** or covert techniques and the acceptance of a degree of political or military [7] **risk** not associated with operations by [8] **conventional** forces. Special Operations deliver [9] **strategic** or operational-level results or are executed where significant political [10] **risk** exists.'

Task 4

Check the prepositions in the table and then tell students to complete the paragraph.

Key	
Famous operations and campaigns [1] **by** Special Forces include the successful anti-communist counter insurgency [2] **in** Malaya (mentioned above), Operation Entebbe – the hostage-rescue mission carried [3] **out** [4] **by** Israeli commandos [5] **at** Entebbe Airport **[6] in** Uganda [7] **on** 4 July 1976, the storming [8] **of** the Iranian Embassy [9] **by** the SAS during the Embassy siege (30 April [10] **to** 5 May 1980), the SAS Bravo Two Zero patrol [11] **in** the 1st Gulf War, the campaign [12] **by** US Special Forces [13] **in** the 2001 war [14] **in** Afghanistan, the SEAL raid to kill Osama bin Laden [15] **in** Abbottabad [16] **in** Pakistan [17] **on** May 2, 2011, and the SEAL rescue [18] **of** Captain Phillips [19] **during** the *Maersk Alabama* hijacking [20] **on**12 April 2009.	

Task 5

Tell the students they will hear a talk about two Special Forces operations and they should make notes about the facts and the speaker's opinion. You could do the listening in two parts in different units.

Key	
Operation 1	Second Gulf War in March 2003, a British Squadron of 60 Special Boat Service and Special Air Service men was sent into northern Iraq. Their mission was to find the Iraqi 5th Army Corps and accept their surrender. Intelligence said that this army did not want to fight and would surrender to the first British or American soldiers who turned up. These sixty men were sent to Iraq to find the 5th Army and make contact and then accept their surrender. Intelligence did not know where the 5th Army was exactly or if they really wanted to surrender but the squadron was sent anyway. They were airlifted into Iraq with their vehicles and then they set off in search of the 5th Army. This was a colossal intelligence failure. Commanders wanted to believe the 5th Army did not want to fight. In fact they did want to fight and the squadron was chased all over northern Iraq before it could be extracted.
Operation 2	The second Special Forces raid was a bit more successful. On the second of May, 2011, at 01:00 Pakistan Standard Time US Special Forces Seal Team Six raided a compound in Abbottabad. This was called Operation Neptune's Spear. The compound contained a large three-storey house and it was surrounded by 4 - 5 m high walls topped with barbed wire. There were two security gates in the wall and there was no Internet or telephone service going into or out of the compound. The compound was located about a kilometre south-west of the Pakistan Military Academy. The 40-minute raid resulted in the death of Osama bin Laden and the seizure of masses of intelligence materials. One of the helicopters crashed but none of the soldiers were killed in the operation.
Opinion:	Op 1: The amazing thing is that they did not lose a man. So, the mission was a failure because the intelligence was wrong. The escape itself was a great success – the unit didn't lose a man and were rescued. The mission itself was a failure. Op 2: But there were two failures in this operation. The first was that a very special helicopter was lost. It crashed during the raid and who knows who got pieces of it. The helicopter was not destroyed in an air strike and it should have been. There should have been a

Predator drone on station with Hellfire missiles and the helicopter should have been hit by missiles to destroy it.

The other big failure was another intelligence failure. A large volume of documents and computer hard drives were recovered from the building but these were not analysed properly and their value was destroyed because President Obama talked about the raid on TV the next day. You <u>never</u> talk about Special Ops raids. You certainly don't do it the very next day. Thirty years later, then maybe you can talk about it. This was another clear and avoidable failure.

Don't forget:

1. Spelling Challenge: World Cities to practice the NATO Alphabet.

2. Test the students on telling the time using the 24 hour clock, and using numbers, and DTG.

Unit 45

About the Unit

This unit is about infantry Fighting Vehicles (IFVs) of different types and is a follow up to **Unit 18 Mechanised Infantry**.

Task 1

Tell the students to look at P45.1 and describe what they can see.

Task 2

Ask the students to answer the questions. Elicit some of their ideas. As this is a pre-reading task do not comment on the quality of their answers.

Task 3

Tell the students to read the text and answer the Task 2 questions. Class check. You might want to deal with some new vocabulary here or leave it until after **Task 4**.

Key	1.	Armoured fighting vehicle; carry infantry squad; at least 20mm cannon.
	2.	An improvised IFV using a modified civilian vehicle

Task 4

Tell the students to read the text again and answer the questions. Deal with new vocabulary here if you did not do it in **Task 3**.

Key	1.	20-40 mm canon; machine guns; ATGMs; smoke and grenade launchers
	2.	unarmoured and lightly armoured vehicles, strong points, infantry, helicopters and low-flying aircraft.
	3.	'They give a squad the ability to manoeuvre more effectively as part of combined arms operations. IFVs transport infantrymen to the fight where they dismount and fight with the support of the IFV cannon and other weapons.'
	4.	' provide speed and mobility for light troop deployment and a degree of fire support, as well as prestige for the users'
	5.	Technicals have tittle no armour; not as tough; less firepower

Check any other unknown words or phrases afterwards. Choose at least one verb phrase, noun phrase and prepositional phrase from the text to explore with the students.

Task 5

Set the Text Analysis tasks in class or for homework.

Suggested Language Focus		
Prepositions	into battle	compromise between mobility, protection,
	from inside	and firepower
	as part of	useful in low intensity conflicts
	transport infantrymen to the fight	by modifying a civilian vehicle
	fight with the support of	on the back of the vehicle
	armed with	a degree of fire support
	armour of various thicknesses	vulnerable to
Collocations	armoured fighting vehicle	low intensity conflicts
	combat infantry squad	peacekeeping operations
	personal weapons	fighting vehicle
	fire support	civilian vehicle
	combined arms operations	support weapon
	modular armour	light troop deployment
	lightly armoured vehicles	air strikes
	strong points	armour protection
	low-flying aircraft	

Task 6

Tell the students to listen to the text to decide which words they need to practice saying. This can be done as homework.

Task 7

Tell the students that they will listen to descriptions of two IFVs and they have to complete the notes. The listening, like many, focuses on hearing and understanding numbers.

Key	
IFV 1	Name: ZBD-04 Weight: 20 tonnes Max speed: 65 km/h on roads Range: 500 km Armour protection: welded steel and applique armour Armament: a 100 mm rifled gun which can fire ATMs. It has a 30 mm autocannon and a 7.62 mm coaxial machine gun Other information: Chinese; fully tracked; designed 1990s; entered service in about 2004; about 7 metres long, almost 3 metres wide and 2.5 metres high; crew of three; 7 passengers
IFV 2	Name: Stridsfordon 90 Weight: 23 and 35 tonnes Max speed: 70 km/h Range: 320 km Armour protection: Ceramic applique armour; cage armour for protection against RPGs Armament: 40mm autocannon. Secondary armament is a 7.62 mm machine gun and it has 6 × 76 mm grenade launchers Other information: Swedish; fully tracked; entered service in 1993; 6.55 m long, 3 metres wide and 2.7 metres high; crew of three ; 8 soldiers

Task 8

Ask the students to discuss which of the IFVs from Task 7 is best and then report to the class. They should give reasons for their answer. Does everyone agree?

Task 9

Consolidation Tasks in Workbook.

Don't forget:

1. Spelling Challenge: World Cities to practice the NATO Alphabet.

2. Test the students on telling the time using the 24 hour clock, and using numbers, and DTG.

Unit 46

About the Unit

This unit is about giving directions in an urban environment – a key skill in urban warfare and peacekeeping ops. The grammar focus is on Present Simple, Present Continuous and modal verbs.

Task 1

Ask the students to look at P46.1 and discuss how to give direction from A to points B, C and D. Monitor and help as required. They can check with P46.2.

Task 2

Check/teach the words in the table.

Task 3

Talk the students through the diagram.

Task 4

Tell the students to look at the map on the next page and find A. They should listen and follow the route. Where do they end up? [Key: E]

Task 5

Check the meaning of the words in the table and ask the students to complete the text while using the map to follow the route.

Key	Start at I. Go [1] **out** of the house and [2] **turn** left down the street. You are heading SSE, almost south. [3] **Turn** left at the junction and head down to the main road. [4] **Turn** right there and [5] **follow** this road to the second [6] **turning** to the right. [7] **Turn** right here and walk [8] **down/along** this road, to the west, to the third [9] **turning** to the right. [10] **Take** the third [11] **turning** to the right and walk [12] **down/along** the road. There are two big buildings [13] **along** the right-[14] **hand** [15] **side** of the road. You want the smaller of these two buildings (Key = B).

Task 6

Tell the students to work in pairs. Each students should draw a route on the map without showing it to their partner. They should take it in turns to describe their route to their partner. They should listen to their partner's description and draw it on the map. Then they can compare. Change partners and practice again.

Don't forget:

1. Spelling Challenge: World Cities to practice the NATO Alphabet.

2. Test the students on telling the time using the 24 hour clock, and using numbers, and DTG.

Unit 47

About the Unit

This unit is about main battle tanks and is a follow-up to **Unit 25 Forces: Armour**

Task 1

Tell the students to look at P47.1 and describe what they can see.

Task 2

Check the meaning of the words in the table. You can use P47.2 and P47.3 to help the students.

Task 3

Tell the students to complete the text with words from Task 2 **and other words.**

Key	Most modern MBTs look very similar with two continuous linked [1] **tracks** on either side of the vehicle rather than wheels, and a [2] **turret** mounted main gun. The [3] **turret** turns on a [4] **ring** which gives it 360 degrees of traverse. The [5] **engine** compartment is usually at the rear of the tank [6] **hull**. Access to the tank is through [7] **hatches** which can be sealed and the tanks provide protection against NBC warfare. Driver, gunner and commander can see through [8] **periscopes** and a range of optical and thermal [9] **sights**. MBT performance is a compromise between the size of the main [10] **armament/gun**, the thickness of the [11] **armour** protection, and speed. The US Abrams, British Challenger 2 and Leopard 2 all have 120 mm main [12] **guns** but the British L30A1 is a rifled [13] **gun** with 49 [14] **rounds**, while both the German and US guns are smooth-bores with 42 [15] **rounds**. All of these tanks have turret mounted main [16] **armament/gun** and 2 (Leopard and Challenger) or three (Abrams) machine guns as [17] **secondary** armament. Most MBT have a [18] **coaxial** machine gun mounted next to the main gun which fires parallel to the main armament. The commander may have a [19] **machine gun** by his [20] **hatch**, or one mounted in a copula and this can be fired remotely. The Challenger 2 weighs 75 tonnes with add-on armour modules, which is [21] **heavier** than the Abrams (65 tonnes) and Leopard 2 (62.3 tonnes). The Leopard 2 emphasises [22] **speed** – 72 km/h – compared to the Challenger 2 (59 km/h) and Abrams (67 km/h). These three tanks all have a [23] **crew** of four (commander, gunner, loader, driver) though some MBTs such as the French AMX Leclerc and Russian T-14 Armata have a [24] **crew** of three and use an auto-loader. The Challenger and Leopard 2 both have an operational [25] **range** of 550 km compared to the Abrams' 426 km. Tank protection is in its [26] **armour**, which can be steel, composite ceramic and alloys, explosive reactive [27] **armour**, or slat [28] **armour**, and electronic countermeasures against missile attack. Most of the armour is concentrated at the front of the vehicle in a sloped glacis plate but the side and tracks can be protected by armoured [29] **skirts/side plates**.

Do a class check and deal with any new vocabulary (or leave until after **Task 4**).

Task 4

Tell the students to read the text again and answer the questions.

Key	1. Challenger is a rifled barrel; other two – smoothbore; all 120 mm
	2. Heaviest: Challenger 2 Lightest: Leopard 2
	3. Fastest: Leopard 2; Slowest: Challenger 2
	4. Longest: Challenger and Leopard 2; shortest: Abrams
	5. Leclerc and Armata

Check any other unknown words or phrases afterwards. Choose at least one verb phrase, noun phrase and prepositional phrase from the text to explore with the students.

Task 5

Tell the students to listen to the text to decide which words they need to practice saying. This can be done as homework.

Task 6

Tell the students that they will listen to descriptions of two MBTs and they have to complete the notes. This listening focuses on numbers.

Key	
MBT 1	Name: Type 99 Weight: 54 - 59 tonnes Max speed: 80 km/h on roads. About 60 km/h off road. Range: 500 km Armour protection: probably welded steel with appliqué and reactive armour Armament: 125 mm smoothbore gun; heavy machine gun and a 7.62 mm coaxial machine gun Other information: Chinese; in service in 2001; over 800 in service; crew of three
MBT 2	Name: Altay Weight: 65 tonnes Max speed: 70 km/h Range: 500 km Armour protection: composite armour Armament: 120 mm smoothbore gun. Secondary armament consists of one 12.7 mm stabilized remote controlled turret and one 12.7 mm coaxial heavy machine gun Other information: Turkish; 2018; 7.3 m long, 3.9 metres wide and 2.6 metres high; crew of four

Task 7

Ask the students to discuss which of the MBTs from T6 is best and then report to the class. They should give reasons for their answer. Does everyone agree?

Task 8

Consolidation Tasks in Workbook.

Don't forget:

1. Spelling Challenge: World Cities to practice the NATO Alphabet.

2. Test the students on telling the time using the 24 hour clock, and using numbers, and DTG.

Unit 48

About the Unit

This unit focuses on knives and other tools, and their uses.

Task 1

Ask students to discuss the questions in pairs and then report.

Task 2

Ask the students to look at the photos (P48.1 and P48.3) and label the parts of the two knives shown. Or you could bring in two knives of the type shown in the photos and elicit the parts of the knives. Check with P48.2-4.

Task 3

Ask students to discuss the questions in pairs and then report. These are opinion questions so there are no right answers. See if the class agrees.

Task 4

Tell the students to read the text and see if they agree with the writer. Class check of any disagreement.

Check any other unknown words or phrases afterwards. Choose at least one verb phrase, noun phrase and prepositional phrase from the text to explore with the students.

Task 5

Set the Text Analysis tasks in class or for homework.

Suggested Language Focus	
Word Order	The knife was one of the first tools invented by man.

Prepositions	to have on you	designed by
	at all times	made of
	attached to	in the handle
	used for	fold in the middle
	set in	folded back into the handle
	carried in	close suddenly on the user's fingers
	to protect	a multitude of
	all the way through the handle	in the field
	come in different shapes	on the main cutting edge
Collocations	useful thing	stabbing point
	at all times	main cutting edge
	traditional military knife	sheath knife
	everyday cutting jobs	full tang blade
	simplest knife	everyday tool
	good quality carbon or stainless steel	in the field
	keep an edge	

Task 6

Tell the students to listen to the text to decide which words they need to practice saying. This can be done as homework.

Task 7

Tell the students to listen to the man describing his knives and to look at P48.5. They should identify the knives he talks about. Then they should listen again and complete the table.

| **Picture Key** | Knife 1: E | Knife 3: B | Knife D is not described |
| | Knife 2: A | Knife 4: C | |

Key	Knife 1	Knife 2	Knife 3	Knife 4
Name	Marttiini Condor fisherman's knife	Arctic Circle knife	No name	Lynx
Description/ Features	a long thin stainless steel blade with a fish descaler on the reverse edge; handle is made of rubber	9 cms long carbon steel blade; curly birch	biggest knife in a way but it is not the longest. It has the shortest blade; The handle is longer than the blade; not a full tang knife	a curly birch handle; The stainless steel bade is 11 cm long and the knife is 22 cm

When does he use it?	For camping/ fishing	When camping	Doesn't say	Doesn't say
Opinion	a pretty good knife and does a good job of filleting the fish and other cutting jobs	a good general purpose knife; Small and handy and good with those magnesium fire starters	stainless steel blade is very thick and strong; the strongest one	I certainly don't need a bigger blade than this, but takes the Arctic Circle instead

Task 8

Ask the students to look at the photos of a multi-tool (P48.6) and check the tools (P48.7). Then they should discuss what each tool can be used for.

Task 9

Ask students to think about the different types of knives and multi-tools (and look at the pictures if necessary) and discuss the questions in pairs and then report. Use the Language Reminder as necessary. You might want to set this task as homework.

Task 10

Consolidation Tasks in Workbook.

Optional Task: You might want the students to bring in a favourite knife to the next unit and talk about it. This could be done as a mingling task.

Note: there are two extra test pictures you can use as revision in future lessons: P48.10 and P48.11.

Unit 49

About the Unit

This unit focuses on artillery – guns, howitzers and mortars – and the work of field artillery teams. The grammar focus is on the Present Simple and modal verbs

Task 1

Tell the students to look at P59.1/2 and describe what they can see.

Task 2

Check the parts of a mortar and field gun using the pictures.

Task 3

The reading is about different types of fire and the students should read the text and translate the terms in bold. Class check of the correct translations.

Task 4

Tell the students to read the text and make notes on the advantages and disadvantages of guns, howitzers and mortars.

Key	advantages	disadvantages
guns	direct fire; longer range than mortars	?
howitzers	Indirect fire ; longer range than mortars	?
mortars	Man-portable; effective from concealed positions	Has to be carried

Check any other unknown words or phrases afterwards. Choose at least one verb phrase, noun phrase and prepositional phrase from the text to explore with the students.

Task 5

Set the Text Analysis tasks in class or for homework.

Suggested Language Focus		
Prepositions	classes of weapons used for fired at a high angle degree of armoured protection consisting of placed as a static part of fortifications provide infantry units with their own artillery set at an angle of between 45 and 85 degrees	to the ground by the gunner used for targets close by from concealed positions disadvantage of mortar use
Collocations	a lower elevation direct fire indirect fire. static part towed gun move around the battlefield armoured protection	a steel tube mortar tube assistant gunner man-portable infantry units concealed positions highly effective

Task 6

Tell the students to listen to the texts to decide which words they need to practice saying. This can be done as homework.

Task 7

Ask the students to listen to the talk about a field artillery team and then describe the diagram. They can explain to their partner before explaining to the class. Being able to describe the diagram is a check of their listening comprehension.

Task 8

Ask the students to brief you on what artillery the students' army uses.

Task 9

Consolidation Tasks in Workbook.

Extra Task: You could ask the students to write a text comparing the performance and use of artillery weapons systems, using the data from P49.7 and P49.8.

Don't forget:

1. Spelling Challenge: World Cities to practice the NATO Alphabet.

2. Test the students on telling the time using the 24 hour clock, and using numbers, and DTG.

Unit 50

About the Unit

This unit focuses on helicopters. The grammar focus is on the Present Simple, modals (can) and comparatives.

Task 1

Tell the students to look at P50.1 and describe what they can see.

Task 2

Check the words in the table, using the pictures (P50.2 – P50.5) to help.

Task 3

Tell the students to read the text and answer the questions.

Key	
1.	Chinook – 33 – 55 troops
2.	Chinook – trick question as it is a transport helicopter.
3.	Black Hawk, Apache and Kiowa
4.	All.
5.	Apache
6.	Chinook
7.	Chinook
8.	Chinook
9.	Kiowa

Check any other unknown words or phrases afterwards. Choose at least one verb phrase, noun phrase and prepositional phrase from the text to explore with the students.

Task 4

Set the Text Analysis tasks in class or for homework.

Suggested Language Focus			
Prepositions	kinds of	armed with	
	defined as	one on the loading ramp	
	such as	shooting through shoulder windows	
	top speed of	crewed by two flight crew	
	carry a load of up to	act as a weapon platform	
	at the rear of the fuselage	equipped with	
	a range of	above the main rotor	
Collocations	transport helicopter	direct fire support	maximum speed
	heavy lift	troop movement	combat radius
	medium lift	ferrying artillery	stub wings
	attack helicopter	battlefield resupply	external tanks
	helicopter gunship	loading ramp	target acquisition
	primary role	personal equipment	night vision systems
	enemy infantry	flight crew	main rotor
	armoured fighting vehicles	weapons platform	

Task 5

Tell the students to listen to the text to decide which words they need to practice saying. This can be done as homework.

Task 6

Tell the students that they will listen to a description of a helicopter and they should complete the table.

Key				
Name	Type	Crew/ passengers	Performance	Armament
Westland Lynx	general pur-pose or mul-ti-role milit-ary heli-copter	a crew of 2 or 3; 8 troops and their equipment	a maximum speed of 324 km/h; a range of 528 km	a naval version can carry two torpedoes *or* four Sea Skua missiles *or* two depth charges; An at-tack variant can carry two 20 mm cannons, two x 70 mm rocket pods or 8 x TOW ATGM. A general purpose variant can carry 7.62 mm General Purpose Machine Guns or a .50 calibre heavy machine gun.

Task 7

Ask the students to work alone and prepare a briefing based on the Fact Files (FF52.1 – F52.5). They can refer to the listening transcript T50.1 to help them prepare. They can present in groups or to the class. Give them feedback on their presentations.

Task 8

Consolidation Tasks in Workbook.

> **Don't forget:**
>
> 1. Spelling Challenge: World Cities to practice the NATO Alphabet.
>
> 2. Test the students on telling the time using the 24 hour clock, and using numbers, and DTG.

Unit 51

About the Unit

This unit focuses on animals and what they can do to you. The grammar focus is on the Present Simple and superlatives.

Task 1

Tell the students to look at P51.1 – 14 and describe what they can see. The students should describe the animals and where they are. They can then check with P51.15– 28 for the names of the animals.

Task 2

Tell students to complete the text with the words *wild, pets* and *domesticated*.

Key	[1] <u>Pets</u> are animals like cats and dogs, and they are tame and are found in the home. [2] <u>Domesticated</u> animals include pets like cats and dogs but also farm animals like cows, pigs and horses; some of these are not really tame (though some are) but they are not wild either. [3] <u>Wild</u> animals live in the [4] <u>wild</u> and are not tame.

Task 3

Tell students to look at the list of animals on the next page and decide if they are *usually* pets, farm animals or wild animals.

Key			
snake	W	lion	W
elephant (African)	W	fox	W
cape buffalo (Africa)	W	rhino	W
goat	F	leopard	W
cow	F	water buffalo (S.E. Asia)	F

jaguar	W	wolf	W
sheep	F	polar bear	W
scorpion	W	spider	W
chimpanzee	W	oryx	W
springbok	W	gorilla	W
giraffe	W	deer	W
cat	P	hyena	W
jackal	W	leech	W
wildebeest	W	dog	P
crocodile	W	hippo	W
mosquito	W	elephant (Asian)	W, F
grizzly/brown bear	W	cheetah	W
tick	W	kangaroo	W

Task 4

Ask students to discuss the questions in pairs and then report. Does the whole class agree with the opinions expressed?

Task 5

Check the meaning of the words given and then ask the students to decide which of the animals in Task 3 can do these things.

Key	Bite: Jaguar, Snake, goat, sheep, chimpanzee, cat, jackal, crocodile, mosquito, grizzly/brown bear, lion, fox, leopard, wolf, polar bear, spider, gorilla, leech, hyena, dog, hippo, cheetah, tick, kangaroo, mosquito, leech
	Sting: scorpion
	Gore: elephant (African), cape buffalo (Africa), cow, rhino, water buffalo (S.E. Asia), oryx, elephant (Asian)
	Trample: elephant (African), cape buffalo (Africa), cow, wildebeest, rhino, water buffalo (S.E. Asia), oryx, gorilla, deer , hippo, elephant (Asian)
	Infect: mosquito, leech, tick

Task 6

Check the words in the table and then tell the students to write out sentences about ten of the animals. This could be done as homework.

Task 7 and **8** are linked. In **Task 7,** ask students to discuss the questions in pairs and then report. As this is a lead in to the listening in **Task** 8 do not comment on the accuracy of their answers.

Task 8

Tell students to listen to the talk and make notes, then check if they agree with the speaker.

Key	
	1. Mosquito – malaria; land mammal – Hippo
	2. Tick – diseases such as Lyme disease
	3. Mosquito – malaria; cobra snakes
	4. Mosquito – malaria; kissing bug – Chagas disease
	5. as above.

Task 9

Ask students to discuss the questions in pairs and then report.

Task 10

Consolidation Tasks in Workbook.

Don't forget:

1. Spelling Challenge: World Cities to practice the NATO Alphabet.

2. Test the students on telling the time using the 24 hour clock, and using numbers, and DTG.

Units 52 - 56 Phase 1 Tests

Units 52 to **56** are tests on the materials in Phase 1. These tests also preview some of the language of Phase 2.

There are five tests to conclude this part of the course. You might want to choose from these tests or do them all.

Decide how long you will give the students for each test based on your knowledge of their capabilities.

Unit 52 Phase 1 Test 1: Grammar Test

This test is a demonstration of their grammatical and lexical knowledge.

Key	
	Lieutenant Colonel Charles Chris Hagemeister (US Army, Retired) [1] **served** the Nation in both the [2] **enlisted** and commissioned ranks. He was both a reserve and [3] **regular** Army officer. His [4] **assignments** included tactical and training units, in peacetime and in combat. He [5] **was drafted** into the United States Army in March 1966 and entered service in May 1966 at Lincoln, Nebraska. He went through [6] **basic** training at Fort Polk, Louisiana, and completed advanced individual training as a [7] **combat** medic at Fort Sam Houston, Texas, in November 1966.
	LTC Hagemeister [8] **was assigned** to the 1st Battalion, 5th Cavalry of the 1st Cavalry Division in the Republic of Vietnam. He was a Specialist 4 (SPC) at the time, supporting a platoon in A Com-

pany in Binh Dinh Province on 20 March 1967 during the Vietnam War. SPC Hagemeister's platoon suddenly came under heavy [9] **attack** from three sides by an enemy force occupying well concealed, [10] **fortified** positions and supported by machine guns and mortars. After SPC Hagemeister saw two of his comrades [11] **seriously** wounded in the initial action, he unhesitatingly and with total disregard for his safety raced through the deadly hail of enemy fire to provide them medical aid. SPC Hagemeister learned that the platoon leader and several other soldiers also had been [12] **wounded**. He continued to brave enemy fire and crawled forward to render lifesaving [13] **treatment**. While attempting to evacuate the seriously wounded soldiers, SPC Hagemeister was taken under fire at close range by an enemy sniper. SPC Hagemeister seized a [14] **rifle** from a fallen comrade and killed the sniper and three other enemy soldiers who were attempting to [15] **encircle** his position. He then silenced an enemy machine gun that covered the area with deadly fire. Unable to remove the [16] **wounded** to a less [17] **exposed** location and aware of the enemy's efforts to isolate his unit, he dashed through the heavy fire to secure help from a nearby platoon. Returning with help, he placed men in positions to [18] **cover** his advance as he moved to evacuate the wounded forward of his location. He then moved to the other [19] **flank** and evacuated additional wounded men, despite the fact that his every move [20] **drew** fire from the enemy. SPC Hagemeister's repeated heroic and selfless actions at the risk of his life saved the lives of many of his comrades and inspired their actions in [21] **repelling** the enemy assault. SPC Hagemeister received the Medal of Honor on 14 May 1968.

After his service in Vietnam, Hagemeister (then Specialist 5) served at McDonald Army Hospital in Fort Eustis, Virginia, and then as a medical platoon sergeant in C Company, 1st Battalion, US Army Medical Training Center at Fort Sam Houston, Texas. Hagemeister received a direct [22] **commission** in the US Army Reserve as an armor officer. After [23] **training** at Fort Knox, Kentucky he was assigned to Fort Hood, Texas where he served as a platoon leader, cavalry troop executive officer, and squadron liaison officer. In 1970 Hagemeister went to Schweinfurt, Germany where he [24] **commanded** Headquarters and Headquarters Troop, 3d Squadron, 7th Cavalry of the 3d Infantry Division where he was also the Squadron Intelligence Officer. After [25] **attending** the Armor Officer Advanced Course and the Data Processing Course Hagemeister [26] **went** back to Fort Hood in September 1977. There he served in the Communications Research and Development Command as the Tactical Operations System Controller. In 1980 he returned to Fort Knox and served as the Chief of Armor Test Development branch and later became the Chief of Platoon, Company, and Troop Training.

Hagemeister became a Regular Army officer on 15 December 1981 and was later [27] **promoted** to Major. Following this promotion, Hagemeister became the executive officer for the 1st Battalion, 1st Training Brigade at Fort Knox. He then [28] **attended** the US Army Command and General Staff College at Fort Leavenworth, Kansas. He [29] **remained** at Fort Leavenworth as the Director of the Division Commander's Course and then as the Author/Instructor for Corps Operations, Center for Army Tactics in the Command and General Staff College. LTC Hagemeister [30] **retired** from the Army in June 1990.

You could check this in class with the students and deal with any problems immediately.

Unit 53 Phase 1 Test 2: Reading Test: Exercise Cambrian Patrol

This test is a demonstration of their grammatical and lexical knowledge.

Key	1. Exercise Cambrian Patrol is an annual international Mission and Task Orientated patrolling exercise
	2. In Wales, in the Cambrian Mountains
	3. Each autumn
	4. All three services (= Army, Navy and Air force; Regular and Reserve) as well as international participants
	5. 25 kg
	6. One of four categories of Awards.
	7. 50-mile (80 km) course in less than 48 hrs
	8. Numerous types of military exercises
	9. Military skills (approx.70% of total marks); Orders (approx.15% of total marks); Debrief (approx.15% of total marks).
	10. Maybe.
	11. Regular army patrols (55)
	12. Seventeen [Norway, New Zealand, Ukraine, Pakistan, Italy, Germany, Denmark, Canada, Albania, Netherlands, Republic of Ireland, India, Australia, Estonia, Poland, Greece and France]

You could check this in class with the students and deal with any problems immediately.

Unit 54 Phase 1 Test 3: Writing Test: PKO Report

In this test the students have to re-read the Peacekeeping Mission reading texts from the Workbook and write a report using the questions in T1 to guide them, and the plan in T2. This test is a demonstration of their writing skills. Collect the writing and correct the scripts and give written feedback on the errors and good points of the response. This test could be done as homework or as a timed writing task in class.

Unit 55 Phase 1 Test 4: Speaking 1: Personnel Biographies

This test is a demonstration of their speaking and listening skills. Follow the instructions and give the students enough time to prepare and practice their presentations. Give them feedback on their presentations. Collect the students' notes about their colleagues' presentations and evaluate their note-taking (and listening) skills.

Unit 56 Phase 1 Test 5: Speaking 2: IFVs

This test is another demonstration of their speaking and listening skills. In this test the students have to brief the class on an IFV. There are ten IFVs to choose from so you might have to test them in batches. Follow the instructions in the Coursebook. T5 is a class discussion task as a follow-up to the presentations and gives the students a reason for watching the presentations. Make sure the students are making notes about the 10 IFVs so they can discuss them after the presentations.

Part 3: Phase 2 Notes and Keys

General Reminder Note about Phase 2 of the Course

Phase 1 of the book was organised into interwoven strands of units and study pages. This phase of the book is organised into blocks of work e.g. **Units 64** to **70** are about the weather. You should decide whether to do the units in blocks or whether to weave them together into strands like Phase 1. Or you might decide that your students only need to do the first unit of weather.

I suggest that you start **Phase 2** by looking at the **Key Tactical Verbs** in Part 21 of the **Workbook**. Check that the students understand these verbs. They might want to translate them, write down the meaning or an example sentence in the table given. Once this is done you can then use these verbs as a random element throughout Phase 2. From time to time, challenge the students to provide an explanation of a verb, or ask them give a synonym or antonym of the verb, or provide an example sentence using the verb. The aim is for the students to be completely familiar with these verbs by the end of Phase 2.

Units 57 – 63 Using the Radio

This series of units is <u>not</u> a complete course in using the radio. It is a set of revision units to remind students about radio procedures, and, for those armies which only train the radiotelephone operator to use radios, to give other students some basic ability in making calls in case the radio operator is wounded or otherwise incapacitated.

Like other sets of units you need to decide if you are going to do them as a block or thread them with other units, and if you need to do all the units.

Unit 57

About the Unit

This first unit is about radio procedures on a <u>radio net</u>. If there are only two stations on a frequency talking to each other then the procedures can be different. Your students will probably be familiar with some of the procedures and PRO words introduced in these units. The purpose of these units are therefore to revise and practice radio procedures.

Task 1

Tell the students to look at P54.1 and describe what they can see.

Task 2 to 9

In each of these tasks procedures and procedure words are introduced, from opening the radio net to closing it down. In each task, introduce the language, listen to the example, and then ask the students to practice the example, and in some case, make their own version of the call and practice and demonstrate.

Unit 58

About the Unit

This second radio unit introduces and practices more PRO words.

Task 1

Key	
WILCO	I have received your signal, understand it and will comply.
ROGER	I have received your last transmission satisfactorily.
OVER	This is the end of my transmission to you and a response is necessary. Go ahead; transmit.
OUT	This is the end of my transmission to you and no answer is required or expected.

Key	
1.	What is the difference between 'over' and 'out'? 'Over' is the end of a turn. 'Out' is the end of the call: goodbye.
2.	Can we say 'over and out'? No.
3.	What is the difference between 'roger' and 'wilco'? Roger = I understand; Wilco = I understand and will do it.
4.	Can we say 'roger wilco'? No.

Task 2 to 5

In each of these tasks one or more PRO word is introduced. Check understanding of the word and then practice it. In Tasks 4, 5 and 6 there is a recording of the example. In **Task 6** you will need maps with a grid to practice giving grid references. This is also a preview of **Unit 93** and you will be able to see how good your students are at giving grid references. You could do **Unit 93** between **Units 57** and **58** if you wanted to, as grids are used quite a lot in the following radio units.

About the Unit

This unit focuses on radio calls based on an incident report form. There is not enough space in the book to practice all the possible calls.

Task 1

Teach/check the language of the form.

Teacher Briefing 1

Precedence is the priority of the message and indicates the timescale of a response or action required.

FLASH: handle as fast as possible – ideally less than 10 minutes.

IMMEDIATE: 30 mins to 1 hour

PRIORITY: 1 to 6 hours

ROUTINE: 3 hours +

Teacher Briefing 2

Classification is a measure of how confidential the message is. There are three main classifications:

SECRET | CONFIDENTIAL | UNCLASSIFIED

You will need multiple copies of this form for this unit. There are copies in the **Workbook** (see pages 165-167) to use.

Task 2

Put the students into pairs and ask them to prepare a model radio call based on an incident. They should script the call, practice in their pairs and then present the call to the class. The students should listen to the presented calls and write down the information from the calls. They should check their notes against the original completed form. How good were their notes? This task will give them a lot of practice making and listening to radio calls.

Options: If you have radios use these to make the calls. Send one party out of the room to make the call. Or all go outside the class: the background noises will make the calls more difficult to hear. Doing it this way will make it more difficult for the listeners to make notes so you will have to adjust the task accordingly.

Don't forget:

1. Spelling Challenge: World Cities to practice the NATO Alphabet.

2. Test the students on telling the time using the 24 hour clock, and using numbers, and DTG.

3. Test the students on the Key Tactical Verbs.

About the Unit

The focus of this unit is on **MEDEVAC/CASEVAC calls.**

Task 1

Teach/check the language of the form. You will need multiple copies of this form for this unit. There are copies in the Workbook (see pages 168-170) to use.

Task 2

Tell the students to listen to the call and complete the form in Task 1. Listen a second time if necessary. Then they can read the transcript to check.

Key		
	1.	ONE, 435970, break
	2.	TWO, 89 decimal 56, A1B, break
	3.	THREE, Alpha 2, Charlie 3, break
	4.	FOUR, Delta 1, break
	5.	FIVE, Lima 1, Alfa 4, break
	6.	SIX, X-Ray, break
	7.	SEVEN, Bravo Yellow, break
	8.	EIGHT, Alfa 5, break
	9.	NINE, Approach from the east; pylons to west.

Task 3

Tell the students to listen to the second call and complete the form in Task 1. Listen a second time if necessary. Then they can read the transcript to check.

Key		
	1.	ONE, 775456, break
	2.	TWO, 72 decimal 27, B2, break
	3.	THREE, Alpha 1, Charlie 1, break
	4.	FOUR, Delta 1, break
	5.	FIVE, Lima 1, Alfa 1, break
	6.	SIX, Papa, break
	7.	SEVEN, Charlie Red, break
	8.	EIGHT, Echo 2, break
	9.	NINE, Tall trees to north and lake to west.

Task 4

Tell the students to complete the radio call and then listen to check.

Key	
Call sign ZY5:	B20, this is ZY5, over.
Call sign B20:	ZY5, this is B20, send. Over.
Call sign ZY5:	B20, this is ZY5, Request urgent CASEVAC, over.
Call sign B20:	ZY5, this is B20, Authenticate Shakespeare, over.
Call sign ZY5:	B20, this is ZY5, I authenticate Macbeth, over.
Call sign B20:	ZY5. Roger, send request over.
Call sign ZY5:	B20. Roger, nine liner as follows, break,
	ONE, 657345, break
	TWO, 69 decimal 45, ZY5, break
	THREE, Alpha 1, Charlie 2, break
	FOUR, Delta 1, break
	FIVE, Lima 1, Alfa 2, break
	SIX, Echo, break
	SEVEN, Bravo White, break
	EIGHT, Alfa 3, break
	NINE, Approach from the south. Over.
Call sign B20:	ZY5. We will send CASEVAC immediately. Over.
Call sign ZY5:	B20. Roger. Out.

Task 5

Put the students into pairs and ask them to prepare a model call call based on a CASEVAC/MEDEVAC situation. They should script the call, practice in their pairs and then present the call to the class. The students should listen to the presented calls and write down the information from the calls. They should check their notes against the original completed form. How good were their notes? This task will give them a lot of practice making and listening to radio calls.

Options: As in **Unit 59**, if you have radios use these to make the calls. Send one party out of the room to make the call. Or all go outside the class: the background noises will make the calls more difficult to hear. Doing it this way will make it more difficult for the listeners to make notes so you will have to adjust the task accordingly.

About the Unit

The focus of this unit is on calls for fire. This is quite a specialised unit and you might want to consider omitting this unless your students have a specific need for it.

Teacher Briefing

In some cases a platoon may be able to call for fire missions. This unit explains how this is done in the US Army.

Calls for fire must include the following three elements: observer identification and warning order; target location and target description as mentioned in Task 2. Task 4 goes into more detail about this warning order. Task 5 explains more about the target description using the acronym SNAP. Task 6 is an example initial radio call for fire.

Then the FDC determines how to attack the target and calls the platoon back in a radio message – see Task 7.

The Observer and FDC will be in radio communication about the effect of the attack and any adjustments to be made, and when to finish the attack. The sequence finishes with a BDA – see Task 8. A sample BDA is 'Four enemy tanks destroyed'.

There are many different permutations which are not practised here. You should practice the basic calls as shown.

In the Workbook on page 198 there is an alternative Call for Fire form. There are some differences from the Coursebook materials. You should note:

In section 3 there are three different ways to give the **Target Location**. In this unit and the radio calls just use the GRID system.

In section 4 the **Target Description** is an alternative to SNAP (Task 5).

In section 9 the Method of Control allows the observer to directly control the firing of mission, or hand over control. 'Time on Target' is used to tell the time you want the target to be hit. 'Time to Target' allows the Observer to specify a precise time counted from a call, like this 'Time to target 1 min 10 seconds, over, Standby, ready, ready, Hack, over'. The FDC counts 1 min and 10 seconds from 'Hack' and then fires. It is not necessary to practice this.

Task 1

Ask students to discuss the questions in pairs and then report.

Task 2

Ask students to read the text and then discuss the question in pairs and then report.

Task 3

Ask students to discuss the questions in pairs and then report. The answers to this question is given in the text in T4.

Task 4

Teach/check the meaning of the words in the table. Then ask the students to complete the text with the words.

Key	**Observer Identification and Warning Order**
	Observer identification tells the fire [1] **direction** center (FDC) who is calling. It also [2] **clears** the net for the duration of the call. The WARNO tells the FDC the [3] **type** of mission and the method of locating the target. The types of indirect fire missions are adjust fire, fire for effect (FFE), suppress, and immediate suppression.
	Adjust Fire Use this command when uncertain of target [4] **Location**. Calling an adjust fire mission means the observer knows he will need to make adjustments prior to calling a fire for effect.
	Fire for Effect: Use this command for rounds on target, no adjustment. An example of this situation is if it is [5] **known** that the target is in building X. Building X is easily [6] **identified** on the map as Grid ML 12345678910.
	Suppress: Use this command to obtain fire [7] **quickly**. The suppression mission is used to initiate fire on a preplanned target (known to the FDC) and unplanned targets.
	Immediate Suppression: Use this command to indicate the platoon is already being [8] **engaged** by the enemy. Target identification is required. The term "immediate" tells the FDC that the friendly unit is in [9] **direct** fire contact with the enemy target.

Task 5

Ask students to read and then match the examples to SNAP.

Key	
Size and/or shape	"one enemy soldier" or "platoon of enemy soldiers"
Nature and/or nomenclature	"T72," "sniper team," "machine gunner"
Activity	"stationary"or"moving"
Protection and/or posture	"in the open,""dug in,"or"on a rooftop"

Task 6

Ask students to read through the radio call and answer the questions 1 – 4.

Key	1. Who is calling the fire mission? 271
	2. What kind of fire mission is it? ADJUST FIRE
	3. What is the target? INFANTRY PLATOON IN THE OPEN
	4. Where is the target? GRID NK180513

Task 7

Ask students to read through the text and then answer the question by reading though the sample call. **Key:** 2 rounds. [Note: '**TARGET IS AF1027**' is the target number from the Target List.]

Task 8

This task shows how to end the attack with a Battle Damage Assessment (BDA).

Task 9

Put the students into pairs and ask them to prepare a model call call based on a call for fire situation. They should script the call, practice in their pairs and then present the call to the class. The students should listen to the presented calls and write down the information from the calls. How good were their notes? This task will give them a lot of practice making and listening to radio calls.

Options: As before, if you have radios use these to make the calls. Send one party out of the room to make the call. Or all go outside the class: the background noises will make the calls more difficult to hear. Doing it this way will make it more difficult for the listeners to make notes so you will have to adjust the task accordingly.

Don't forget:

1. Spelling Challenge: World Cities to practice the NATO Alphabet.

2. Test the students on telling the time using the 24 hour clock, and using numbers, and DTG.

3. Test the students on the Key Tactical Verbs.

Unit 62

About the Unit

The focus of this unit is on patrol calls. It is a preview of the patrol units later in **Phase 2**. You could do this unit later in the course as well, after the patrol units **Units 153 – 160**.

Task 1

Ask the students to use their maps to plan a patrol according to the instructions.

Task 2

In this task the class is briefed about each patrol. Students should make notes about the patrol and then check their notes. How good are the notes?

Task 3

Ask the students to prepare and then demonstrate radio calls during the patrol. Ask the students to give feedback on the calls.

Unit 63

About the Unit

The focus of this unit is on convoy calls. It is a preview of the convoy units later in Phase 2. You could do this unit later in the course, after the convoy units – **Units 137-142**.

Task 1

Ask the students to use their maps to plan a convoy according to the instructions.

Task 2

In this task the class is briefed about each convoy. Students should make notes about the convoy and then check their notes. How good are the notes? This task will give you a good idea of how well they can talk about convoys in English.

Task 3

Ask the students to prepare and then demonstrate five radio calls during the convoy. Ask the students to give feedback on the calls.

Units 64 – 70 Weather and Climate

This series of units is about weather and climate. **Unit 64** is about basic weather and climate words. **Unit 65** is about weather forecasts. **Units 66** to **69** are about climate zones around the world. In **Unit 70** students have to give group briefings on extreme weather and/or the climate in different parts of the word.

Like other sets of units you need to decide if you are going to do them as a block or thread them with other units, and if you need to do all the units. You might decide to just do **Units 64** and **65**. It depends on your students' needs.

Unit 64

About the Unit

The focus in this unit is on weather vocabulary and the typical weather in seasons in your students' country.

Task 1

Tell the students to look at P61.1 – P61.3 and describe what they can see: snow, fog and sunshine/cloud.

Task 2

Teach/check the words in the table and then ask the students to sort them into rain, windy, sunny, and winter weather.

Key			
Rainy Weather	**Windy Weather**	**Sunny Weather**	**Winter Weather**
raining	windy	Sunny	freezing
cloudy	gust	hot	snowing heavily
spitting	(a) light/strong breeze	clear blue skies	sleet
damp	prevailing (wind)	boiling	slush
heavy / light	biting	humid	(a) blizzard
showers	(a) monsoon	dry	cold
pouring down	(a) gale		freezing (rain) [also rainy
torrential	light		weather]
monsoon			drifting snow
drizzling			chilly
humid			icy
(a) downpour			bitterly (cold)
			frosty

Task 3

Ask the students to describe the annual weather/climate for their country by completing the table on the next page. Check as a class. Does everyone agree?

Task 4

This task is a preview task for the next unit. Use it to see how good the students are at describing the weather for one typical day in a season.

Unit 65

About the Unit

This is the second unit on weather and climate. The focus is on the language of weather forecasts.

Task 1

Use this task as revision for the vocabulary of **Unit 64**. You could do an open class round where they test each other as a class.

Task 2

This task is a preview task for the main listening task in Task 5. The students should listen to the extracts and mark the pauses and main stresses. There may be some differences and the students may have trouble hearing which words are stressed most. Do not worry too much about getting this exactly right: it is an awareness raising task.

Key		
1.	/In <u>Astana</u> at the moment it's <u>clear</u> and <u>sunny</u>/
2.	<u>Cape Town</u> is <u>waking</u> up to a <u>beautiful</u> <u>day</u>.
3.	It is <u>4 degrees</u> in <u>Shanghai</u> and <u>overcast</u>.
4.	<u>Today</u> is forecast to be <u>nearly</u> the same <u>temperature</u> as <u>yesterday</u>.
5.	It's <u>clear</u> and <u>19 degrees</u> at the <u>moment</u> but this <u>afternoon</u> should see <u>26 degrees</u> and <u>yesterday's sunshine</u> <u>will</u> continue.

Task 3

Tells students to listen to the complete weather forecasts for the four cities and complete the table. Listen a second time if necessary. Class check.

Key	1. Astana	2. Cape Town	3. Shanghai	4. London
Weather now	clear and sunny; minus 21 degrees; Winds are from the south-south-east: 15 to 30 km/h	It's sunny and warm: 20 degrees; 55% humidity.	4 degrees; overcast.	Clear; 19 degrees
Weather later today	minus 12 degrees in the mid-afternoon; clouding over; night snow showers; 2 -3 cms of snow	25 degrees this afternoon, 83% humidity this evening. Tonight will be clear, about 18 degrees,; southerly winds of up to 50 km/h	Occasional rain showers later this morning; 2 mm of rain; northerly winds with gusts up to 30 km/h. The rain should end about 7 pm and the clouds should clear later tonight. The temperature will drop to about minus 1 overnight.	this afternoon: 26 degrees; sunshine will continue. Winds from the north-east at 15 to 25 km/h. Wednesday night: mostly clear and the winds will veer east-north-east and drop to 10 to 15 km/h.
Weather tomorrow	minus 8 in the morning, windy, 30 to 50 km/h, and with more snow showers; minus 22 degrees in the evening.	Thursday: warm, 28 degrees, and clear but still windy, with gusts up to 50 km/h again.	Thursday: sunny all day; high of 6 degrees; north west winds gusting up to 40 km/h	Thursday: warm; 28 degrees; cloud and sunshine. Scattered thunderstorms in the evening.

Task 4

Tells the students to complete the transcript tasks for the first three forecasts. They can listen to check and then check with the transcripts.

Task 5

Ask students to discuss the questions in pairs and then report on what each other said.

Don't forget:

1. Spelling Challenge: World Cities to practice the NATO Alphabet.

2. Test the students on telling the time using the 24 hour clock, and using numbers, and DTG.

3. Test the students on the Key Tactical Verbs.

Unit 66

About the Unit

This is the third unit on weather and climate. The focus is on the climate in three cities: London (Temperate Oceanic); Timbuktu (Dry Continental); Singapore (Tropical).

Task 1

Ask students to discuss the questions in pairs and then report.

Task 2

In this task the students have to unravel three texts which have been merged together. Make sure you and the students understand how to do this task before you start. The first three sentences are the start of the three texts. Then the sentences are mixed up between the texts but are still **in** the correct order. The students should decide which city text the sentence is for.

Key	
	London, the capital of England and the United Kingdom, has a temperate oceanic climate. It has regular but light precipitation (40 to 68 mm per month) throughout the year (total: 600 mm) with most rain falling from October to January. June to August are the warmest months with average highs of 22 – 23 °C and average lows of 14 – 15 °C. Summer temperatures rarely exceed 33 °C, though the highest temperature ever recorded in London was 38.1 °C one August. Winter temperatures range from average lows of 2 °C to average highs of 8 °C December – February.
	Timbuktu, a city in Mali, Africa, has a hot desert climate. The weather is hot and dry throughout much of the year. Average daily maximum temperatures in the hottest months of the year – April, May and June - are over 40 °C. The lowest temperatures occur during the Northern hemisphere winter – December, January and February but even then, the average maximum temperatures do not drop below 30 °C. The average annual rainfall is 182.8 millimetres; June to September are the wettest months with from 16 to 73 mm of rain per month.
	Singapore, the city-island state in South-east Asia, lies 1 degree north of the equator and it has a tropical rainforest climate with no distinctive seasons. It has uniform temperature (usually ranging from 22 to 36 °C), and high humidity, which averages around 79% in the morning and 73% in the afternoon. March, April and May are the hottest months with average high temperatures of 31.6 /7 °C. November to January are the wetter monsoon season with 19 rainy days per month on average.

Check the meaning of the words and phrases in the texts.

Task 3

Tell the students to listen to the texts to decide which words they need to practice saying. This can be done as homework.

Task 4

Ask the students to discuss the questions in pairs and then report on their partner's preference. They can bring in other ideas apart from the weather to justify their choice.

Task 5

Consolidation Tasks in Workbook.

Don't forget:

1. Spelling Challenge: World Cities to practice the NATO Alphabet.

2. Test the students on telling the time using the 24 hour clock, and using numbers, and DTG.

3. Test the students on the Key Tactical Verbs.

Unit 67

About the Unit

This unit builds on the vocabulary introduced in **Unit 66** and explores climate zones in more detail through a series of listenings.

Task 1

Ask the students what they remember about the climate in the three cities from **Unit 66**. You could get them to work in pairs first and then report or do it as an open class task.

Task 2

Ask the students to look at the diagram and see if they can complete any of the labels. Then they listen to the talk and complete the diagram. They can check with the key P67.1 and read the transcript T67.1

Task 3

This listening task goes into some detail about the four climate types in the table. Students should listen and make notes about the characteristics of such climates. You could also ask them to listen for the locations such climates are found. You should check with the transcript for the key. Decide how many times you are going to allow the students to listen. There are transcript tasks to follow in Task 4 and they can listen again to check these. Do not let them read the transcripts until after they have done the transcript tasks.

Task 4

Ask the students to complete the transcripts. They can listen to check and then read the transcripts.

Task 5

Ask the students to prepare a two day forecast for one the three cities, without mentioning which city it is. They should read their forecasts to the class; the class should guess which city the forecast is for.

Task 6

Ask the students to write out a another weather forecast for a city of their choice. This could be set as homework. Collect the texts and correct them and give feedback.

Task 7

Ask the students to discuss the questions in pairs and then report on their partner's answers.

Unit 68

About the Unit

This is the fifth unit on weather and climate. The focus is on the climate in three more cities: Washington (Subtropical); Churchill (Subarctic); Tripoli (Semi-arid).

Task 1

Ask students to discuss the questions in pairs and then report.

Task 2

This task is exactly the same as Task 2 in **Unit 66**. In this task the students have to unravel three texts which have been merged together. Make sure you and the students understand how to do this task before you start. The first three sentences are the start of the three texts. Then the sentences are mixed up between the texts but are still in the correct order. The students should decide which city text the sentence is for.

Key	**Washington D. C.**, the capital of the USA, is in the humid subtropical climate zone. Winter is usually chilly with light snow, spring is mild, summer is hot and humid, and autumn (or fall) is mild to warm. Average winter temperatures range from 4 °C in December to 1 °C in January and 3 °C in February, with record lows of – 26 °C recorded. Snowfall is highest in January and February while the highest average rainfall occurs in May, June and August with 93 mm, and 96 mm and 99 mm respectively. June to August is the hottest and most humid time of year with average temperatures of between 24 and 26 °C but with highs of 29 – 30 °C.
	Churchill, a small town in northern Canada on the Hudson Bay, has a borderline subarctic climate. It has long very cold winters, and short, cool to mild summers. The shallow Hudson Bay freezes in winter making the winters colder than expected for its latitude. Prevailing northerly winds from the Arctic cool the town to a –26.0 °C January daily average, with lows of – 30 °C, and a record low of – 45 °C . In summer, when the Hudson Bay thaws, Churchill's temperature is an average of 12.7°C in July, though the record high is 36.9 °C. Most rain falls in the summer months (June: 44 mm; July 60 mm; August and September: 70 mm), while in October and November 30 to 40 cms of snow falls.
	Tripoli, the capital of Libya, lies on the North African coast of the Mediterranean sea. It has a hot semi-arid climate with long, hot and extremely dry summers and relatively wet and warm win-

ters. Summer high temperatures often exceed 38 °C, while the record high is 48.3 °C. Average July temperatures are between 22 and 33 °C. Temperatures can reach as low as 0 °C December to February but the average lows are around 9 °C for these months. The average annual rainfall is less than 400 millimetres; October to January are the wettest months with 46 to 67 mm of rain per month.

Check the meaning of the words and phrases in the texts.

Task 3

Tell the students to listen to the texts to decide which words they need to practice saying. This can be done as homework.

Task 4

Ask the students to discuss the questions in pairs and then report on their partner's preference. They can bring in other ideas apart from the weather to justify their choice.

Task 5

Consolidation Tasks in Workbook.

Don't forget:

1. Spelling Challenge: World Cities to practice the NATO Alphabet.

2. Test the students on telling the time using the 24 hour clock, and using numbers, and DTG.

3. Test the students on the Key Tactical Verbs.

Unit 69

About the Unit

This unit builds on the vocabulary introduced in **Units 66 - 68** and explores more climate zones in more detail through a series of listenings.

Task 1

Ask the students what they remember about the climate in the three cities from **Unit 66**. You could get them to work in pairs first and then report or do it as an open class task.

Task 2

This listening task goes into some detail about the five climate types in the table. Students should listen and make notes. You should check with the transcript for the key. Decide how many times you are going to allow the students to listen. There are transcript tasks to follow in Task 3 and they can listen again to check these. Do not let them read the transcripts until after they have done the transcript task.

Task 3

Ask the students to complete the transcripts. They can listen to check and then read the transcripts.

Task 4

Ask the students to prepare a two day forecast for one the three cities, without mentioning which city it is. They should read their forecasts to the class; the class should guess which city the forecast is for.

Task 5

Divide the class into groups and allocate one city from **Units 65 - 69** to each group. Ask them to prepare a ten day weather forecast for their city. They should prepare and practise a presentation of the weather forecast.

The whole class should listen to all the presentations and make notes to answer the questions 1 -5.

Unit 70

About the Unit

This is the final unit on weather and climate. The focus is on Weather Systems And Extreme Weather.

Task 1

Put the students into pairs or groups and tell them to prepare briefings using **Unit 70 Briefing Slides 1.** They should script their presentation and then practice giving it, before giving it to the class. Give the students feedback on their presentations.

Task 2

Repeat the procedure for **Unit 70 Briefing Slides 2.**

> **Extra Task:** Use the Severe Weather Warning from the Workbook (page 197) to practice issuing a severe weather warning as a radio call. Students script the calls and demonstrate them.

Units 71 - 92 Terrain

This sequence of units is about Terrain and has units on mountains (**Units 71-73**), deserts (**Units 74-76**), temperate hills, lowlands and rivers (**Units 78-79**), tropical forests (**Units 80-82**), estuary and coasts (**Units 83-84**), urban terrain (**Units 85-90**), bridges, dams and airfields (**Unit 91**), and expressing uncertainty (**Unit 92**). You might want to choose to omit units based on your students' needs.

About the Unit

This unit focuses on the language used to describe mountain terrain.

Task 1

Tell the students to look at P71.1 and describe what they can see. Do they know what A – F are? Check with P71.2

Task 2

Check that the students understand the meaning of the words in the table. You can use the pictures to help.

Task 3

Ask students to complete the text with words from Task 2. Check any other unknown words or phrases after-wards. Choose at least one verb phrase, noun phrase and prepositional phrase from the text to explore with the students.

Key	A mountain [1] **range** is a series or chain of mountains that are close together. Mountains them-selves are landforms which are higher than the surrounding area. There might be lower [2] **foot-hills** near the mountain range itself. Some mountains form an [3] **escarpment** ridge which rises up sharply from the lowlands. Mountains usually have steep, sloping [4] **slopes** and sharp or rounded [5] **ridges**. Mountain slopes can have steep [6] **cliffs** or rocky outcrops on them and some slopes are covered with [7] **scree** which makes walking difficult. The side of a mountain is known as the flank. This might rise up to a rounded [8] **shoulder** or up to a steeper ridge. The ridge will run to the highest point of the mountain called the [9] **peak** or summit, or might run further as a ridge line which includes several peaks. Some summits are called [10] **horns** or pyr-amidal peaks. Mountain peaks have [11] **faces** which are referred to by the direction they face e.g. the north face faces north.
	There might be [12] **saddles** (or cols) in the ridge line where the elevation drops between two summits and this can be used as a [13] **pass** to cross over the mountains. A [14] **spur** is a lower summit of a mountain closely connected to the summit on the same ridge line. A small steep val-ley between two spurs is known as a [15] **re-entrant** or draw. A [16] **plateau** is an area of relat-ively flat highland, also called a high plain or tableland.

Task 4

Tell the students to listen to the text to decide which words they need to practice saying. This can be done as homework.

Task 5

Now ask the students to identify some mountain features on a map. Look at M71.1. Check with the key: M71.2. If you have other maps of mountain areas, you might want to extend this task.

Task 6

Ask students to work in pairs and then go into a group with another pair. You might want to do a class check if you can project the photos onto a screen.

Task 7

Ask the students to discuss the questions in pairs and then report on their partner's preference.

Don't forget:

1. Spelling Challenge: World Cities to practice the NATO Alphabet.

2. Test the students on telling the time using the 24 hour clock, and using numbers, and DTG.

3. Test the students on the Key Tactical Verbs.

Unit 72

About the Unit

This unit focuses on language used to describe alpine mountain terrain.

There is quite a lot of material in this unit and you might want to split it into two.

Task 1

Tell the students to look at P72.1 and describe what they can see. [Note: This is a picture from the Rwenzori Mountains, which are described in Task 5.]

Task 2

Check that the students understand the meaning of the words in the table. You can use the pictures to help.

Task 3

Ask students to complete the text with words from Task 2. Check any other unknown words or phrases after-wards. Choose at least one verb phrase, noun phrase and prepositional phrase from the text to explore with the students.

Key   Many mountain ranges still have active glacier systems on them and these [1] **glaciers** are still shaping the mountains by eroding the rock. A glacier can carve out a [2] **U-shaped** valley, while a river carves a [3] **V-shaped** valley. If an alpine glacier melts, an alpine lake can form in the [4] **cirque** left behind. The mountain side above the lake (or glacier) is known as the [5] **headwall**. An [6] **arête** is a steep-sided, sharp-edged bedrock ridge formed by two glaciers eroding away on opposite sides of the ridge.

Mountain ranges can act as [7] **watersheds** – water flows either side of the mountain ridge line into different river basins. Streams might cut deep [8] **ravines** into the rock as they flow down the mountainside and there migth be high [9] **waterfalls**.

Some mountains are covered in trees while others are higher in altitude and have a [10] **treeline** above which trees will not grow. Above this line there might be [11] **moorland** with grasses and heather plants. Above this there will be [12] **lichen** covered rocks. The permanent snowline is the point above which snow and ice cover the ground throughout the year.

Task 4

Tell the students to listen to the text to decide which words they need to practice saying. This can be done as homework.

Task 5

Ask the students to cover up Task 6 before they look at Task 5.

Ask students to listen to the recording and make notes about the mountains being described. Check with T65.1 for the key. Decide how many times they can listen.

Task 6

Ask the students to complete the transcript and then listen to check. Check with T72.1

Task 7

Ask students to work in pairs and then groups to identify mountain features from the maps. There is no key given. Ask the students to work in pairs and identify features, then check with another pair. If there is disagreement, discuss as a class. Note: these maps are from the First World War (1914-18) where the Germans and Austrians fought the Italians.

Task 8

Ask students to work in groups to prepare presentations based on the slides **Unit 72 Briefing Slides Mountain Features.** Remember to give them feedback on their presentations.

Task 9

Consolidation Tasks in Workbook.

Unit 73

About the Unit

This unit brings together material about climate, animals and mountain terrain.

Task 1

Put students into groups and ask them to prepare a briefing based on one of the slides in the **Unit 73 Briefing Slides Mountain Ranges**. They should talk about the different geographical and biological features of the mountain ranges. Give them feedback on their briefings. You could also do this as individual work if you have 15 students, or pairs if you have 30.

About the Unit

This unit focuses on basic vocabulary to do with deserts.

Task 1

Tell the students to look at P74.1 and describe what they can see. Do they know what A – F are? Check with P74.2

Task 2

Check that the students understand the meaning of the words in the table. You can use the pictures to help.

Task 3

Ask students to complete the text with words from Task 2. Check any other unknown words or phrases afterwards. Choose at least one verb phrase, noun phrase and prepositional phrase from the text to explore with the students.

Key	Sand and sand [1] **dunes** cover only about 20 percent of the Earth's deserts. Nearly 50 percent of desert surfaces are [2] **plains** where the wind has exposed loose gravels consisting predominantly of pebbles. The remaining surfaces of arid lands are composed of exposed bedrock outcrops, desert soils, and fluvial deposits including alluvial fans, playas, desert lakes, and oases. [3] **Bedrock** outcrops commonly occur as small mountains surrounded by extensive plains. An [4] **oasis** is a vegetated area fed by springs, wells, or by irrigation. Most desert plants are drought- or salt-tolerant. Some store water in their leaves, roots, and stems. Other desert plants have long tap roots that penetrate the water table, anchor the soil, and control erosion. Rain does fall occasionally in deserts. Normally dry stream channels, called arroyos or [5] **wadis**, can quickly fill after heavy rains, and flash floods make these channels dangerous. Desert [6] **lakes** are generally shallow, temporary, and salty. When small lakes dry up, they leave a salt crust or hardpan. The flat area of clay, silt, or sand encrusted with salt that forms is known as a [7] **playa**.

Task 4

Ask the students to discuss the questions in pairs and then report on their partner's preference. You could extend this to a discussion about mountains and deserts, and about mountain deserts. Which do/would they prefer to operate in? Which are harder/easier to operate in? Which has more dangers? What are they? What are the problems of each? You could ask groups to make posters about mountains and/or deserts, display them on the walls and ask for comments.

Task 5

Consolidation Tasks in Workbook.

About the Unit

This unit focuses on more vocabulary to do with deserts.

Task 1

Tell the students to look at P75.1 and describe what they can see. Do they know what A – F are? Check with P75.2

Task 2

Make sure your students are clear on the difference between the skyline and horizon. 'To skyline' is to appear on the skyline, and this is a bad thing to do in military terms.

Task 3

Ask students to match the three words and definitions.

Key	
outcrop	An area of bedrock above the surrounding land surface, not covered in soil or sand.
bedrock	The solid rock which is found under soil or sand.
salt marshes	A flat wet area where water has evaporated leaving a salt crust on the surface

Tasks 4 – 8 are text completion tasks. Check the meaning of the words in the table before the students complete the short texts. Check any other unknown words or phrases after each section.

Task 4

Key	**Mountain Deserts** are characterised by scattered ranges or areas of barren hills or mountains separated by dry, flat [1] **basins.** High ground may rise gradually or abruptly from flat areas to several thousand meters above sea level. Most of the infrequent rainfall occurs on high ground and runs off rapidly in the form of [2] **flash** floods. These floodwaters erode deep gullies and ravines and deposit sand and gravel around the edges of the basins. Water rapidly [3] **evaporates**, leaving the land as barren as before, although there may be [4] **short-lived** vegetation. If more water enters the basin than evaporates, shallow lakes may develop: most of these lakes have a high [5] **salt** content.

Task 5

Key	**Rocky Plateau Deserts** have relatively low [1] **relief** separated by extensive [2] **plains** with quantities of solid or broken rock at or near the surface. There may be [3] **steep-walled**, eroded ravines, known as [4] **wadis** in the Middle East and arroyos or canyons in the United States and Mexico.

Task 6

Key	**Sandy or Dune Deserts** are extensive flat areas covered with sand or [1] **gravel**. Some areas may contain sand dunes that are over 300 meters high and 16 to 24 kilometers long. Ease of [2] **movement** in such [3] **terrain** will depend on the windward or [4] **leeward** slope of the dunes and the texture of the sand. Plant [5] **life** may vary from none to scrub over 2 meters high.

Task 7

Key	**Salt Marshes**
	Salt marshes are flat, [1] **desolate** areas, sometimes studded with clumps of grass but devoid of other vegetation. They occur in [2] **arid** areas where rainwater has collected, evaporated, and left large [3] **deposits** of alkali salts and water with a high salt concentration. The water is so salty it is [4] **undrinkable**. A crust that may be 2.5 to 30 centimeters [5] **thick** forms over the saltwater.

Task 8

Key	**Broken Terrain**
	All arid areas contain [1] **broken** or highly dissected terrain formed by [2] **rainstorms** that erode the soft sand and carve out [3] **canyons** or wadis. A wadi may [4] **range** from 3 meters wide and 2 meters deep to several hundred meters [5] **wide** and deep.

Task 9

Tell the students to listen to the texts to decide which words they need to practice saying. This can be done as homework.

Task 10

Ask students to discuss the question in pairs and then report to the class.

Task 11

Ask the students to look at the two photos and write short descriptions about them. Collect the writing to mark, and give feedback; or the texts could be displayed on the walls for comments. This could be set as a homework task.

Task 12

Consolidation Tasks in Workbook.

Unit 76

About the Unit

This is a revision unit based on five listenings about deserts.

Task 1 - 5

Ask students to listen and make notes from the listenings. They can check their notes with the transcripts.

This is a self evaluation task – how much can they note down? Which words do they still need to learn?

You could do this a class listening task or as an individual listening task, with the students listening to the texts on their mobile phones through head or earphones. If they are listening on their own, suggest that they can stop and start/review but give them an overall time limit to complete the tasks.

Unit 77

About the Unit

This is a consolidation unit about deserts.

Task 1

There are eight briefings about desert regions. Put the students into pairs or groups and tell them to prepare briefings using **Unit 77 Briefing Slides: Deserts**. They should script their presentation and then practice giving it, before giving it to the class. Ask the students, as they listen to the briefings, to make notes on the desert areas and then compare the deserts – which is the biggest etc.? Give the students feedback on their presentations.

Don't forget:

1. Spelling Challenge: World Cities to practice the NATO Alphabet.

2. Test the students on telling the time using the 24 hour clock, and using numbers, and DTG.

3. Test the students on the Key Tactical Verbs.

4. Test the students about mountains.

Unit 78

About the Unit

This terrain unit is focused on temperate hills and lowlands.

Task 1

Tell the students to look at P78.1 and describe what they can see. Do they know what A – F are? Check with P78.2.

Task 2

Check that the students understand the meaning of the words in the table. You can use the pictures to help.

Task 3

Ask students to complete the text with words from Task 2. Check any other unknown words or phrases afterwards. Choose at least one verb phrase, noun phrase and prepositional phrase from the text to explore with the students.

Key	Temperate lowland and hilly rural areas are characterised by farmland and forest areas with small settlements.
	Farms are cultivated areas of [1] **fields** with farm buildings. These [2] **fields** are bordered by hedges or wire [3] **fences**, or by drainage ditches, or left without a boundary marker. [4] **Forests** are large areas of trees, while [5] **woods** are smaller areas. The trees might be coniferous or [6] **deciduous** trees. [7] **Copses** are small isolated collections of trees.
	Paths or [8] **tracks** can cross across the countryside linking roads and [9] **villages**, which are smaller than towns.
	Hilly areas may be wooded or they may be covered in treeless moorland characterised by low-growing vegetation like heather and grasses.
	[10] **Scrubland** is rough ground with bushes and some trees. It is not farmed and may be forest regrowth after felling.
	There might be different kinds of [11] **quarries** used to extract building materials.
	Temperate lowland rural areas often seem safe but there are dangers – bears and snakes and ticks for example.

Task 4

Tell the students to listen to the text to decide which words they need to practice saying. This can be done as homework.

Task 5

Check that the students are clear about the differences between the words in the table. Use the photos to help.

Task 6

Ask the students to explain the terms.

Task 7

Ask the students to choose a photo or assign a photo to a student; ask them to write a detailed description of what they can see.

Task 8

Ask students to discuss the questions in pairs and then report to the class.

Task 9

Consolidation Tasks in Workbook.

Unit 79

About the Unit

This terrain unit is focused on rivers and lakes.

Task 1

Tell the students to look at P79.1 and describe what they can see. Do they know what A – M are? Check with P79.2

Task 2

Check that the students understand the meaning of the words in the table. You can use the pictures to help.

Task 3

Ask students to complete the text with words from Task 2. Check any other unknown words or phrases afterwards. Choose at least one verb phrase, noun phrase and prepositional phrase from the text to explore with the students.

Key　　[1] **Springs** in hills feed [2] **streams** which join together to form rivers. [3] **Tributary** streams and rivers join the main river of a river [4] **basin**. The joining of two rivers is known as the [5] **confluence**. Rivers may have water meadows which flood in the spring when the [6] **banks** of the rivers burst. Rivers may be crossed by [7] **road** bridges or by [8] **footbridges** for pedestrians. Rivers can be fast flowing with dangerous [9] **rapids** and waterfalls, or slow flowing with [10] **meanders**. A canal is a kind of man-made river – they usually have a straight channel.

Lakes are also fed by streams and sometimes rivers, and are sometimes the main source of rivers which start at the [11] **lake** mouth. Wooded lake [12] **shores** are good habitats for wildlife. [13] **Reservoirs**, artificial lakes, are made by constructing a [14] **dam** and the water is used for hydro-electric power generation or as a water supply. Other wetland areas include [15] **marshes**, areas of grasses, rushes or reeds found on the edges of lakes and rivers, and [16] **swamps**, forested wetland.

A river's catchment area is all the land where water falls and flows into that one river. The watershed is the division between two catchment areas.

Task 4

Tell the students to listen to the text to decide which words they need to practice saying. This can be done as homework.

Task 5

Now ask the students to identify some terrain features on a map. Look at M79.1. Check with the key: M79.2

Task 6

Ask students to work in pairs and then go into a group with another pair. You might want to do a class check if you can project the photos onto a screen.

Task 7

Ask students to discuss the questions in pairs and then report to the class.

Task 8

Consolidation Tasks in Workbook.

> Do the **Revision: Key Collocations** task or set it for homework.

> **Don't forget:**
>
> 1. Spelling Challenge: World Cities to practice the NATO Alphabet.
>
> 2. Test the students on telling the time using the 24 hour clock, and using numbers, and DTG.
>
> 3. Test the students on the Key Tactical Verbs.
>
> 4. Test the students about mountains and deserts.

Unit 80

About the Unit

This terrain unit is focused on tropical forests.

Task 1

Tell the students to look at P80.1 and describe what they can see. Check with P80.2

Task 2 - 8 are text completion tasks. Check that the students understand the meaning of the words in the table above each text extract. Check any other unknown words or phrases afterwards. Choose at least one verb phrase, noun phrase and prepositional phrase from the text to explore with the students.

Task 2

Key	The climate varies little in tropical rain forests. Up to 3.5 meters of rain falls evenly throughout the year. Temperatures [1] **range** from about 32 degrees C in the day to 21 degrees C at night. The forest [2] **floor**, the bottom-most layer, of the forest only receives 2% of the [3] **sunlight** through the canopy. This means the forest floor is relatively clear of [4] **vegetation**. The understory layer lies between the canopy and the forest floor. It is home to numbers of birds, small mammals, insects, reptiles, and predators. The canopy is the [5] **primary** layer of the forest, forming a [6] **dense** roof of vegetation over the two lower layers. It contains the majority of the largest trees, which are typically 30–45 m in height. The emergent layer, above the canopy, contains a small [7] **number** of very large trees, called *emergents*, which reach heights of 45–55 m.

Task 3

Key	**Secondary growth rain forest** is very similar to rain forest but has [1] **denser** vegetation as more [2] **sunlight** reaches the lower levels of the forest. Secondary jungle is often [3] **regrowth** of areas of forest which have be burned, cut or cultivated and then abandoned. It is also found along the edges of the jungle or on river [4] **banks.**

Task 4

Key	**Semi-evergreen seasonal and monsoon forests** have two [1] **strata** of trees. Those in the upper story average 18 to 24 meters; those in the lower [2] **story** average 7 to 13 meters. The diameter of the trees averages 0.5 meter. Their leaves fall during a seasonal [3] **drought**.

Task 5

Key	In tropical scrub and thorn forests there is a definite dry [1] **season** when the trees are [2] **leafless**. The ground is [3] **bare** except for a few plants in bunches; grasses are uncommon. Most plants have [4] **thorns**. A *wait-a-while* tree will force you to stop and unhook your clothing.

Task 6

Key	**Tropical savannahs** are found within the tropical zones in South America and Africa. They look like a broad, [1] **grassy** meadow, with trees spaced at wide [2] **intervals**. Savannah [3] **soils** are frequently red.

Task 7

Key	Saltwater swamps are common in coastal areas subject to [1] **tidal** flooding. Mangrove trees, which can reach up to 12 m high, [2] **thrive** in these swamps and their tangled roots are an [3] obstacle to movement. Visibility in this type of swamp is [4] **poor**, and movement is extremely difficult. Tides in saltwater swamps can [5] **vary** as much as 12 meters.

Task 8

Key	Freshwater swamps are found in [1] **low-lying** inland areas. There are masses of thorny [2] **undergrowth**, reeds, grasses, and occasional short palms that reduce [3] **visibility** and make travel difficult. There are often [4] **islands** that dot these swamps, allowing you to get out of the water. Wildlife is [5] **abundant** in these swamps.

Task 9

Ask the students to re-read the texts they have completed and answer the questions:

Key	1.	Up to 3.5 meters
	2.	From about 32 degrees C in the day to 21 degrees C at night
	3.	Tropical Forest or secondary forest? Secondary
	4.	Saltwater or freshwater swamps? Saltwater.
	5.	Savannah.

Task 10

Tell the students to listen to the texts to decide which words they need to practice saying. This can be done as homework.

Task 11

Ask students to discuss the questions in pairs and then report to the class.

Task 12

Consolidation Tasks in Workbook.

Unit 81

About the Unit

This is a revision unit based on four listenings about tropical forests.

Task 1 - 4

Ask students to listen and make notes from the listening. They can check their notes with the transcripts.

This is a self evaluation task – how much can they note down? Which words do they still need to learn?

You could do this a class listening task or as an individual listening task.

Unit 82

About the Unit

This is a consolidation unit about tropical jungles.

Task 1

Ask students to work in pairs or small groups to prepare a briefing about an area of tropical forest from **Unit 82 Briefing Slides Tropical Regions**. There are 15 briefings, including the first one which is a presentation of the location of the regions. Ask the students as they listen to the briefings to make notes on the tropical areas and then compare them – which is the biggest etc.? Give feedback on their briefings.

Note: there are two versions of the briefings: individual versions for preparation (Standard size only), and a complete version of all the presentations together for the final briefing itself (Standard and Widescreen). The students can use the single briefings on their phones to prepare, and then present using the complete briefing on the larger screen, if that is possible.

About the Unit

This unit focuses on the language of terrain features associated with river estuaries and the coast.

Task 1

Tell the students to look at P83.1 and describe what they can see. Check with P83.2

Task 2

Teach/check the words in the table. Use the pictures indicated to help the students.

Task 3

Tell the students to look at M83.1 and identify the features A- O. They can check with their partner, then check with M83.2.

Task 4

Ask students to complete the text which describes the map in Task 3 with words from T2.

Key	The map show the [1] **estuary** of the North River. The river runs from the west into Massachusetts Bay. The Herring River joins the North River as it turns south-east towards the bay and the South River runs north to meet the North river as it joins the sea. The [2] **confluence** of the two rivers is exactly where the main [3] **channel** to the sea is. The main river channel is open at low tide. Smaller creeks also join the rivers and there are extensive [4] **marshes** in the estuary, together with a number of [5] **islands** like Bear Island and Wills Island. You can see the tidal [6] **mud flats** which are revealed at low tide and covered at high tide. There is a sand [7] **spit** running south along the coastline from Rivermoor into the North River channel, and this spit has pushed the river south. North of Rivermoor the coast is mainly a [8] **cliff** until Pegotty [9] **Beach.** There is a second cliff before the [10] **harbour** at Scituate. The harbour is protected by a [11] **breakwater** and there is a lighthouse on Cedar Point.

Task 5

Tell the students to listen to the text to decide which words they need to practice saying. This can be done as homework.

Task 6

Ask students to work in pairs and then go into a group with another pair. You might want to do a class check if you can project the photos onto a screen.

Task 7

Ask the students to test each other with M83.3, M83.2 and M83.3. They should identify features from T2 and test their partner on these using grid references: *What feature is at GRID 123456?*

Task 6 Teach/check the words in the table. Use the pictures to help.

Task 7 Ask the students to discuss the questions in pairs and then report.

Task 8

Consolidation Tasks in Workbook.

Do the **Revision: Key Collocations** task or set it for homework.

Don't forget:

1. Spelling Challenge: World Cities to practice the NATO Alphabet.

2. Test the students on telling the time using the 24 hour clock, and using numbers, and DTG.

3. Test the students on the Key Tactical Verbs.

4. Test the students about mountains, deserts, rivers and lakes.

Unit 84

About the Unit

This unit focuses on the language of transport associated with rivers, estuaries and the coast.

Task 1

Tell the students to look at P84.1 and describe what they can see.

Task 2

Teach/check the words in the table. Use the pictures indicated to help the students.

Task 3

Ask the students to discuss the questions in pairs and then report.

Task 4

Ask the students to make notes about the man's experiences. See transcript for key.

Do the students have similar anecdotes about travelling on water?

Task 5

Ask the students to discuss the questions in pairs and then report.

About the Unit:

This is the first of six units on urban terrain – the most complex terrain the students will operate in.

Task 1

Tell the students to look at P85.1 and describe what they can see. [Note: the photograph is from Prague, Czech)

Task 2

As a lead in to this task write these terms on the board and discuss the differences in meaning: e*state | compound | housing estate.*

Teach/check the words in the table. Use the pictures to help. Then discuss the question.

Task 3

Teach/check the words in the table. Use the pictures to help.

Task 4

Check the students are clear on the difference in meaning between the words.

Task 5

Ask the students to look at **P85.34** and complete the text. Check any other unknown words or phrases afterwards. Choose at least one verb phrase, noun phrase and prepositional phrase from the text to explore with the students.

Key	The picture shows a block of [1] **flats** or an [2] **apartment** block. It is made of [3] **bricks**. It is a five [4] **storey** building. There are four [5] **entrances** to the building. There are [6] **steps** up to each entrance. There are sixteen [7] **balconies** and you can see three [8] **drainpipes**.

Ask: What other details could be added to the description?

Task 6

Ask the students to look at **P85.35** and complete the text. Check any other unknown words or phrases afterwards. Choose at least one verb phrase, noun phrase and prepositional phrase from the text to explore with the students.

Key	The picture shows two buildings. On the left there is a pink two [1] **storey** wooden [2] **detached** house. It has a [3] **wooden** door in the centre of the ground [4] **floor** and two [5] **windows** on each side of the door. On the second storey there are probably five [6] **windows** – two are hidden by a tree. It has grey asbestos [7] **roof** and two [8] **chimneys**. The building on the right is a [9] **brick** three [10] **storey** building. It also has an asbestos [11] **roof** and two [12] **chimneys**. There are four satellite dishes. This building is a corner [13] **building**. Across the street from the pink building there is a park bench and rubbish bin. Between the two buildings there is a narrow street or a passageway to a [14] **courtyard** where a car is parked.

Ask: What other details could be added to the description?

Task 7

Ask the students to write a description of P85.36. This could be done for homework. Collect their descriptions and give feedback.

Task 8

Make sure the students can explain the difference between the terms.

Task 9

Ask the students to discuss the questions in pairs and then report.

Options: Bring in more photos of urban terrain to describe.

Don't forget:

1. Spelling Challenge: World Cities to practice the NATO Alphabet.

2. Test the students on telling the time using the 24 hour clock, and using numbers, and DTG.

3. Test the students on the Key Tactical Verbs.

4. Test the students about mountains, deserts, rivers and lakes.

Unit 86

About the Unit:

This unit focuses on describing positions on buildings – useful if you are receiving fire from a building and want to suppress it.

Task 1

Tell the students to look at P86.1 and describe what they can see.

Task 2

Look at the two systems to describe floors, and talk about storeys. Which floor system is used in your country?

Task 3

Look at how to describe which window is which.

Key   1 First story, fourth **from** the right: 2   3 Third story, first **from** the left: 11

2 Second storey, third **from** the left: 8

Task 4

Ask the students to practise in pairs. You might want to do an open class practice if you can project the photos.

Task 5

Now ask the students to practice describing the whole buildings from the same photographs. You might want to assign a photo to each student and ask them to write a description for homework.

> **Don't forget:**
>
> 1. Spelling Challenge: World Cities to practice the NATO Alphabet.
>
> 2. Test the students on telling the time using the 24 hour clock, and using numbers, and DTG.
>
> 3. Test the students on the Key Tactical Verbs.
>
> 4. Test the students about mountains, deserts, rivers and lakes, jungles, and coastal areas.

Unit 87

About the Unit

This unit focuses on the language of road features.

Task 1

Tell the students to look at P87.1 and describe what they can see. Check with P87.2.

Task 2

Teach/check the words in the table. Use the pictures indicated to help the students.

Task 3

Ask students to complete the text which describes P87.20 with words from T2. Check any other unknown words or phrases afterwards. Choose at least one verb phrase, noun phrase and prepositional phrase from the text to explore with the students.

Key	The picture shows a [1] **river** running through a city. The [2] **river** is running through a stone-lined channel. In the centre of the picture there is a stone [3] **bridge** crossing the river. There are some people walking across the [4] **bridge**. On the right bank of the river there is a [5] **road** with tram tracks and a tram. Between the road and the river there is a [6] **pavement/sidewalk**. There are street [7] **lights** lining the road. Cars and buses are also using this road. It is a [8] **one-way** street. On the other side of the river there is another [9] **road** and there is a glass fronted [10] **building**. In the background there are trees – there is a small [11] **park**. By there trees there seems to be a small [12] **market**. And on this side of the river in the [13] **background** there are some tall [14] **buildings**.

Ask: What other details could be added to the description?

Task 4

Ask students to complete the text which describes P87.21 with words from T2. Check any other unknown words or phrases afterwards. Choose at least one verb phrase, noun phrase and prepositional phrase from the text to explore with the students.

Key	The picture shows a complicated road [1] **junction**. There is a road coming in from the left, meeting a road from the right to make a [2]**T-junction**. Just before the junction, on each road there is a zebra crossing. There are no [3] **traffic** lights.
	To the left of this junction there is another [4] **turning** to the right. Just after the turning there is another zebra crossing. The road from the right continues to the left of the photograph and there is a fourth zebra crossing there.
	In the [5] **background** there are some trees and low [6] **buildings** on the left, and on the right there is a white two [7] **storey** building.
	The road junction is protected with [8] **barriers** to stop [9] **pedestrians** crossing except at the zebra crossings.
	In the foreground there are two flower beds with red flowers and there is a [10] **manhole** cover in the bottom right-hand corner of the photograph.

Ask: What other details could be added to the description?

Task 5

Ask the students to write descriptions of one or more of the photos P87.22-4.

Task 6

Check the students understand the differences between the words for different kinds of roads etc.

Task 7

This task is a revision task – revising language from **Unit 46**. You might want to do this task with other maps you have of town centres.

Task 8

Consolidation Tasks in Workbook.

Don't forget:

1. Spelling Challenge: World Cities to practice the NATO Alphabet.

2. Test the students on telling the time using the 24 hour clock, and using numbers, and DTG.

3. Test the students on the Key Tactical Verbs.

4. Test the students about mountains, deserts, rivers and lakes, jungles, and coastal areas.

Unit 88

About the Unit

This unit focuses on the language of forms of transport.

Task 1

Tell the students to look at P88.1 and describe what they can see.

Task 2

Teach/check the words in the table. Use the pictures indicated to help the students.

Task 3

Ask students to discuss the questions and report to the class on their partner's experiences and opinions.

Task 4

Teach/check the words in the table. Use the pictures indicated to help the students.

Task 5

This is a task to revise the language from **Units 85 – 88**.

Unit 89

About the Unit

This unit focuses on the three dimensions of urban areas.

Task 1

Tell the students to look at P89.1 and discuss the two questions. Do a class check.

Task 2

Teach/check the words in the table.

Task 3

Ask students to complete the text which describes P89.1 with words from T2. Check any other unknown words or phrases afterwards. Choose at least one verb phrase, noun phrase and prepositional phrase from the text to explore with the students.

Key	The urban environment is the most complex [1] **environment** soldiers will operate in. Urban areas have three dimensions to consider. Streets afford avenues of [2] **approach** and are the primary means for rapid ground movement in a [3] **built-up** area. Forces travelling along [4] **streets**, however, are often channeled by [5] **buildings** and have little space for maneuver off of the main thoroughfares. Buildings themselves provide cover and [6] **concealment**. They limit or enhance [7] **fields** of observation and fire, and they restrict or block movement of [8] **ground** forces. Upper floors and roofs

provide the urban threat forces excellent observation [9] **points** and battle [10] **positions** above the maximum elevation of many [11] **weapons** of troops at ground level. Shots from upper floors can strike friendly armored vehicles in [12] **vulnerable** points. Conventional lateral boundaries ([13] **lines**) will often not apply as threat forces control some stories of the same building while friendly forces control others. Below street [14] **level**, building [15] **basements** can also provide firing points below many weapons' minimum depressions and strike at weaker armor on the underside of the vehicle. Subterranean systems, such as [16] **sewers**, subways, connected [17] **cellars**, and utility systems, like electric cable tunnels, can provide covered and concealed access throughout the area of [18] **operations**. They can easily be employed as avenues of approach for dismounted elements. Both attacker and defender can use subterranean routes to [19] **outflank** or turn enemy positions and to conduct ambushes, [20] **counterattacks**, infiltration, and sustainment operations.

Task 4

Ask the students to explain to their partner the collations from the text; class check.

Task 5

Tell the students to listen to the text to decide which words they need to practice saying. This can be done as homework.

Task 6

Ask the students to prepare a talk on the difficulties of operating in the urban areas shown in the photographs. This could be done as a pair work or group work task. The students can use the language reminder to help them.

Task 7

Consolidation Tasks in Workbook.

Don't forget:

1. Spelling Challenge: World Cities to practice the NATO Alphabet.

2. Test the students on telling the time using the 24 hour clock, and using numbers, and DTG.

3. Test the students on the Key Tactical Verbs.

4. Test the students about mountains, deserts, rivers and lakes, jungles, and coastal areas.

Unit 90

About the Unit

This unit continues the focus on the three dimensions of urban areas with a series of listening tasks.

Task 1

Ask the students what they can remember from **Unit 89**. They could work in pairs before the class check or do it as an open class exercise.

Task 2

Teach/check the words in the table. Use the pictures indicated to help the students.

Task 3

Ask students to make notes about the different urban areas talked about. See transcript for key.

Task 4

Ask students to complete the transcript on the next page, then listen to check. You could let them check with the transcript.

Task 5

Ask students to make notes about the other dimensions talked about talked about. See transcript for key.

Task 6

Ask students to complete the transcript on the next page, then listen to check. You could let them check with the transcript.

Task 7

Ask students to discuss the questions and report to the class on their partner's opinions.

Task 8

Ask the students to work in pairs and role play they are intelligence officers. Before they do the task, ask them to specify what information they would expect to hear in such a briefing. Evaluate them on how well they present this expected information. They should present an intelligence briefing about the town shown on the map in the slides.

Unit 91

About the Unit

This unit focuses on the language of bridges, dams and airfields.

Task 1

Tell the students to look at P91.1 and describe what they can see.

Task 2

Teach/check the words in the table. Use the pictures indicated to help the students.

Task 3

Ask students the differences between the types of bridges. Then let them look at the photographs to check. Which types do they have in their country?

Task 4

Teach/check the key words about dams using the photograph.

Task 5

Teach/check the key words about airfields using the photograph.

Task 6 -8

Ask the students to prepare a briefing on one of the slides from **Unit 91 Briefing Slides**. Do not forget to give them feedback on their briefings.

Don't forget:

1. Spelling Challenge: World Cities to practice the NATO Alphabet

2. Test the students on telling the time using the 24 hour clock, and using numbers, and DTG.

3. Test the students on the Key Tactical Verbs.

4. Test the students about mountains, deserts, rivers and lakes, jungles, and coastal areas.

Unit 92

About the Unit

This unit focuses on how to express uncertainty. Students need to understand how to show they are uncertain about something and to understand when someone else is uncertain about something.

As there is a lot of material in this lesson you might want to split it into two.

Task 1

Tell the students to look at P92.1 and describe what they can see. They will have to guess what is shown in the photo.

Task 2 and 3

Look at how we present things as facts and how we hedge if we are not sure.

Key				
	1.	Fact.	7.	Uncertain.
	2.	Uncertain.	8.	Uncertain.
	3.	Fact.	9.	Uncertain.
	4.	Uncertain.	10.	Uncertain.
	5.	Fact.	11.	Uncertain.
	6.	Uncertain.	12.	Uncertain.

Task 4

Teach/check the key words about describing shapes.

Task 5

Ask the students to describe the building parts in P92.2.

Task 6

Ask the students to complete the description of P92.2.

Key	On the [1] **left** there is a light grey structure made out of [2] **concrete**. It is [3] **cylindrical** and has a dark grey [4] **conical** roof. Behind it, and slightly to the left, is another building which looks exactly the same. They are joined together by a metal [5] **structure** which runs from the tip of each roof. Next to these two structures, on the left, is a square white [6] **building** with a dark grey roof. On the right side of this building there is a a dark grey rectangular [7] **sloping** structure which runs up to the tip of the first building with the conical roof. There is a similar structure running to the tip of the roof of the second cylindrical building. Behind the square white building is the largest building. It is a big [8] **square** building with a blue [9] **rectangular** structure on the right on the wall facing us, as well as a tall, grey [10] **cylindrical** structure. On this same wall but on the left. Behind the building is a dark grey [11] **platform** and another blue rectangular structure. In front of these are two large silver [12] **cylindrical** structures. The one of the left is slightly taller than the one on the right.

Task 7

Ask the students to work in pairs and look at the photos in sequence and discuss what they can see. The pictures are all of the same thing, which gradually reveals itself as a table.

Task 8

Ask students to look at P92.9 and listen to how the speaker describes what he can see. This is a preview of what they have to do in Task 9. They can check with the transcript.

Task 9

Ask the students to present one of the photos from **Unit 92 Briefing Slides**. They could do this in pairs, or in groups or as a class. Remember to give them feedback on their breifings.

Units 93 – 98 Land Navigation

This series of units is focused on land navigation. Like other sets of units you need to decide if you are going to do them as a block or thread them with other units, and if you need to do all the units.

The map tasks and radio calls units will have given you some idea of how good your students are at giving grid references. The work here focuses on 6 figure grid references but you might want them to give you 8 figure references, which are, of course, more exact.

Unit 93

About the Unit

This unit is focused on the differences between the three norths, and on using grid references.

Task 1

Ask the students to discuss the question in pairs or small groups and report on their discussion.

Task 2

Ask the students to draw a compass rose and then check with P93.1. Drill the pronunciation of the compass points.

Task 3

Ask the students to complete the text.

Key	A compass points to **magnetic** north. This is different from **true** north and **grid** north, the north of the northing lines on a map. The difference between **true/magnetic** north and **true/magnetic** north is known as the magnetic declination.

Task 4

There are different kinds of compasses – check the students know the parts of the two kinds pictured.

Task 5

Ask the students to prepare a presentation for another group on one kind of compass. They should talk about the parts of the compass and explain what they are used for and how they are used.

Task 6 and 7

Ask the students to work through the explanation in pairs about grid references. Monitor and help as required.

Task 8

In this task the students test themselves on what they learnt from T6 and T7.

Key	1. 588828	5. 587823	9. 585825
	2. 585827	6. 584820	10. 589829
	3. 584824	7. 580826	
	4. 588828	8. 589821	

Task 9

In this task, ask the students to test each other on grid references using other maps. Make sure they give the references clearly and slowly. You could do it using radios if you have them.

Unit 94

About the Unit

This unit revises and extends the students knowledge of how terrain is represented on maps. There is a presentation of the diagrams, pictures and maps for Task 2, Task 3, Task 4 and Task 5 to use if you prefer.

Task 1

Ask the students to work in pairs and write down all the words they remember from the units on mountainous terrain (**Units 71** and **72**).

Task 2

Ask students to look at the diagrams and compare the photo/drawing with the map representation.

Task 3

In this task the students test themselves by finding mountain features on the map on the next page. They can check in groups and look at the sample key in M94.2.

Task 4

Check the students know the words in the table and then see if they can find them on the maps. Note that each map series has different conventions. These map sections are taken from old Soviet maps.

Task 5

This task gives more practice in seeing how features are represented on maps.

P94.1 shows features A – E. Students should look at Map M94.11 and try to identify the features A – E. They can check with P94.10. This might not work as it will depend on how well they can see the features on the map.

Repeat the task with P94.11 and features A – H. Use M94.12, Check with P94.12.

Task 6

This is further practice in a more formal setting of a map presentation. The briefer should point out significant features, from a military perspective, on the maps to the audience.

Task 7

This task combines the vocabulary from this unit and map references from **Unit 93**. Good quality maps are essential for this task.

Don't forget:

1. Spelling Challenge: World Cities to practice the NATO Alphabet.

2. Test the students on telling the time using the 24 hour clock, and using numbers, and DTG.

3. Test the students on the Key Tactical Verbs.

4. Test the students about all terrain features.

Unit 95

About the Unit

This unit focuses on the use of route cards to describe routes e.g. patrol routes.

Task 1

Check the students understand the route card.

Task 2

Ask the students to use maps and prepare a 5 leg route. They should prepare a route card and brief the class (or another pair or group) on their route.

Unit 96

About the Unit

This unit focuses on the military considerations when analysing terrain.

Task 1

Ask students to discuss and then report on why **OAKOC** is important.

Task 2

Teach/check the words in the table.

Task 3

Ask students to complete the text with words from T2. Check any other unknown words or phrases afterwards. Choose at least one verb phrase, noun phrase and prepositional phrase from the text to explore with the students.

Key	**Observation and Fields of Fire**. The purpose of observation is to see the enemy (or various [1] **landmarks**) but not be seen by him. Anything that can be seen can be hit. Therefore, a field of fire is an area that a weapon or a group of weapons can [2] **cover** effectively with fire from a given [3] **position**.
	Avenues of Approach. These are [4] **access** routes. They may be the routes you can use to get to the enemy or the routes they can use to get to you. Basically, an identifiable route that approaches a position or location is an avenue of approach to that location. They are often terrain [5] **corridors** such as [6] **valleys** or wide, open areas.
	Key Terrain. Key terrain is any locality or area that the seizure or [7] **retention** of affords a marked advantage to either combatant. Urban areas that are often seen by higher headquarters as being key terrain because they are used to control [8] **routes**. On the other hand, an urban area that is destroyed may be an [9] **obstacle** instead. High ground can be key because it dominates an area with good observation and fields of fire. In an open area, a draw or [10] **wadi** may provide the only cover for many kilometers, thereby becoming key. You should always attempt to locate any area near you that could be even remotely considered as key terrain.
	Obstacles. Obstacles are any [11] **obstructions** that stop, delay, or [12] **divert** movement. Obstacles can be natural (rivers, swamps, cliffs, or mountains) or they may be artificial (barbed wire entanglements, pits, concrete or metal anti-mechanized traps). They can be ready-made or constructed in the [13] **field**. Always consider any possible obstacles along your movement [14] **route** and, if possible, try to keep obstacles between the enemy and yourself.

> **Cover and Concealment**. Cover is shelter or [15] **protection** (from enemy fire) either natural or [16] **artificial.** Always try to use covered routes and seek [17] **cover** for each halt, no matter how brief it is planned to be. Unfortunately, two [18] **factors** interfere with obtaining constant cover. One is time and the other is terrain. Concealment is protection from observation or surveillance, including concealment from enemy air observation. Before, trees provided good [19] **concealment**, but with modern thermal and infrared imaging equipment, trees are not always effective. When you are moving, concealment is generally [20] **secondary**; therefore, select routes and positions that do not allow covered or concealed enemy near you.

Task 4

Ask students to explain the collocations from the text. They can do this in pairs before a class check.

Task 5

Tell the students to listen to the text to decide which words they need to practice saying. This can be done as homework.

Task 6

This task repeats T2 from **Unit 95** but in more detail.

Task 7

Consolidation Tasks in Workbook.

Don't forget:

1. Spelling Challenge: World Cities to practice the NATO Alphabet.

2. Test the students on telling the time using the 24 hour clock, and using numbers, and DTG.

3. Test the students on the Key Tactical Verbs.

4. Grid references: test the students, or ask them to test each other, on grid references and terrain features, using a good map.

Unit 97

About the Unit

This unit focuses on more military considerations when analysing terrain.

Task 1

Ask students to discuss and then report on why **METT-T** is important.

Task 2

Teach/check the words in the table.

Task 3

Ask the students to complete the text with words from T2. Check any other unknown words or phrases afterwards. Choose at least one verb phrase, noun phrase and prepositional phrase from the text to explore with the students.

Key	**Mission**. This refers to the specific task assigned to a unit or individual. Soldiers must get to the right place, at the right time, and in good [1] **fighting** condition. Patrol missions are used to conduct combat or [2] **reconnaissance** operations. During the map reconnaissance, the mission leader determines a primary and [3] **alternate** route to and from the objectives. Movement to contact is conducted whenever an element is moving toward the enemy but is not in contact with the enemy. Delays and [4] **withdrawals** are conducted to slow the enemy down without becoming decisively [5] **engaged**, or to assume another mission. To be effective, the element leader must know where he is to move and the route to be taken.
	Enemy. This refers to the strength, status of training, disposition (locations), doctrine, capabilities, equipment (including night vision devices), and probable courses of [6] **action** that impact upon both the planning and execution of the [7] **mission**, including a movement.
	Terrain and Weather. The leader conducts a map reconnaissance to determine key terrain, obstacles, cover and concealment, and likely avenues of approach. Weather has little [8] **effect** on dismounted land navigation. Rain and snow could possibly slow [9] **down** the rate of march, that is all. But during mounted land navigation, the navigator must know the effect of weather on his vehicle.
	Troops. Consideration of your own troops is equally important. The size and type of the unit to be moved and its capabilities, physical [10] **condition**, status of training, and types of equipment assigned all affect the selection of routes, positions, fire plans, and the various decisions to be made during movement. On ideal terrain such as relatively [11] **level** ground with little or no woods, a platoon can defend a [12] **front** of up to 400 meters. The leader must conduct a thorough map reconnaissance and terrain analysis of the area his unit is to defend. Heavily wooded areas or very hilly areas may [13] **reduce** the front a platoon can defend. The size of the unit must also be taken into [14] **consideration** when planning a movement to contact. During movement, the unit must retain its ability to [15] **maneuver**. A small draw or stream may reduce the unit's maneuverability but provide excellent concealment. All of these factors must be considered.
	Time Available. At times, the unit may have little time to reach an [16] **objective** or to move from one point to another. The leader must conduct a map reconnaissance to determine the quickest [17] **route** to the objective; this is not always a straight route. From point A to point B on the map may appear to be 1,000 meters, but if the route is across a large [18] **ridge**, the distance will be greater. Another route from point A to B may be 1,500 meters—but on flat [19] **terrain**. In this case, the quickest route would be across the flat terrain; however, [20] **concealment** and cover may be lost.

Task 4

Tell the students to listen to the text to decide which words they need to practice saying. This can be done as homework.

Task 5

This task repeats T2 from **Unit 95** and T6 from **Unit 96** but with more complexity.

Task 6

Consolidation Tasks in Workbook.

Don't forget:

1. Spelling Challenge: World Cities to practice the NATO Alphabet.

2. Test the students on telling the time using the 24 hour clock, and using numbers, and DTG.

3. Test the students on the Key Tactical Verbs.

4. Grid references: test the students, or ask them to test each other, on grid references and terrain features, using a good map.

Unit 98

About the Unit

This is the last unit on land navigation and is about navigation techniques and about the difficulties of navigating in different terrains.

The students have to give presentations and this will give them the opportunity to use their soldiering knowledge in English.

Be ready to give feedback on the language they use. Let the other soldiers give feedback on military issues.

Units 99 – 103 The Disposition of Forces

This series of units is about the disposition of forces as represented on maps with symbols.

The symbols used here are adapted from US Marine symbols but these might differ from the ones used by your soldiers in some ways. This is not a problem as they should be used to adapting to slight differences in the symbols used. They will need to be able to learn the symbols on missions which might be different again so this is good practice for them.

Each lesson follows roughly the same pattern – vocabulary introduced in words, then symbols, then a map description task, then a briefing task. You will need other maps for these units.

You should encourage the students to only use the symbols which have been taught in that unit and the previous ones. They will probably know other symbols but you should suggest that they concentrate on the set being presented in the unit.

Like other sets of units you need to decide if you are going to do them as a block or thread them with other units, and if you need to do all the units. This sequence of units would probably be better threaded with other units instead of doing them as a block. You could intersperse them with the following survival units or with the medical units.

Unit 99

About the Unit

This is the first of five units on the disposition of forces. The others are: **Units 100, 101, 102. 103**. The grammar focus is on present tenses and passive verb forms.

Task 1

Tell the students to look at P99.1 and P99.2 and describe what they can see.

Tasks 2 – Task 4 are linked.

Task 2

Check the meaning of the words in the table.

Task 3

Tell students to look at the set of Symbols and Meaning, or in P99.3 or **Unit 99 Presentation**.

Task 4

Then tell them to look at the text and Map and Overlay, or in P99.4 or **Unit 99 Presentation** and complete the description of the disposition of the forces.

Key	We have a [1] **platoon** of 4 light tanks in defensive positions north of Pelican Creek just east of Vermilion Springs. There are two light [2] **howitzers** on a hill at Grid 377878. South of the Creek there is an infantry [3] **platoon** with two [4] **machine guns,** with two [5] **mortars** in support at Grid 373871, and two light [6] **anti-tank missiles** on the left flank on the Pelican Creek Trail. The enemy is in defensive positions to the west. An armoured [7] **platoon** with three light [8] **tanks** is in position to the east of Ebro Springs, between the Sulphur Hills and Pelican Creek. South of the Creek there is an [9] **infantry** platoon with three light [10] **machine guns**. Just north of the East Service Road, north of Squaw Lake there is another light armoured [11] **platoon** with three [12] **tanks.**

Task 5

Tell the students to use their maps and prepare an overlay of disposition of forces using the symbols from T3. They should brief the class on the disposition of forces. Give feedback on their briefings. You might want to provide them with photocopies of their maps so they can draw on them, or provide overlay materials.

Unit 100

About the Unit

This is the second of five units on the disposition of forces. The grammar focus is on present tenses and passive verb forms.

Task 1

Ask the students to work in pairs and test each other with symbols from previous units on the disposition of forces.

Task 2

Check the meaning of the words in the table and check the words from the previous units.

Task 3

Tells students to look at the set of Symbols and Meaning, or in P100.1 or **Unit 100 Presentation**.

Task 4

Then tell them to write a description of the forces . When everyone has finished, display the descriptions on the walls and everyone should read the descriptions and correct any mistakes.

Task 5

Tell the students to use their maps and prepare an overlay of disposition of forces using the symbols from T3. They should brief the class on the disposition of forces. Give feedback on their briefings.

Unit 101

About the Unit

This is the third of five units on the disposition of forces. The grammar focus is on present tenses and passive verb forms.

Task 1

Ask the students to work in pairs and test each other with symbols from previous units on the disposition of forces.

Task 2

Check the meaning of the words in the table and check the words from the previous units.

Task 3

Tells students to look at the set of Symbols and Meaning, or in P101.1 or **Unit 101 Presentation**.

Task 4

Then tell them to write a description of the forces. When everyone has finished, display the descriptions on the walls and everyone should read the descriptions and correct any mistakes.

Task 5

Tell the students to use their maps and prepare an overlay of disposition of forces using the symbols from T3. They should brief the class on the disposition of forces. Give feedback on their briefings.

Unit 102

About the Unit

This is the fourth of five units on the disposition of forces. The grammar focus is on present tenses and passive verb forms.

Task 1

Ask the students to work in pairs and test each other with symbols from previous units on the disposition of forces.

Task 2

Check the meaning of the words in the table and check the words from the previous units.

Task 3

Tells students to look at the set of Symbols and Meaning, or in P102.1 or **Unit 102 Presentation**.

Task 4

Then tell them to write a description of the forces . When everyone has finished, display the descriptions on the walls and everyone should read the descriptions and correct any mistakes.

Task 5

Tell the students to use their maps and prepare an overlay of disposition of forces using the symbols from T3. They should brief the class on the disposition of forces. Give feedback on their briefings.

Don't forget:

1. Spelling Challenge: World Cities to practice the NATO Alphabet.

2. Test the students on telling the time using the 24 hour clock, and using numbers, and DTG.

3. Test the students on the Key Tactical Verbs.

4. Grid references: test the students, or ask them to test each other, on grid references and terrain features, using a good map.

Unit 103

About the Unit

This is the fifth of five units on the disposition of forces. The grammar focus is on present tenses and passive verb forms.

Task 1

Ask the students to work in pairs and test each other with symbols from previous units on the disposition of forces.

Task 2

Check the meaning of the words in the table and check the words from the previous units.

Task 3

Tells students to look at the set of Symbols and Meaning, or in P103.1 or **Unit 103 Presentation**.

Task 4

Then tell them to write a description of the forces. When everyone has finished, display the descriptions on the walls and everyone should read the descriptions and correct any mistakes.

Task 5

Tell the students to use their maps and prepare an overlay of disposition of forces using the symbols from T3. They should brief the class on the disposition of forces. Give feedback on their briefings.

Units 104 – 110 Survival

This series of units is about survival kits and situations.

Unit 104 is about survival kits.

Unit 105 is about the steps to take in survival situations.

Units 106 – 109 are survival simulations. There are no separate Teacher's Notes for these units.

Unit 110 is a survival quiz.

Like other sets of units you need to decide if you are going to do them as a block or thread them with other units, and if you need to do all the units.

Unit 104

About the Unit

This unit focuses on the contents of survival kits and the uses of the equipment found in them.

Task 1

Ask students to discuss the question in pairs and report to the class on their discussion.

Task 2

Use the photographs to check items commonly found in survival kits.

Task 3

Ask students to take notes about what the man says the pieces of equipment are and what they are used for. You can use the transcript to focus on the language the man uses to talk about what things are used for.

Task 4

Ask students to talk about the other items of equipment in the kit from T2. What can each thing be used for? How inventive can your students be?

Task 5

This task focuses on a so-called 'military survival kit'. Ask students to look at the picture first and then listen, make notes and answer the question.

This can be extended into a writing task by asking the students to compare the two kits. Use the language reminder box to help.

Task 6

Ask the students to work in pairs to devise and then present their ideal survival kit.

Extra Task: You could present this imaginary problem situation to your students and see how creative and inventive they are. Put the students into teams. The teams are put into different parts of the room and given a large blank piece of poster paper and a pen. Tell the students they will be given a problem to solve and they have to compete to see who can give the most solutions to the problem after five minutes. The students work together to brainstorm solutions. A secretary writes the ideas on the poster paper. All ideas must be written up. No questions or discussion until the brainstorm is over.

Describe the situation to the students: *Imagine we are survivors from a plane crash in the Pacific ocean. We have swum to a desert island and here we are sitting on the beach thinking of what to do next. We have absolutely nothing apart from the clothing we are wearing. Suddenly we see something floating in the water! We run to get it. It is a case. What's inside?...Twenty-four cans of Coca-cola! The problem is, what are we going to do with them? How may uses for them can you think of in five minutes?*

After the brainstorming phase the students have some time to clarify and justify their answers. Then check as a class. Which team has the most original answers?

Acknowledgement: This task is taken from Richard and Marjorie Baudains (1990) Alternatives, Longman.

Don't forget:

1. Spelling Challenge: World Cities to practice the NATO Alphabet.

2. Test the students on telling the time using the 24 hour clock, and using numbers, and DTG.

3. Test the students on the Key Tactical Verbs.

4. Grid references: test the students, or ask them to test each other, on grid references and terrain features, using a good map.

About the Unit

This unit focuses on the priority steps you should take in a survival situation.

> **Important Note:** Make sure you ask students to cover up the text in Task 5 at the beginning of the lesson.

Task 1

Ask the students to look at the photos and describe what they can see.

Task 2

This second Talk and Report task is a prediction task for the listening in Task 3. Elicit ideas of what they think they should do in a survival situation. Do not comment on their ideas.

Task 3

Ask students to listen to the talk and make notes, and see if they agree with the speaker.

Task 4

This is a prediction task for the reading task in Task 5. Elicit ideas.

Task 5

Ask students to read the text to see if their ideas in Task 4 were correct. Check any other unknown words or phrases afterwards. Choose at least one verb phrase, noun phrase and prepositional phrase from the text to explore with the students.

Task 6

Ask students to explain the collocations from the text. They can do this in pairs before a class check.

Task 7

Tell the students to listen to the text to decide which words they need to practice saying. This can be done as homework.

Task 8

Ask the students to make notes on what the speaker says about temperate lowlands. This listening is presenting some language they can use in Task 9.

Task 9 - 11

Ask the students to prepare a presentation on survival in the three situations – desert, tropical and cold weather survival.

Units 106 – 109 Survival Simulations

There are detailed notes on how to use the four survival simulations in the Coursebook.

You might want to consider appointing one member of each group secretly to act as 'Devil's Advocate'. Their role is to challenge the other members of the group to justify their ideas. They would ask questions like: 'Do you think that is a good idea?'; 'Is that the best way?'; 'Why do you think that?'

Remember, you might not want to do these four units as a block but spread them out over the remainder of the course.

Unit 110

About the Unit

This is a Survival Quiz, which test the student's survival knowledge, not just from the material in this book, and the use of should/shouldn't and would/wouldn't etc. Follow the instructions in the Coursebook.

Units 111 – 110 Medical Units

This series of units is about parts of the body, medical problems and treatment, and Tactical Casualty Combat Care (TCCC/TC3). TC3 vocabulary is necessary for specialised training in this area.

Like other sets of units you need to decide if you are going to do them as a block or thread them with other units, and if you need to do all the units.

Soldiers at an HQ or working in logistics would only need the general medical units (**Units 111-114**). Soldiers involved in active patrolling, or who are based at an FOB will also need TC3.

Unit 111

About the Unit

This unit focuses on parts of the body and common medical problems.

Task 1

Check the students know the parts of the body using the photos. Add your own exercises to practise/test their knowledge. In each of the following units there will be revision of this vocabulary.

Task 2

Check the students know the difference between these commonly confused terms. Ask them to work in groups and produce model sentences to show the differences.

Task 3

Ask the students to match the ailment and the definition.

Key	1. a headache	a pain in the head or neck
	2. high blood pressure	elevated blood pressure in arteries
	3. a migraine	a severe long-lasting headache
	4. sun/heat stroke	when the body temperature is greater than 40.6 °C; with dry skin, rapid, strong pulse and dizziness [hyperthermia; compare with hypothermia]
	5. hypothermia	when the body core temperature is below 35.0 °C; with shivering and mental confusion
	6. a fracture	a break in a bone
	7. a haemorrhage	bleeding
	8. backache	pain in the back
	9. a twisted/sprained ankle	torn ligaments in an ankle
	10. a pulled muscle	an overstretched muscle
	11. an allergy	immune system hypersensitivity to an environmental factor e.g. dust or pollen; with sneezing, runny nose and eyes
	12. a heart attack	when blood flow stops to a part of the heart causing damage to the heart muscle, and possible death due to cardiac arrest
	13. food poisoning	vomiting, fever, and aches, and may include diarrhoea due to contaminated food.
	14. diarrhoea	loose or liquid bowel movements leading to dehydration
	15. stroke	poor blood flow to the brain resulting in cell death; due to lack of blood flow or bleeding.
	appendicitis	inflammation of the appendix
	concussion	a head injury with a temporary loss of brain function.
	frostbite	Frozen skin and tissue

Task 4

Students practice asking and answering questions using the Present Perfect and Simple Past to ask about their partner's medical history. This practise the distinction between sometime before now (Present Perfect) and a specific known time in the past (Simple Past). Ask them to report on what their partner has suffered from and when it happened. In this kind of exercise the students do not have to just tell the truth. They could make up an eventful medical history just to practice the words and grammar.

Unit 112

About the Unit

This unit revises the language presented in **Unit 111** and extends it with treatments.

Task 1

Students test each other on parts of the body and ailments from **Unit 111**.

Task 2

Students discuss and then report on the standard treatment for three medical problems.

Task 3

Ask students to match the ailments from T3 **Unit 111** with the suggested treatments.

Key	1. a headache	take some painkillers
	2. high blood pressure	eat healthier, quit smoking, exercise more
	3. a migraine	take some painkillers, lie down and sleep
	4. sun/heat stroke	remove excess clothing, reduce body temperature with water or ice packs
	5. hypothermia	warm the victim's trunk gradually and give warm fluids if awake
	6. a fracture	have an x-ray, splint the limb or use a plaster cast
	7. a haemorrhage	clean the wound and stop the bleeding
	8. backache	do exercises to strengthen muscles
	9. a twisted/sprained ankle	apply cold compress, bandage and rest
	10. a pulled muscle	rub the muscle to warm it and then rest it
	11. an allergy	take anti-histamine tablets
	12. a heart attack	perform CPR if necessary; go to hospital, take medicine to reduce blood clots
	13. food poisoning	avoid solid food until vomiting stops; prevent dehydration
	14. diarrhoea	drink plenty of clean water and rehydration fluids
	15. stroke	go to hospital for scans, possible surgery and medicine
	appendicitis	hospitalisation for an operation to remove the affected organ
	concussion	Observation and rest; CT or MRI scan.
	frostbite	Heating treatment on affected areas or surgery if necessary.

Task 4

In this task the students take the suggested treatments from Task 3 and make it into advice or suggestions as in the Language Reminder box.

Don't forget:

1. Spelling Challenge: World Cities to practice the NATO Alphabet.

2. Test the students on telling the time using the 24 hour clock, and using numbers, and DTG.

3. Test the students on the Key Tactical Verbs.

4. Grid references: test the students, or ask them to test each other, on grid references and terrain features, using a good map.

Unit 113

About the Unit

This unit extends the students' knowledge of medical language into a more formal medical history, which they may need to give if seeking medical attention.

Task 1

Again, students test each other on parts of the body, ailments and treatments from **Unit 111/2**

Task 2

Check the students understand the difference between the five five words and then ask them to do a short Q and A practice using 'Have you ever had...?'

Task 3

Teach/check the words in the table and then ask the students to complete the text. Check any other unknown words or phrases afterwards. Choose at least one verb phrase, noun phrase and prepositional phrase from the text to explore with the students.

Key	When I was a boy I [1] **broke** my upper right arm playing in the school playground. My nose was [2] **broken** in a pub fight. I've never had to wear a [3] **plaster cast** though. I used to have a lot of migraine [4] **headaches** but now I don't as I don't drink so much coffee. Sometimes I have a [5] **bad** back, if I twist it, but if I do regular exercise I can lift things without any problems. I have hay [6] **fever** – I'm allergic to grass and dust. I had the usual childhood [7] **diseases** – measles and mumps but I've never had a serious [8] **infectious** disease like TB. I don't smoke, or drink too much. I've had food poisoning (acute [9] **gastroenteritis**) once or twice and ended up in hos-

pital because I had [10] **diarrhoea** and was [11] **vomiting** a lot. The most serious medical problem I've ever had was when I had [12] **viral** meningitis. That meant two weeks in hospital and two months [13] **convalescence** leave. My most serious [14] **operation** was to remove my appendix. Generally, I'm fit and active, and healthy. I have a good diet and get regular exercise and go out in the sunshine for [15] **vitamin** D when I can.

Task 4

It would be a good idea to analyse the use of verbs in this text to highlight the use of Simple Present, Present Perfect and Simple Past forms in particular.

Task 5

Tell the students to listen to the text to decide which words they need to practice saying. This can be done as homework.

Task 6

This task is preparation for the speaking task in Task 7. These kinds of tasks work best if the students use their imagination and invent a history of medical problems. This preserves privacy as well.

Task 7

This is an extended version of the task in Task 2 of this unit and Task 4 in **Unit 111**. You should expect your students to show better grammatical and lexical control over this repeated practice.

Task 8

Students report on their partner's medical history.

Do the **Revision: Key Collocations** task or set it for homework.

Don't forget:

1. Spelling Challenge: World Cities to practice the NATO Alphabet.

2. Test the students on telling the time using the 24 hour clock, and using numbers, and DTG.

3. Test the students on the Key Tactical Verbs.

4. Grid references: test the students, or ask them to test each other, on grid references and terrain features, using a good map.

About the Unit

This is the last of the general medical units. The focus is on visiting a doctor and answering the doctor's questions.

Task 1

Again, students test each other on parts of the body, ailments and treatments from **Unit 111/2**. Repeated (but short) practice of this is very necessary.

Task 2

Check the students understand the difference between the five five words and then ask them to do a short Q and A practice using *'Have you ever had something which was...?'* Suggest the students ask for more details: *'When did it happen? Did you go to the doctor?'* Etc.

Task 3

Teach/check the words in the table and then ask the students to complete the text. Check any other unknown words or phrases afterwards. Choose at least one verb phrase, noun phrase and prepositional phrase from the text to explore with the students.

Key	The doctor's role is to [1] **diagnose** and [2] **treat** patients. Patients trust doctors to make a correct [3] **diagnosis**, to be up to date with medical [4] **knowledge** and be capable of deciding on the most appropriate treatment, and they expect the doctor to [5] **act** in the patient's best interest. Diagnosis is a key part of a doctor's [6] **expertise**. It involves [7] **evaluating** the first signs of the [8] **illness**, and asking for and assessing [9] **information** from the patient. Then the doctor decides on treatment based on the diagnosis.
	Doctor's should take a medical [10] **history** of the patient, do a [11] **physical** examination and authorise tests such as blood work and various [12] **scans** (e.g. USG) to reach the proper diagnosis. The doctor may then [13] **prescribe** different types of treatment such as a course of antibiotics, surgery, physiotherapy and so on.
	Doctors should be able to explain and discuss the [14] **risks**, benefits and uncertainties of various tests and [15] **treatments** so that the patient can make informed decisions about their care.

Task 4

In this task the students sort the terms according to verb (have/feel) use.

Key	Have: a cold | a temperature | a disease | a heart attack [nouns]
	Feel: cold | tired | exhausted | stressed [adjectives]

Task 5

Teach/check the key words in the table and then ask the students to complete the sentences, which are things a doctor might say.

Key	1. I'll just [1] **prescribe** some sleeping [2] **pills** for you. You should take them two hours before going to bed with food. 2. I'd like to run some [3] **tests**. We'll do an [4] **x-ray** and an [5] **ultrasound** scan.

Task 6

Ask the students to match the beginnings and ends to make a dialogue.

Key	Good morning Mr Harrison. How are you feeling today? Well, I've been having trouble sleeping. How long has this lasted? For a couple of weeks now. I feel very tired when I wake up Do you manage to get to sleep? Do you wake up in the middle of the night. It takes me a long time to get to sleep. Then I wake up two or three times in the night. Are you worried about something? Do you have problems at work? Nothing more than usual. No. Have there been any changes in your routine? Or your diet? No, everything is normal. Well, let's do some blood tests and see what that tells us. I'll just call the nurse.

Task 7

Ask students to practice the dialogue in pairs, and then to change the dialogue for a different medical problem and practice that. You might want to ask them to perform the dialogue in groups or open class.

Task 8

Ask the students to brief you on the medical tests and check-ups in their army.

Task 9

This writing task could be set for homework.

Task 10

Consolidation Tasks in Workbook.

About the Unit

This is the first of the TCCC units and not all your students will need to do these units. This unit focuses on medical kits and TCCC in general. You should have done the more general medical units before doing these units though.

Task 1

Again, students test each other on parts of the body, ailments and treatments from **Unit 111/2**.

Task 2

Discuss the difference in the words used to describe pain.

Then look at which words can be used to describe an ache.

Key	chronic/dull/continuous + ache

Task 3

Ask students to discuss and then report on the question.

Task 4

Ask students to list what should be in a medical kit. You could ask them for reason why.

Task 5

This task focuses on a civilian style first aid kit. Discuss with the class the differences between this kit and the kit they are/should be issued with.

Task 6

This is a prediction task for the reading in Task 7.

Task 7

Ask the students to read the text and see if they agree with the writer. Discuss any new words etc.

Task 8

Ask the students to read the text again and answer the questions.

Key	1. Only what the medic is carrying.
	2. The same as 1.
	3. The equipment/supplies in the vehicle used for CASEVAC.
	4. In Phase 1 you should win the firefight. In Phase 2 you can give more care. In Phase 3 there might be more resources and personnel to help.

Choose at least one verb phrase, noun phrase and prepositional phrase from the text to explore with the students.

Task 9

Set the Text Analysis tasks in class or for homework.

Task 10

Tell the students to listen to the text to decide which words they need to practice saying. This can be done as homework.

Task 11

Ask the students to brief the teacher on what training they receive and what training they should receive (if you think this is culturally appropriate).

Task 12

Consolidation Tasks in Workbook.

Don't forget:

1. Spelling Challenge: World Cities to practice the NATO Alphabet.

2. Test the students on telling the time using the 24 hour clock, and using numbers, and DTG.

3. Test the students on the Key Tactical Verbs.

4. Grid references: test the students, or ask them to test each other, on grid references and terrain features, using a good map.

Unit 116

About the Unit

This unit is wholly focused on learning the vocabulary necessary to understand TCCC.

Task 1

Ask the students to describe what they can see in the photo.

Task 2 - 7

In each task the students have to match words and definitions.

Task 2

Key	Airway: breathing tubes to the lungs
	haemorrhage: bleeding from the body
	hypovolemic shock: shock due to decreased blood pressure
	shock: the body's response to a severe event
	tourniquet: bandage or strap of some kind applied above a wound to stop the blood flow from the wound

---

Task 3

Key	cervical spine immobilization: stopping the neck from moving because of injury
	penetrating injury: an injury caused when the skin is pierced.
	Painkillers: medicine taken to control pain
	antibiotics: medicine taken to control infections by bacteria
	clinical assessment: an evaluation of the medical condition of a patient

Task 4

Key	treatment rendered: the steps taken to solve a medical problem
	pulse: the signal that the heart is beating
	respiration: breathing
	hypothermia: a body core temperature below 35.0 °C
	electrocution: injury or death caused by electricity

Task 5

Key	traumatic: adjective describing a serious injury
	intravenous (IV): within a vein
	trunk: the body of a person but not head, arms or legs
	wound: an injury where the skin is torn, broken or penetrated e.g. by a knife or bullet
	radial pulse: the heartbeat felt through the veins on the wrist

Task 6

Key	hemostasis: a process which causes bleeding to stop
	infection: invasion of the body by bacteria or viruses
	blood pressure: how strongly the blood moves around the body
	pulse oximetry: measurement of the amount of oxygen in the blood
	chest wound: a penetrating injury to the upper front of the trunk

Task 7

Key	splint: a device to support or immobilize a limb i.e. an arm or a leg.
	cardiopulmonary resuscitation: an emergency procedure of chest compression and mouth-to-mouth resuscitation
	unconscious: lack of consciousness
	morphine: an opiate based painkiller

Task 8

Ask students to listen to the words from T2 – T6 and practice saying them.

Task 9

Ask the students to test each other on the terms.

Task 10

This task focuses on the terms from T2 to T7 by not focusing on them.

Key		
	1.	If you have a headache you **can** take painkillers.
	2.	High blood pressure is **bad** for you.
	3.	Morphine **is** a very strong painkiller.
	4.	You **shouldn't** use antibiotics to treat a viral infection.
	5.	A knife wound **is** a penetrating injury.
	6.	When a patient is bleeding heavily from a limb you **should** apply a tourniquet.
	7.	After a serious injury for traumatic experience a patient **will** go into shock.
	8.	If someone has a heart attack you **should** attempt cardiopulmonary resuscitation.
	9.	A broken bone e.g. in your arm **should** be immobilised with a splint.
	10.	Loss of blood **might** lead to hypovolemic shock.

Task 11

Again, students test each other on parts of the body, ailments and treatments from **Unit 111/2**.

Don't forget:
1. Spelling Challenge: World Cities to practice the NATO Alphabet.
2. Test the students on telling the time using the 24 hour clock, and using numbers, and DTG.
3. Test the students on the Key Tactical Verbs.
4. Grid references: test the students, or ask them to test each other, on grid references and terrain features, using a good map.

Unit 117

About the Unit

This is the first unit focusing exclusively on TCCC/TC3.

Task 1

Ask the students to describe what they can see in the picture.

Task 2

This is a prediction task for the reading in Task 3. Elicit ideas but do not comment on the correctness of them. You might want the students to justify their answers.

Task 3

Ask the students to read the text and see if they agree with the writer. Check which students agree/disagree with the writer.

Task 4

Students re-read the text to answer the questions.

Key	1.	Because it is more important to win the firefight.
	2.	To protect yourself.
	3.	Play dead.
	4.	Not at this stage.
	5.	Because you can bleed out very quickly.
	6.	Ponchos, doors, dragging or manual carries
	7.	Rucksack if it contains valuable information, weapons and ammunition.

Check any other unknown words or phrases afterwards. Choose at least one verb phrase, noun phrase and prepositional phrase from the text to explore with the students.

Task 5

Set the Text Analysis tasks in class or for homework.

Task 6

Tell the students to listen to the text to decide which words they need to practice saying. This can be done as homework.

Task 7

This is a revision task of the main points of the text. Do individually, then in pairs and then as open class.

Task 8

Consolidation Tasks in Workbook.

Unit 118

About the Unit

This is the second unit focusing exclusively on TCCC.

Task 1

Ask the students to describe what they can see in the picture.

Task 2

This is a revision/prediction task for the reading in Task 3. Elicit ideas but do not comment on the correctness of them. You might want the students to justify their answers.

Task 3

Ask the students to read the text and see if they agree with the writer. Check which students agree/disagree with the writer.

Task 4

Students re-read the text to answer the questions.

Key		
	1.	Massive Haemorrhage, Airway, Respiration, Circulation, Head.
	2.	If the victim does not have a pulse.
	3.	For non-traumatic disorders.
	4.	In case they injure you or themselves.
	5.	The minimum.
	6.	To stop contamination and help hemostasis.
	7.	To make up for blood loss.
	8.	No.
	9.	Splint the leg.
	10.	Yes; to stop infections.
	11.	To reassure him.
	12.	To help care at the next level.

Check any other unknown words or phrases afterwards. Choose at least one verb phrase, noun phrase and prepositional phrase from the text to explore with the students.

Task 5

Set the Text Analysis tasks in class or for homework.

Task 6

Tell the students to listen to the text to decide which words they need to practice saying. This can be done as homework.

Task 7

This is a revision task of the main points of the text.

Task 8

Consolidation Tasks in Workbook.

About the Unit

This is the third unit focusing exclusively on TCCC.

Task 1

Ask the students to describe what they can see in the picture.

Task 2

This is a revision/prediction task for the reading in Task 3. Elicit ideas but do not comment on the correctness of them. You might want the students to justify their answers.

Task 3

Ask the students to read the text and see if they agree with the writer. Check which students agree/disagree with the writer.

Task 4

Students re-read the text to answer the questions.

Key		
	1.	3; primary, secondary and tertiary.
	2.	MEDEVAC vehicles are specially designed vehicles for casualty evacuation. CASEVAC vehicles are fighting vehicles.
	3.	These are vehicles which are used by several units/formations.
	4.	Availability of assets, weather, tactical situation and mission.
	5.	Those in shock, unconscious, with a traumatic brain injury or chest wound.

Check any other unknown words or phrases afterwards. Choose at least one verb phrase, noun phrase and prepositional phrase from the text to explore with the students.

Task 5

Set the Text Analysis tasks in class or for homework.

Task 6

Tell the students to listen to the text to decide which words they need to practice saying. Can be set as homework.

Task 7

This is a revision task of the main points of the text.

Task 8

Consolidation Tasks in Workbook.

Don't forget:
1. Spelling Challenge: World Cities to practice the NATO Alphabet.

2. Test the students on telling the time using the 24 hour clock, and using numbers, and DTG.

3. Test the students on the Key Tactical Verbs.

4. Grid references: test the students, or ask them to test each other, on grid references and terrain features, using a good map.

Unit 120

About the Unit

This is a revision unit where students practice giving a briefing on TCCC. This can be done in groups or as a whole class.

After the briefing you can ask the briefers to evaluate the audiences' notes. This can be done by the audience sticking their notes on the walls of the room and the briefer going around giving the notes marks.

Unit 121

About the Unit

This unit has two parts.

Task 1 is a listening task where students listen to a talk on TCCC.

Task 2 is a game where students have to answer questions about medical problems.

Task 1

This is a note-taking task. Ask the students to make notes and then check how good their notes are by reviewing their partner's notes and the transcript T121.1.

Task 2

These are the questions for the Medic! Game.

Situation 1

You have a headache. What should you do?

Situation 2

You have diarrhoea. What should you do?

Situation 3

You have an allergy. What should you do?

Situation 4

You have a migraine. What should you do?

Situation 5

One of your soldiers twist his ankle while on patrol. What should you do?

Supplementary Question:

Would you call for MEDEVAC?CASEVAC? Why? Why not?

Situation 6

One of your soldiers is bitten by a snake while on patrol. What should you do?

Supplementary Question:

Would you call for MEDEVAC?CASEVAC? Why? Why not?

Situation 7

One of your soldiers develops frostbite while on patrol in a mountain area in the winter. What should you do?

Supplementary Question:

Would you call for MEDEVAC?CASEVAC? Why? Why not?

Situation 8

One of your soldiers develops hypothermia while on patrol in a mountain area in the winter. What should you do?

Supplementary Question:

Would you call for MEDEVAC?CASEVAC? Why? Why not?

Situation 9

One of your soldiers is dizzy and disorientated while on patrol on a very hot day. What should you do?

Supplementary Question: Would you call for MEDEVAC?CASEVAC? Why? Why not?

Situation 1

One of your soldiers pulls a muscle in one of his legs while on patrol. What should you do?

Supplementary Question: Would you call for MEDEVAC?CASEVAC? Why? Why not?

Situation 11

One of your soldiers falls and hits his head while on patrol. He is unconscious for about 1 minute. What should you do?

Supplementary Question: Would you call for MEDEVAC?CASEVAC? Why? Why not?

Situation 12

One of your soldiers complains of being out of breath while on patrol in a mountainous area at an altitude of 4,000 metres. What should you do?

Supplementary Question: Would you call for MEDEVAC?CASEVAC? Why? Why not?

Situation 13

On a patrol through a jungle area you stop and check each other for leeches. You find several leeches on some soldiers. What should you do?

Supplementary Question: Would you call for MEDEVAC?CASEVAC? Why? Why not?

Situation 14

A soldier puts on a boot but is stung by a scorpion inside. What should you do?

Supplementary Question: Would you call for MEDEVAC?CASEVAC? Why? Why not?

Situation 15

On a patrol through a jungle area you are attacked by bees. Several soldiers are stung badly on their hands and face. One cannot see due to the swelling from the stings. What should you do?

Supplementary Question: Would you call for MEDEVAC?CASEVAC? Why? Why not?

Situation 16

A sniper shoots one of your patrol in the chest. What should you do?

Supplementary Question: Would you call for MEDEVAC?CASEVAC? Why? Why not?

Situation 17

A roadside IED explodes and your unarmoured vehicle is badly damaged. Two soldiers have been wounded in their legs by shrapnel from the bomb. They are bleeding badly from the wounds. What should you do?

Supplementary Question: Would you call for MEDEVAC?CASEVAC? Why? Why not?

Situation 18

One of your soldiers is hit by a speeding car when crossing the road. He is conscious, lying down, clutching his stomach where the car hit him. What should you do?

Supplementary Question: Would you call for MEDEVAC?CASEVAC? Why? Why not?

Situation 19

One of your soldiers starts vomiting and has uncontrollable diarrhoea while at camp on patrol. What should you do?

Supplementary Question: Would you call for MEDEVAC?CASEVAC? Why? Why not?

Situation 20

One of your soldiers fractures his wrist in a fall while on patrol. What should you do?

Supplementary Question: Would you call for MEDEVAC?CASEVAC? Why? Why not?

Unit 122

About the Unit

This unit is a simulation to bring together a lot of vocabulary from Phase 1 and Phase 2. The focus is on terrain, weather, equipment, training and emergency procedures. It is also a kind of practice for the final test of Phase 2 (see **Unit 175**).

The students should plan and prepare a briefing, and then brief on their 'Island Adventure' training exercise, using the prepared **Unit 122 Briefing Slides**.

Don't forget:

1. Spelling Challenge: World Cities to practice the NATO Alphabet.

2. Test the students on telling the time using the 24 hour clock, and using numbers, and DTG.

3. Test the students on the Key Tactical Verbs.

---

4. Grid references: test the students, or ask them to test each other, on grid references and terrain features, using a good map.

5. Test your students on a random medical problem. See who can answer the quickest.

Unit 123

About the Unit

This is the first of two units on Rules of Engagement. It is quite a long unit and you should consider splitting it into two if necessary, or think about what you might set as homework.

Task 1

Ask the students to discuss and then report on the three questions.

Task 2

This task focuses on the different verb forms which might be found in ROE.

Key	All can be found in ROE.

Task 3

Key	Active: 2, 3, 5
	Passive: 1, 4, 6

Task 4

The difference is in the subject and if the subject is doing something (active) or something is being done (etc.) to the subject (passive).

Task 5

Students complete the text with the verbs given. The numbers indicate how many times they can use the verbs.

Key	All enemy military personnel and vehicles transporting enemy personnel or their equipment [1] **may be** engaged subject to the following restrictions:
	A. When possible, the enemy [2] **will be** warned first and asked to surrender.
	B. Armed force is the last **resort**.
	C. Armed civilians [3] **will be** engaged only in self-defense.
	D. Civilian aircraft [4] **will not be** engaged, except in self-defense, without approval from division level.
	E. All civilians [5] **should be** treated with respect and dignity. Civilians and their property [6]

should not be harmed unless necessary to save US lives. If possible, civilians [7] should be evacuated before any US attack. Privately owned property may be used only if publicly owned property is unavailable or its use is inappropriate.

F. If civilians are in the area, artillery, mortars, AC-130s, attack helicopters, tube-launched or rocket-launched weapons, and main tank guns [8] should not be used against known or suspected targets without the permission of a ground maneuver commander (LTC or higher).

G. If civilians [9] are in the area, all air attacks [10] must be controlled by FAC or FO, and close air support, white phosphorus weapons, and incendiary weapons are prohibited without approval from division.

H. If civilians [11] are in the area, infantry [12] will shoot only at known enemy locations.

I. Public works such as power stations, Water treatment plants, dams, and other public utilities [13] may not be engaged without approval from division level.

J. Hospitals, churches, shrines, schools, museums, and other historical or cultural sites [14] will be engaged only in self-defense against fire from these locations.

K. All indirect fire and air attacks [15] must be observed.

L. Pilots [16] must be briefed for each mission as to the location of civilians and friendly forces.

M. Booby traps [17] are not authorized. Authority to emplace mines [18] is reserved for the division commander. Riot control agents [19] can be used only with approval from division level.

N. Prisoners [20] should be treated humanely, with respect and dignity.

O. Annex R to the OPLAN provides more detail. In the event this card conflicts with the OPLAN, the OPLAN [21] should be followed.

DISTRIBUTION: ONE FOR EACH SOLDIER DEPLOYED (ALL RANKS)

Task 6

Ask the students to reread the text and answer the questions. The letters in brackets below mark the section.

Key	
	1. Can you aim artillery over a hill to a target you cannot observe? No. [K]
	2. Can a platoon leader order mines to be placed? No [M]
	3. Can you attack a church if you see the enemy have entered it? No [J]
	4. Can a company commander order a mortar barrage in an area with civilians? No [F]
	5. Can a platoon leader order an attack on a dam? No [I]
	6. If you see an armed civilian, can you engage them? No [C].
	7. Can you defend yourself? Yes [first line] but...rest of ROE.
	8. How should you treat prisoners? Humanely, with respect and dignity [E]
	9. When can you use riot control agents? With divisional approval [M].
	10. How does the presence of civilians affect a firefight? Infantry will shoot only at known enemy locations [H]

Check any other unknown words or phrases afterwards. Choose at least one verb phrase, noun phrase and prepositional phrase from the text to explore with the students.

Task 7

Tell the students to listen to the text to decide which words they need to practice saying. This can be done as homework.

Task 8

Consolidation Tasks in Workbook.

Do the **Revision: Key Collocations** task or set it for homework.

Don't forget:

1. Spelling Challenge: World Cities to practice the NATO Alphabet.

2. Test the students on telling the time using the 24 hour clock, and using numbers, and DTG.

3. Test the students on the Key Tactical Verbs.

4. Grid references: test the students, or ask them to test each other, on grid references and terrain features, using a good map.

5. Test your students on a random medical problem. See who can answer the quickest.

Unit 124

About the Unit

This is the second unit on ROE, and focuses on RAMP, and a short simulation.

Task 1

This is a revision task on **Unit 123**.

Task 2

This is a prediction task for the listening in Task 3. Elicit ideas, perhaps to the board. Use these to focus the listening in Task 3.

Task 3

Students listen and complete the text.

Key	R – [1] **Return** Fire with Aimed Fire. [2] **Return** force with force. You always have the right to repel hostile acts with necessary force.
	A – [3] **Anticipate** Attack. Use force if, but only if, you see clear indicators of hostile intent.
	M - [4] **Measure**. You should carefully calibrate the amount of Force that you use, if time and circumstances permit. Use only the amount of force necessary to protect lives and accomplish the

---

> mission.
>
> P - [5] **Protect** with deadly force only human life, and property designated by your commander. Stop short of deadly force when protecting other property.

Task 4 and 5

Ask the students to work in groups and draft ROE for the situation given. You could collect them and mark/correct them, or display on the walls of the classroom and ask the other students to go around the room and read the other ROE. They could write comments/give feedback.

Task 6

Consolidation Tasks in Workbook.

Don't forget:

1. Spelling Challenge: World Cities to practice the NATO Alphabet.

2. Test the students on telling the time using the 24 hour clock, and using numbers, and DTG.

3. Test the students on the Key Tactical Verbs.

4. Grid references: test the students, or ask them to test each other, on grid references and terrain features, using a good map.

5. Test your students on a random medical problem. See who can answer the quickest.

Unit 125

About the Unit

This is the first of two units about position. It is a relatively short unit focused on the word 'position'. You should supplement the unit materials with some map work and disposition tasks (to revise **Units 99 – 103**).

Note: Ask students to cover up T3 at the start of the lesson.

Task 1

Students describe the two pictures.

Task 2

Students brainstorm words which collocate with 'position'. Elicit the words to the board and ask students to explain what they mean.

Task 3

Students match the collocations with the definitions.

Key	
1. in position	preposition + position (d)
2. fortified position	a position hardened ready for attack (a)
3. concealed position	a hidden position (h)
4. move into position	go into position (b)
5. defensive position	a position you will defend (o)
6. prepared position	a position you have made ready (j)
7. firing position	a position which you will fire from (n)
8. take up position	go into position (m)
9. attack a position	assault a position (k)
10. enemy position	a position held by the enemy (e)
11. fighting position	a position you will fight from (g)
12. current position	your position now (i)
13. bypass an enemy position	to go around an enemy position (c)
14. alternate position	a secondary position (l)
15 hold in position	remain in position (f)

Ask students to agree on a translation with their partner, if your students share the same first language.

Task 4 and 5

These two tasks are sentence completion tasks.

Task 4

Key		
	1.	Make sure you are **in** position by 1600.
	2.	**Move** into position just after dark.
	3.	**Take** up your positions.
	4.	We will need to **attack/bypass** the enemy's fortified/prepared.....
	5.	You should **hold** in position until relieved.
	6.	I want you to **attack/move into** these positions here, here .... 0430.
	7.	Can you see the **enemy's** positions?

Task 5

Key	1.	This hill is a strong **defensive** position.
	2.	I want you to dig **concealed/fortified/defensive/fighting/alternate/ prepared** positions in this area.
	3.	Where are you? What is your **current** position?
	4.	If we have to withdraw, we will move to these **alternate** positions.
	5.	We need to dig trenches to connect the **fortified/firing/concealed/ prepared/fighting** positions.
	6.	Soldiers who attack **fortified/prepared** positions should expect to encounter planned enemy fires.
	7.	A soldier must be able to use hasty **fighting** positions when attacked.

Options and Decisions: As mentioned above, supplement this unit with work using maps and the language of dispositions. Ask students to prepare maps of defensive positions and to explain <u>why</u> they chose to site the positions where they did. Remember OAKOC from **Unit 96**.

Don't forget:

1. Spelling Challenge: World Cities to practice the NATO Alphabet.

2. Test the students on telling the time using the 24 hour clock, and using numbers, and DTG.

3. Test the students on the Key Tactical Verbs.

4. Grid references: test the students, or ask them to test each other, on grid references and terrain features, using a good map.

5. Test your students on a random medical problem. See who can answer the quickest.

Unit 126

About the Unit

This is the second unit about position – focused on defensive positions and attacks on fortified positions.

Task 1

This is a revision task from **Unit 125**. Ask the students to brainstorm the collocations from **Unit 125** and then test each other.

Tasks 2 and **Task 3** are note taking tasks. After the first listening ask them to check with their partner. Elicit the main points they noted. Then decide if they need to listen again.

Task 4

Ask the students to complete the transcripts, then listen to check.

Task 5

Ask the students to discuss and then report back to the class for a group discussion.

Do the **Revision: Key Collocations** task or set it for homework.

Don't forget:

1. Spelling Challenge: World Cities to practice the NATO Alphabet.

2. Test the students on telling the time using the 24 hour clock, and using numbers, and DTG.

3. Test the students on the Key Tactical Verbs.

4. Grid references: test the students, or ask them to test each other, on grid references and terrain features, using a good map.

5. Test your students on a random medical problem. See who can answer the quickest.

Unit 127

About the Unit

This unit looks at what kinds of buildings are found on bases and how to describe their position. This revises language from **Units 4** and **46**.

Task 1

Ask students to cover up Task 2 and then brainstorm all the kinds of buildings. Elicit them to the board and ask the students to explain what they are.

Task 2

Check any words in the table which did not come up in Task 1.

Language Note: PX = Post Exchange – US military base shop; NAFFI is the same for British military bases.

Task 3

Look at the plan and ask students to speculate what the unlabelled buildings are. Then students listen and label the buildings. Let them check with their partner before listening a second time if necessary. Check with P127.1. Listen again for confirmation if necessary.

Task 4

Ask the students to listen yet again and see what was not marked on the diagram. Check with P127.2.

Task 5

Ask students if they remember what kind of language the speaker used to describe location. Elicit to the board. Listen for more if necessary.

Task 6

Ask students to discuss the base in pairs and then report on their discussion. Use the Language Reminder box.

Task 7

Ask students to draw a base plan and then describe to their partner. They can discuss whose base is best.

Task 8

Use the base plans to practice giving directions (see **Unit 46**).

Task 9

Ask students to write a description of their base. Collect, correct and ask student to rewrite. You could then display the plans and descriptions on the walls of your classroom.

Task 10

Consolidation Tasks in the Workbook.

Units 128 – 133 Fundamentals of Base Security

This series of units is focused on base security and guard duty. Depending on your students needs you should decide which units to do.

Each unit is quite a short unit in terms of the material it contains. You should decide to either combine the units together, or to use the extra time you might have to revise the material from previous units, especially medical English.

Unit 133 is a Forward Operating Base simulation based on these units (and **Unit 127**) and you need to carefully consider which of these units (**Units 128-132**) you need to do before you do **Unit 133**.

Unit 128

About the Unit

This unit introduces some ideas behind base security.

Note: Ask students to cover up T5 at the start of the lesson.

Task 1

Ask the students to describe what they can see in the photo.

Task 2

This is a prediction task. Ask the students to discuss and report to the class.

Task 3

This is a quick check of Task 2. Discuss if they agree with the key. Are there other factors?

Task 4

Discuss the students' ideas of the defender's advantage. This is a prediction task for T5.

Task 5

Check the words in the table and then ask the students to complete the text. Check the key and then check their predictions from T4.

Key	**Use of the Defenders' Advantages.**
	Defenders' advantages may permit a [1] **numerically** inferior force to defeat a much larger one. Some of these advantages are:
	The ability to fight from [2] **cover**;
	More detailed knowledge of local [3] **terrain** and environment;
	The ability to prepare [4] **positions**, routes between them, obstacles, and [5] **fields** of fire in advance;
	The ability to plan communications, control measures, [6] **indirect** fires, and logistic support to fit any predictable situation;
	and the ability to [7] **deceive** enemy forces about friendly [8] **defensive** capabilities, [9] **dispositions**, and execution of [10] **operations**.

Check any other unknown words or phrases afterwards. Choose at least one verb phrase, noun phrase and prepositional phrase from the text to explore with the students.

Task 6

Discuss the perimeter defences the students' army uses around bases. Use P128.3 to help. What other defence measures are there?

Don't forget:

1. Spelling Challenge: World Cities to practice the NATO Alphabet.

2. Test the students on telling the time using the 24 hour clock, and using numbers, and DTG.

3. Test the students on the Key Tactical Verbs.

4. Grid references: test the students, or ask them to test each other, on grid references and terrain features, using a good map.

5. Test your students on a random medical problem. See who can answer the quickest.

Unit 129

About the Unit

This unit is mainly about a text about intelligence, firepower, attacks and counter-attacks, coordination and legal issues with regards to base defence.

Task 1

This is a revision question about **Unit 128**.

Task 2

This a pre-reading prediction set of questions. Ask the students to discuss and report on these questions. They will read the text in Task 3 to check their answers.

Task 3

Key		
	1.	You always need to understand the enemy
	2.	To get an accurate picture of the battlespace, to anticipate battlespace events.
	3.	To gain local superiority at critical points.
	4.	To add depth to the battlespace
	5.	To produce a combined arms effect. By synchronizing forces and fires a smaller force can be capable of defeating a larger enemy force.
	6.	Political and legal constraints restrict how and when force can be used
	7.	This is a legal requirement.

Check any other unknown words or phrases afterwards. Choose at least one verb phrase, noun phrase and prepositional phrase from the text to explore with the students.

Task 4

Set the Text Analysis tasks in class or for homework.

Task 5

Tell the students to listen to the text to decide which words they need to practice saying. This can be done as homework.

Task 6

Check the collocations from the text.

Task 7

Consolidation Tasks in Workbook.

Unit 130

About the Unit

This unit revises **Units 128/9** and previews **Unit 131**.

Note: Ask students to cover up T4 at the start of the lesson.

Task 1

Ask the students to describe what they can see in the photo.

Task 2

This is a revision question about **Unit 128**.

Task 3

This is a prediction task about actions of defence forces.

Task 4

Ask the students to complete the text with a suitable word.

Key	1.. Detect	3. Deny	5. Delay
	2. Warn	4. Destroy	

Task 5

This is a revision/preview task which explores a lot of vocabulary from the book. Check the meaning first and then ask the students to work together through the list and talk about why these things are important.

Task 6

Ask the students to write ten sentences based on the language from these units.

Task 7

Ask students to talk about what they can see in the pictures. You could elicit descriptions and also turn it into a writing task.

Don't forget:

1. Spelling Challenge: World Cities to practice the NATO Alphabet.

2. Test the students on telling the time using the 24 hour clock, and using numbers, and DTG.

3. Test the students on the Key Tactical Verbs.

4. Grid references: test the students, or ask them to test each other, on grid references and terrain features, using a good map.

5. Test your students on a random medical problem. See who can answer the quickest.

Unit 131

About the Unit

This unit is about patrols and previews much of the work done in **Units 153-160**.

Task 1

Ask the students to describe what they can see in the photo.

Task 2

Ask the students to read the text to answer the questions. You might want them to answer the questions first and then read the text to check.

Key	1. To provide additional base security
	2. Reconnaissance and combat
	3. Dismounted: able to interact with local inhabitants but still should be ready to conduct combat operations. Mounted: especially useful in an economy of force mission where the unit has a large sector to cover and few personnel to patrol
	4. The whole of Organization and Preparation. Paragraph.

Check any other unknown words or phrases afterwards. Choose at least one verb phrase, noun phrase and prepositional phrase from the text to explore with the students.

Task 3

Set the Text Analysis tasks in class or for homework.

Task 4

Tell the students to listen to the text to decide which words they need to practice saying. This can be done as homework.

Task 5

Check the collocations from the text.

Task 6

Consolidation Tasks in Workbook.

Do the **Revision: Key Collocations** task or set it for homework.

Unit 132

About the Unit

This unit is about the language of guard duty. It is longer than the other base defence units.

Task 1

Ask the students to describe what they can see in the photos.

Task 2

Ask the students to complete the collocations with a word.

Key	on duty/guard/alert	all passes must be shown	duty roster

Task 3

Ask the students to complete the sentences with a preposition.

Key		
	1.	I will meet you **at** the entrance.
	2.	Stand **at (by)** the barrier.
	3.	I am **on** duty from 1800.
	4.	Who is **in** charge here?
	5.	You must stop **at** the barrier.
	6.	Slow **down** as you approach the entrance.
	7.	Keep alert **at** all times.
	8.	Lift the barrier **up** to let the vehicles **in** and out.
	9.	The guard house is over there next **to** that tree.
	10.	There is concertina wire behind and **in** front of the wall.

Task 4

Check what physical perimeter defence measures the students remember from **Unit 128**.

Check with P128.3.

Task 5 and Task 6

Ask the students to work with a partner and draw a plan of an entrance to a base that they are familiar with, and then follow the instructions in the coursebook. They could make up the entrance to a base if there are security implications of talking about a real base.

Task 7 and Task 8

These are preparation tasks for the Role Play in Task 9.

Task 9

Follow the instructions and do the Role Play. Monitor carefully and give feedback on the language used and how they behaved.

Task 10

Ask the students to describe what they can see in the photo.

Don't forget:

1. Spelling Challenge: World Cities to practice the NATO Alphabet.

2. Test the students on telling the time using the 24 hour clock, and using numbers, and DTG.

3. Test the students on the Key Tactical Verbs.

4. Grid references: test the students, or ask them to test each other, on grid references and terrain features, using a good map.

5. Test your students on a random medical problem. See who can answer the quickest.

About the Unit

This unit is a simulation about a Forward Operating Base. It brings together all the language from **Units 127 – 132**. Follow the instructions in the coursebook. Give feedback on the language they use, both positive and negative.

Unit 134

About the Unit

This unit is about Observation Posts.

Task 1

Ask the students to describe what they can see in the photos.

Task 2

Ask the students to discuss and then report about OPs.

Task 3

This is a reading task but the task is to find the mistakes in the text. The mistakes are underlined in the key below.

Key   **OP Guidelines**

OPs are used to watch and listen for enemy activity and provide security and intelligence for the platoon. OPs <u>shouldn't</u> be sited to allow observation of the designated area. They <u>shouldn't</u> be sited to take advantage of natural cover and concealment to provide protection for the soldiers manning it and OPs should <u>never</u> be located within small-arms range of the platoon positions. When selecting observation posts, you <u>should</u> chose the most prominent position. Avoid obvious terrain such as hilltops and <u>use</u> easily identifiable terrain features such as water towers, church steeples, tallest buildings, lone buildings or trees, or isolated groves. A selected observation post should be observed for 10 to 15 minutes to ensure it is not occupied. <u>Do not</u> select a covered and concealed route to and from the OP: <u>use</u> routes or positions that skyline soldiers. If the post is located on a hill, crawl to a position where the skyline is broken. If a tree is used, the position should have a background so as not to be silhouetted against the sky while climbing or observing. At least two soldiers must man each OP. A fire team may man the OP if it will remain in place or not be relieved for long periods. All soldiers should prepare fighting positions at the OP for protection and concealment. Additionally, each soldier must have a prepared position to return to in the platoon position. An observation post <u>should always be</u> manned for more than 24 hours. As a guide, OPs should be relieved every two to four hours. When leaving the observation post, <u>the same route</u> from that of the approach should be used. If a radio is used, its antenna should be located to provide clear communication to the controlling commander but masked from enemy observation and direction-finding equipment. Upon departure, scouts <u>shouldn't</u> remove the antennae from the observation post so as not to give away the position.

Discuss the errors and why the corrected version is better.

Check any other unknown words or phrases afterwards. Choose at least one verb phrase, noun phrase and prepositional phrase from the text to explore with the students.

Task 4

Ask the students to justify this information being given to the soldiers.

Key	challenge and password: so they can challenge.
	running password: so they will not be shot on their return to the lines.
	when to engage and when not to engage the enemy: so they do not make mistakes and give away the position unnecessarily.
	conditions when the OP can withdraw: so they know when to withdraw.
	When to expect relief: so they are prepared/know how long they will be in the OP.
	contingency plans for loss of communications: so they can cope in this situation.

Task 5

Key	All of this equipment

Task 6

This is a self-check listening task. Students listen, make notes, check with their partner, listen again if necessary. They can check the quality of their notes with the transcript.

Task 7

This is a gap-fill task supported by two pictures.

Key	The observer makes an [1] **overall** search of the entire area for [2] **obvious** targets, unnatural colors, outlines, or movement. To do this quickly, he raises his eyes from just in front of his [3] **position** to the greatest range he wants to observe. If the sector is wide, he observes it in [4] **sections**. Then he observes [5] **overlapping** 50-meter wide [6] **strips**, alternating. from left to right and right to left until he has observed the [7] **entire** area. When he sees a [8] **suspicious** spot, he searches it well.

Task 8

Consolidation Tasks in Workbook.

About the Unit

This is the first of two units about overwatch. This unit is about different kinds of overwatch during tactical movement.

Task 1

Ask the students to describe what they can see in the photo.

Task 2

Ask students to discuss and report on their ideas about the three terms.

Task 3

Students listen to make notes about the differences. They will probably need to copy the table to their notebooks to give them space to write notes.

Key

MOVEMENT TECHNIQUE	WHEN NORMALLY USED	CHARACTERISTICS			
		CONTROL	DISPERSION	SPEED	SECURITY
TRAVELLING	Contact not expected.	Good.	Less than other techniques	fast	Not good; vulnerable to ambush.
TRAVELLING OVERWATCH	Contact possible but not expected	Less than travelling	More dispersed than travelling	Slower than travelling	More security than travelling because overwatch
BOUNDING OVERWATCH	Contact is expected	Most control	Most dispersion	slowest	highest

Task 4

Check the words in the table then ask the students to complete the text. Do a pair check before a class check.

Key	**Travelling Overwatch**
	Travelling Overwatch is used when contact is [1] **possible** but speed is [2] **required** . The platoon leader moves where he can best [3] **control** the platoon. The platoon sergeant travels with the [4] **trailing** squad, though he is free to move through the [5] **formation** to enforce security, noise and light [6] **discipline** and distances. The lead squads use travelling overwatch, and the trailing squad use travelling. The [7] **distance** between the lead squad and the platoon HQ element [8] **extends** from the normal 20m out to 50 – 100m.

> **Bounding Overwatch**
>
> Bounding overwatch is used when [1] **contact** is expected, when the unit leader feels the enemy is [2] **near**, or when a large open danger area must be [3] **crossed**. Platoons conducting bounding overwatch using successive or [4] **alternate** bounds. One squad (the trail fire team) bounds [5] **forward** to a chosen position, then it becomes the overwatching [6] **element** unless contact is made en route. The bounding squad can use either travelling overwatch, or individual techniques (low and high crawl, and short [7] **rushes** by the fire team or pairs). While this squad moves forward another squad [8] **overwatches** from covered [9] **positions** from which it can see and [10] **suppress** likely enemy positions. The unit leader usually stays with this overwatch team. The trail fire team [11] **signals** the unit leader when his team completes its bound and is prepared to [12] **overwatch** the movement of the other team.

Check any other unknown words or phrases afterwards. Choose at least one verb phrase, noun phrase and prepositional phrase from the text to explore with the students.

Task 5

Ask the students to draw a diagram to illustrate travelling and bounding overwatch. This is a comprehension check of Task 4. Each student could do a diagram for one technique, or for both. Use the space given in the coursebook for a draft and then give paper for a finished diagram. You could display the diagrams on the wall for feedback. Who has the clearest and most informative diagram(s).

> **Don't forget:**
>
> 1. Spelling Challenge: World Cities to practice the NATO Alphabet.
>
> 2. Test the students on telling the time using the 24 hour clock, and using numbers, and DTG.
>
> 3. Test the students on the Key Tactical Verbs.
>
> 4. Grid references: test the students, or ask them to test each other, on grid references and terrain features, using a good map.
>
> 5. Test your students on a random medical problem. See who can answer the quickest.

Unit 136

About the Unit

This is the second unit on overwatch, and is about crossing large open areas.

Task 1

This is a revision question about **Unit 135**.

Task 2

Ask students to look at the picture and then complete the orders.

Key	First squad, [1] **overwatch** from this [2] **position**. Second squad, [3] **move** through those trees to the left and [4] **clear** that small hill one hundred meters to our front and [5] **set up** an [6] **overwatch** on the hill. [7] **signal** with your [8] **mirror** when in position. I will move [9] **up** with the first and third squad, and give you your next [10] **orders**. Third squad , move [11] **up** behind first squad and [12] **await** orders. Platoon sergeant, [13] **position** your machine guns and antitank weapon to the right of the first squad. I will [14] **position** mine to the [15] **left** of the first squad.

Task 3

This is a prediction task for Task 4.

Task 4

Ask students to listen to the text and label the diagram. You might want them to copy the diagram out larger first. Listen and then pair check and listen again if necessary. Check with P136.2.

Task 5

Consolidation Tasks in Workbook.

Don't forget:

1. Spelling Challenge: World Cities to practice the NATO Alphabet.

2. Test the students on telling the time using the 24 hour clock, and using numbers, and DTG.

3. Test the students on the Key Tactical Verbs.

4. Grid references: test the students, or ask them to test each other, on grid references and terrain features, using a good map.

5. Test your students on a random medical problem. See who can answer the quickest.

Units 137 – 142 Convoys

This series of units is about convoys. The first two units are about convoy organisation and control, and could be combined. The other units are about convoy driving and briefings.

You will need maps to do the convoy briefings in **Unit 142**.

About the Unit

This unit introduces the topic of convoys and the elements of a convoy.

Task 1

Ask the students to describe what they can see in the photos.

Task 2

Options and Decisions: Use this discussion question to elicit ideas about the use of convoys (and experience of convoys), and then extend the discussion into the dangers a convoy might face and what can be done to protect a convoy. This will usefully preview the following units.

Task 3

Students read the text and answer the questions. Discuss if this way of organising convoys is the same in their army.

Key	1. A six vehicle march unit.
	2. To match units size and enable effective control.
	3. For effective command and control.

Task 4

Students listen and note down the composition of the convoys.

Key	1. 5 APCs
	2. A one serial convoy with two march units. One tank and an APC for the advance guard. Each march unit will be 1 APC, 5 trucks, 1 APC, 5 trucks. The rearguard is another tank and two APCs.
	3. Advance guard of two tanks and APCs Commander's APC. 1st serial of two march units. Second serial; also of two march units. Each march unit will be one APC, five trucks, one APC, five trucks, one APC, 5 trucks, one tanker, one APC. Between the two serials we'll have two tanks in the middle of the convoy. The trail will be three tanks and two APCs.

Options and Decisions 1: On a second listening you could ask the students to note down more details like the route etc. Ask them to check the transcript after this listening.

Options and Decisions 2: Extend this task if you have time by asking the students to create their own convoys and to brief the class on them. Students make notes on the composition of the convoys. Do not spend too long on this though.

Task 5

Consolidation Tasks in Workbook.

About the Unit

This unit focuses on convoy control.

Task 1

Ask the students to describe what they can see in the photo.

Task 2

This is a lead-in/prediction task for Task 3.

Task 3

Ask the students to complete the text with the terms from Task 2.

Key	A: Pacesetter	C: Trail Maintenance Officer
	B: Trail Officer	D: Guides

Check any other unknown words or phrases afterwards. Choose at least one verb phrase, noun phrase and prepositional phrase from the text to explore with the students.

Task 4

Unit 137 looked at the main divisions of the convoy. This task looks within these elements.

Check the words in the table and then ask students to complete the text.

Key	**Convoy Sections**
	All columns, serials, and march units, regardless of size, have three parts: a head, a main body, and a trail Each of these parts has a specific function.
	Head. The head is the [1] **first** vehicle of each column, serial, and march unit. Each head should have its own [2] **pacesetter.** The [3] **pacesetter** rides in this vehicle and sets the pace needed to meet the scheduled itinerary along the route. The officer or non-commissioned officer at the head ensures that the column follows the proper [4] **route**. He may also be required to report arrival at certain [5] **checkpoints** along the route. With the head performing these duties, the convoy commander has the flexibility to move up and down the column to enforce [6] **march** discipline.
	Main body. The main body follows immediately after the head and consists of the [7] **majority** of the vehicles moving as part of the convoy. This is the part of the convoy that may be [8] **subdivided** into serials and [9] **march** units for ease of control.
	Trail. The trail is the [10] **last** sector of each march column, serial, and march unit. The trail officer/NCO is responsible for recovery, maintenance, and medical support. The recovery vehicle, maintenance vehicles, and medical support vehicles/teams are located in the trail. The trail officer/NCO assists the convoy commander in maintaining march [11] **discipline**. He may also be required to report [12] **clear** times at checkpoints along the route. In convoys consisting of [13] **multiple** march units and serials, the convoy commander may direct minimum support in the trail of

each serial or march unit and a larger trail party at the [14] **rear** of the column. As the trail party may be left behind to conduct repairs or recovery, the convoy commander should provide trail [15] **security** and communications.

Check any other unknown words or phrases afterwards. Choose at least one verb phrase, noun phrase and prepositional phrase from the text to explore with the students.

Task 5

This task is a self-check listening task about convoy security. Ask students to listen and make notes. Ask them to check with their partner, then ask them if they want to listen again. Listen again if necessary, then do a class check. If they have not got enough details listen again. Then ask them to check with the transcript. Ask them to rate their notes.

Task 6

Consolidation Tasks in Workbook.

Unit 139

About the Unit

This is a briefing unit about convoy driving. There are three briefings to give. Ask the students to work in groups to prepare briefings based on the prepared slides. Follow the procedure as outlined in the Coursebook. Give feedback on the how they briefed and the language they used. The audience should make notes during the briefing. Then ask the briefers to rate the audiences' notes. How good are the notes?

Don't forget:

1. Spelling Challenge: World Cities to practice the NATO Alphabet.

2. Test the students on telling the time using the 24 hour clock, and using numbers, and DTG.

3. Test the students on the Key Tactical Verbs.

4. Grid references: test the students, or ask them to test each other, on grid references and terrain features, using a good map.

5. Test your students on a random medical problem. See who can answer the quickest.

Unit 140

About the Unit

This unit looks in detail at what you might hear in a convoy briefing. It is preparation for the following two units.

Note: Ask students to cover up T2 and T3 at the start of the lesson.

Task 1

Ask students to brainstorm what they might hear in a briefing.

Task 2

Uncover T2 but keep T3 covered and ask students to compare their lists with the list given.

Task 3

Ask the students to work through the table and put the items from the right-hand column into the correct position in the left-hand column. You might want to check the words in the right-hand column before doing this. The numbers in brackets indicate how many things are required in each section.

They listen to check: **Task 4** . If there are any questions they can check with the transcript.

Key	Situation
	Friendly forces.
	Enemy situation.
	Support units.
	Mission
	Type of cargo.
	Origin.
	Destination.
	Execution
	General organization of the convoy.
	Time schedule.
	Routes.
	Convoy speed.
	Catch-up speed.
	Vehicle distance.
	Execution: Emergency measures
	Accidents.
	Breakdowns.
	Obstacles
	Separation from convoy.
	Ambush.
	Action of convoy personnel if ambushed.
	Action of security forces during ambush.

Medical support.
Administration and Logistics
Control of personnel.
Billeting arrangements.
Messing arrangements.
Refueling and servicing of vehicles, complying with spill prevention guidelines.
Command and Signal
Location of convoy commander.
Succession of command.
Action of security force commander.
Serial commander's responsibility.
Arm and hand signals.
Other prearranged signals.
Radio frequencies and call signs for:
Control personnel.
Security force commander.
Fire support elements.
Reserve security elements.
Medical evacuation support.
Safety
Hazards of route and weather conditions.
Defensive driving.
Environmental protection
Spill prevention.
Transporting HAZMAT.

Task 5

In this task they discuss why this information is important. You could assign sections to each student to justify the importance of the information.

Unit 141

About the Unit

This unit is basically one listening task as preparation for **Unit 142**.

Task 1

Ask the students to describe what they can see in the photos.

Task 2

Ask students to listen and mark the route on the map. They can check with P141.3.

Then they can listen again and note key information about the convoy composition, route etc. They can check their notes with the transcript.

Task 3

This gives the students an opportunity to evaluate the convoy briefing from a professional perspective, and using the form from **Unit 140**.

Don't forget:

1. Spelling Challenge: World Cities to practice the NATO Alphabet

2. Test the students on telling the time using the 24 hour clock, and using numbers.

3. Test the students on the Key Tactical Verbs.

4. Grid references: test the students, or ask them to test each other, on grid references and terrain features, using a good map.

5. Test your students on a random medical problem. See who can answer the quickest.

Unit 142

About the Unit

This unit is a briefing unit which brings together all the language of the previous units about convoys. Follow the procedure as outlined in the Course book. Do not forget to give feedback on the briefings.

Units 143 – 144 IEDS and UXO

These two units (and the following Study Page) are about IEDs and UXO.

IEDs are improvised explosive devices; UXO – unexploded ordinance.

See PX 143.1.

About the Unit

This unit introduces IEDs and UXO and the 5Cs technique.

Task 1

Ask the students to describe what they can see in the photos.

Task 2

This is a lead-in to the topic. Find out how much students know about IEDs and UXO.

Tasks 3 to **6** are linked tasks in that they are based on five sections of text with questions to answer..

Task 3

Key	1. to target soldiers, civilians, NGOs and government agencies.
	2. timed, remotely or on impact.

Check any other unknown words or phrases afterwards. Choose at least one verb phrase, noun phrase and pre-positional phrase from the text to explore with the students.

Task 4

Key	1. Confirm; Clear; Call in; Cordon; Control.
	2. To simply awareness and reaction to IEDs.

Check any other unknown words or phrases afterwards. Choose at least one verb phrase, noun phrase and pre-positional phrase from the text to explore with the students.

Task 5

Key	Projectiles, thrown and dropped ordnance: Enemy and friendly force ordnance: HE (High explosive), chemical rounds, illumination rounds, mortar rounds, rockets, guided missiles, rifle grenades, different kinds of grenades and mines; and bombs – dropped ordnance.

Check any other unknown words or phrases afterwards. Choose at least one verb phrase, noun phrase and pre-positional phrase from the text to explore with the students.

Task 6

Key	To go off unexpectedly and also to protect IEDs

Check any other unknown words or phrases afterwards. Choose at least one verb phrase, noun phrase and pre-positional phrase from the text to explore with the students.

Task 7

Tell the students to listen to the text to decide which words they need to practice saying. This can be done as homework.

Task 8

This task is a self-check listening task about IEDs. Ask students to listen and make notes. Ask them to check with their partner, then ask them if they want to listen again. Listen again if necessary, then do a class check. If they have not got enough details listen again. Then ask them to check with the transcript. Ask them to rate their notes.

Task 9

Consolidation Tasks in Workbook.

Unit 144

About the Unit

This units looks at the 10-line UXO/IED report.

Task 1

Ask the students to describe what they can see in the photos.

Task 2

This is a revision task from **Unit 144**: answer – follow the 5Cs. Elicit what these are.

Task 3

Check the language of the 10-line report.

Task 4

Ask the students to work in pairs to prepare a radio call based on the report form in T3. Ask them to demonstrate their call to the class once they have had a chance to practise. If you have radios, use these to make it more realist-ic.

Options and Decisions: You can then run the task again but unscripted this time. Assign call signs and roles and ask the soldiers 'on the ground' to call in an IED or UXO.

This page is to raise awareness of some of the collocations possible with explosives. The students match the words in the diagram with the term 'explosives'.

Key	verb + noun	conceal explosives use explosives	
	adjective + noun + noun	crude home-made explosives	
	noun + noun	plastic explosives	
	adjective + noun	high explosives	high-yield explosives
		lethal explosives	vehicle-delivered explosives
		hazardous explosives	
	noun + verb + preposition + noun	vehicles loaded with explosives	
	noun + verb + to + verb + noun	dogs trained to detect explosives	

Units 145 – 152 checkpoints and Roadblocks

This series of seven units is focused on checkpoints and roadblocks.

To do these units well you will need things to model checkpoints, like Cuisenaire rods, or Lego bricks, or coloured pencils, as well as toy cars and soldiers.

Unit 145

About the Unit

This unit considers four kinds of checkpoint.

Task 1

Ask the students to describe what they can see in the photos.

Task 2

This is a prediction task for the reading in Task 3. Ask the students to discuss in pairs and then elicit answers and see if everyone agrees or has different answers.

Task 3

Students should read the text to check their answers from Task 2.

Make sure students are clear on the differences between the four types of checkpoint.

Task 4

Key   1. Hasty, triggered and reactionary.

         2. The text clearly mentions covert protection forces for hasty and triggered roadblocks but they should also be used for the other two types as well.

         3. Deliberate probably, if you do not count helicopters.

         4. Triggered and reactionary.

Check any other unknown words or phrases afterwards. Choose at least one verb phrase, noun phrase and prepositional phrase from the text to explore with the students.

Task 5

Set the Text Analysis tasks in class or for homework.

Task 6

Tell the students to listen to the text to decide which words they need to practice saying. This can be done as homework.

Task 7

Ask the students to look at the terms in the table and discuss their meaning with their partner. Class check. These words are used in the Task 8 listening.

Task 8

Ask the students to listen to the description of the checkpoint and complete the diagram. Check with P154.3.

Task 9

Consolidation Tasks in Workbook.

Extra Task: Ask students to use their maps and choose sites for different kinds of roadblock. This previews **Unit 147**.

Don't forget:

   1.   Spelling Challenge: World Cities to practice the NATO Alphabet.

2. Test the students on telling the time using the 24 hour clock, and using numbers, and DTG.

3. Test the students on the Key Tactical Verbs.

4. Grid references: test the students, or ask them to test each other, on grid references and terrain features, using a good map.

5. Test your students on a random medical problem. See who can answer the quickest.

6. Check the composition of a convoy and the role of key personnel.

7. Check the different kinds of IEDs and UXO, 5Cs, and 10-liner report.

Unit 146

About the Unit

This unit considers how checkpoints and roadblocks are manned. Depending on the time available and your students, you might want to split the unit into 2 parts e.g. Tasks 1 – 7; Tasks 8 – 11.

Task 1

Ask the students to describe what they can see in the photo.

Task 2

These questions are revision questions from **Unit 145**.

Task 3

Teach/check the words in the table and then ask the students to complete the text.

Key	The number of troops required will depend upon the number of roads and expected [1] volume of traffic. If searching women, forces must have women searchers, and provide [2] special accommodation. The military commander should have, where possible, the rank of [3] sergeant or above. Keep a police [4] presence at a military roadblock, whenever possible, especially when military powers of [5] search, arrest, or control of movement is limited. Interpreters are also useful. Normally, [6] man a control point with at least a platoon, but relate the strength required to the number of roads controlled and the anticipated traffic. At a [7] minimum, man the roadblock at the following:
	Control point headquarters. Commander, [8] signaler, and runner.
	Barrier Sentries. One non-commissioned officer (NCO) for each road or lane of traffic blocked, and one [9] sentry for each barrier.
	Covering party. Two military personnel [10] covering each set of barrier sentries.
	Assault Force. A designated unit is critical in the event an [11] element breaks through a roadblock or CP.
	Overwatch. Where possible, man an [12] overwatch on a nearby rooftop.

Check any other unknown words or phrases afterwards. Choose at least one verb phrase, noun phrase and prepositional phrase from the text to explore with the students.

Task 4

Set the Text Analysis tasks in class or for homework.

Task 5

Ask the students to listen and make notes. Elicit what they heard/understood and decide if they need to listen again. Then check again.

Task 6

Check the words in the table and then ask the students to complete the transcript. Check this task with the transcript.

Task 7

Ask the students to complete the collocations and then listen again to check.

Note: Tasks 8, 9 and 10 preview **Unit 150.**

Task 8

This is a brainstorming task before Task 9. **Make sure students have covered up T9 before you do this task.** Elicit some ideas from the students before they do Task 9.

Task 9

Key
Who
Command and Control
<ul><li>Exercises C2</li><li>Maintains communications with HQ</li><li>Maintains a log of all activities</li><li>Co-ordinates RIP as required</li><li>Co-ordinates linkups as required</li><li>Co-ordinates the role of civil authorities</li><li>Co-ordinates local patrols</li><li>Integrates reserve /QRF</li><li>If available, uses a vehicle for patrolling, moving elements etc.</li></ul>
Security Element
<ul><li>Provides early warning to CP</li><li>Prevents ambush</li><li>Able to reinforce position as necessary</li><li>Observes and reports suspicious activity</li><li>Monitors traffic flow up to and through the checkpoints</li></ul>
Search Element
<ul><li>Halts vehicles at the checkpoint</li></ul>

• Guides vehicles to the search area • Conducts vehicle searches: passenger and cargo • Conducts personnel searches: male and female • Directs cleared vehicles out of the CP • Detains personnel as directed
Assault Element
• Destroys escaping personnel and vehicles • Able to reinforce as necessary

Task 10

Key
Do's
• Speak to the driver; driver speaks to occupants • have the driver open all the doors and compartments before the soldier searches the vehicle • ask politely to follow your instructions • speak naturally and no louder than necessary • allow driver to observe the search • all vehicle occupants are required to exit vehicle • be courteous when searching • use scanners and metal detectors when possible • stay calm and make a special effort to be polite • maintain a high standard of dress, military bearing, and stay in uniform
Don'ts
• be disrespectful or give any hint of dislike • put your head or arm in the vehicle without permission • shout or show impatience • frisk women or ask them to put their hands up • become involved in a heated argument • become careless or sloppy in appearance • use force unless as directed by ROE

Task 11

Consolidation Tasks in Workbook.

Unit 147

About the Unit

This unit looks at checkpoint equipment and its uses, and the construction of a checkpoint.

Task 1

Ask the students to describe what they can see in the photos.

Task 2

These are revision questions. See what the students remember from the previous units.

Task 3

Check the meaning of the terms and, if appropriate, ask the students to agree on translations.

Task 4

Ask the students to listen to the instructor explaining the use of the items in T3. He makes two mistakes – what are they?

Key	**Mistake 1:** 'Tire/Tyre puncture chains are very useful in repairing any punctures you might get in tires. You don't want your IFV to get a puncture and not be able to repair it.' Tire puncture chains <u>cause</u> punctures.
	Mistake 2: 'A knife rest is very useful for putting your knife on when you are eating your dinner.' This is true at a formal dinner but at a checkpoint a knife rest is a portable defensive barrier consisting of a frame covered in barbed wire.

Task 5

This is a pre-reading prediction task.

Task 6

Students read the text to check their answers from Task 5.

Key	Security: protection from attacks.
	Concealment: so people cannot avoid or bypass the roadblock.

Task 7

Ask the students to reread the text and answer the questions.

Key	1. Up to 7.
	2. For obvious reasons.
	3. It should not be visible from a distance. It should be concealed.
	4. To protect the roadblock and soldiers operating it.
	5. As sentries (backstops); as a backup force.

Check any other unknown words or phrases afterwards. Choose at least one verb phrase, noun phrase and prepositional phrase from the text to explore with the students.

Task 8

Set the Text Analysis tasks in class or for homework.

Task 9

Tell the students to listen to the text to decide which words they need to practice saying. This can be done as homework.

Task 10

Ask the students to explain, in English, or translate these terms.

Task 11

Consolidation Tasks in Workbook.

Extra Task: Ask students to use their maps and choose sites for different kinds of roadblock as in **Unit 145**.

Don't forget:

1. Spelling Challenge: World Cities to practice the NATO Alphabet.

2. Test the students on telling the time using the 24 hour clock, and using numbers, and DTG.

3. Test the students on the Key Tactical Verbs.

4. Grid references: test the students, or ask them to test each other, on grid references and terrain features, using a good map.

5. Test your students on a random medical problem. See who can answer the quickest.

6. Check the composition of a convoy and the role of key personnel.

7. Check the different kinds of IEDs and UXO, 5Cs, and 10-liner report.

Unit 148

About the Unit

This unit looks in more detail at the different kinds of roadblock and how to describe them. It is reading and writing preparation for the speaking tasks in **Unit 149**.

Task 1

This is a revision task.

Task 2

This is a lead-in/speculation task. You might want to suggest courses of action for a bit of fun. Should the person in the photo be shot on sight? Invited in for a cup of tea? Questioned? Arrested and sent to be questioned at HQ. What might innocent explanations be for his proximity to the checkpoint?

Task 3

Examine the diagram of the mobile checkpoint. Ask the students if there are any errors, or if they would arrange things differently. If yes, ask them to justify the differences.

Then students should listen to the description. What mistakes are made by the speaker.

Key	This roadblock consists of three vehicles. The front and rear vehicles block traffic in one lane each, while the command vehicle is parked by the side of the road. Search Protection is placed out of sight on one side of the road. The 2IC runs the checkpoint on the road **while the commander waits in the front vehicle (not true – in a stand off position). Vehicles can be stopped in one direction only (not true – in both directions according to the diagram).** The two traffic sentries direct traffic to the search areas. There are two searchers waiting in the search areas. There are four cut offs – two at either side of the roadblock – down the road before vehicles reach the roadblock.

Task 4

Ask the students to listen again and tick the prepositions they hear.

Key	The students should have ticked al but *under, between* and *above.*

Task 5

Ask the student to complete the text with the correct prepositions.

Key	This roadblock consists [1] **of** two vehicles. The front and rear vehicles block traffic [2] **on** one lane each. Search Protection is placed [3] **out** of sight [4] **on** both sides [5] **of** the road. The 2IC runs the checkpoint [6] **on** the road while the commander waits [7] **in** a standoff position. Vehicles can be stopped [8] **in** both directions. The two traffic sentries direct traffic [9] **to** the search areas. There are two Searchers waiting [10] **in** the search areas. There are four Cut Offs – two [11] **on** either side [12] **of** the roadblock – [13] **down** the road before vehicles reach the roadblock.

Task 6

Ask the students individually, in pairs or groups to write out descriptions of the other two roadblock diagrams. You might want to display the descriptions and ask for feedback from the other students before you make corrections.

Task 7

Ask the students to write sentences comparing the roadblocks. Display for comments and/or collect and correct.

Don't forget:
1. Spelling Challenge: World Cities to practice the NATO Alphabet.

2. Test the students on telling the time using the 24 hour clock, and using numbers, and DTG.

3. Test the students on the Key Tactical Verbs.

4. Grid references: test the students, or ask them to test each other, on grid references and terrain features, using a good map.

5. Test your students on a random medical problem. See who can answer the quickest.

6. Check the composition of a convoy and the role of key personnel.

7. Check the different kinds of IEDs and UXO, 5Cs, and 10-liner report.

Unit 149

About the Unit

This is a presentation unit where the students prepare models of the three kinds of roadblocks shown in the diagrams in **Unit 148** (using Lego, Cuisenaire rods, pencils, toy cars and soldiers etc.), and then they present their model to the group. Follow the instructions and guidance in the Coursebook. Give the students plenty of time to prepare and practise their presentations. Give feedback during the preparation time, and feedback after the presentations.

Unit 150

About the Unit

The students should now be clear on the construction and layout of checkpoints. **Unit 150** focuses on body searches, while **Unit 151** looks at vehicle searches. You might want to change the order of these two units but make sure you do both before doing **Unit 152**. If you do switch the units you will not be able to do Task 2 of **Unit 151**.

Task 1

Ask the students to describe what they can see in the photos.

Then elicit ideas about what you would say when you want to conduct a body search.

Task 2

Students complete the text with 'total check' or 'spot check'.

Key	A [1] **total check** occurs when everyone passing the CP is searched. This form of checking is hard on resources (both time and personnel) and is often performed only when the CP is located on borders, frontiers, etc. (e.g., national frontiers or cease fire lines).
	A [2] **spot check** refers to a certain number of persons/vehicles being searched. The remainder

can pass freely, be briefly questioned, or will have to show their identity cards. Over a period, [3] **spot check** should prove effective in curtailing illegal movement of people or material in the AO. This method conserves resources compared with the [4] **total check** method.

Task 3

Ask the students to reorder the words in these requests and instructions.

Remember that 'please' can often be put at the beginning and end of the sentences.

Key		
	1. Do you agree to be searched?	7. Stand there please.
	2. Is this your bag?	8. Please take off your coat/jacket.
	3. Come over here please.	9. We need to search you.
	4. Please empty your pockets.	10. What is your name?
	5. Get out of the car/vehicle please.	11. Whose bag is this?
	6. Please stand like this.	12. Put your feet apart and your arms out.

Check, then ask the students to suggest a sequence. There are many possible sequences.

Task 4

Drill the sentences with the students.

Task 5

Teach/check the words in the table and then ask students to complete the text.

Key

Quick Body Searches

[1] **Do not** stand directly in front or behind the subject to avoid confrontation.

[2] **Do not** become distracted. Avoid eye contact with the subject.

[3] **Watch** for non-verbal communications, e.g., increased nervousness or silent gestures to others.

[4] **Do not** cross the line of fire of the cover man.

[5] **Position** the subject with legs slightly apart and arms extended parallel to the ground. Do not spread-eagle the subject as this may interfere with the collection of forensic evidence.

[6] **Conduct** the search quickly and systematically from head to toe, down one side and up the other, covering all body parts, front, and back. [7] **Pay attention** to pockets and waistbands. [8] **Pay attention** when searching the small of the back, armpits, crotch areas and closed hands.

[9] **Use** a stroking squeezing movement when searching. When searching limbs, both hands are used with thumbs and index fingers touching. This method increases the chances of detecting foreign object through the clothing.

[10] **Search** and be respectful of any baggage or removed clothing.

The use of metal detectors or X-ray machines can be a force multiplier especially when searching large groups (i.e. CP operation).

Detailed Body Search Considerations

[12] **Establish** the identity of the subject and the ownership of baggage and other articles.

Invite the subject to empty all pockets and remove all items.

If necessary to remove clothing, the subject may do so voluntarily (should be recorded) or powers exist to require the removal of certain items in or out of the public eye. Typically, the outer coat, jacket, and gloves may be removed in public. In private, there may be grounds to remove other clothing. Note that only outer clothing may be removed.

[13] **Pay attention** to every detail i.e. clothing seams, waistbands, belts, collars, lapels, padding, shirt, and trouser cuffs. Socks and shoes provide easily missed hiding places. Medical dressings are always suspected and medical personnel should examine dressings if necessary. Clothing nametags, manufactures labels, and laundry tags can be valuable.

[14] **Do not show emotion** upon finding illegal or prohibited items. [15] **Significant** articles should not be separated from others but all should be out of reach of the subject.

Check any other unknown words or phrases afterwards. Choose at least one verb phrase, noun phrase and prepositional phrase from the text to explore with the students.

Task 6

Set up a role-play of a body search to practice the language of Task 3 and the do's and don'ts of Task 5.

Task 7

Ask the students to discuss the question and report.

Task 8

Consolidation Tasks in Workbook.

Don't forget:

1. Spelling Challenge: World Cities to practice the NATO Alphabet.

2. Test the students on telling the time using the 24 hour clock, and using numbers, and DTG.

3. Test the students on the Key Tactical Verbs.

4. Grid references: test the students, or ask them to test each other, on grid references and terrain features, using a good map.

5. Test your students on a random medical problem. See who can answer the quickest.

6. Check the composition of a convoy and the role of key personnel.

7. Check the different kinds of IEDs and UXO, 5Cs, and 10-liner report.

About the Unit

This unit is about the language and procedures for searching vehicles. This is all preparation for the extended simulation of **Unit 152**.

Task 1

Ask the students to describe what they can see in the photos

Task 2

This is a revision question from **Unit 151**, which you can obviously not do if you switched the order of units.

Task 3

Ask the students to reorder the words in these instructions.

Remember that 'please' can often be put at the beginning and end of the sentences.

Key		
	1. Please drive over there to be searched.	5. Please open the boot/trunk.
	2. Get out of the vehicle please.	6. Please stand/wait over there.
	3. Please keep your hands where I can see them.	7. Please set away from the vehicle.
	4. Please open the bonnet/hood.	8. Please turn the engine off.

Check, then ask the students to suggest a sequence. There are many possible sequences.

Task 4

Drill the sentences with the students.

Task 5

Teach/check the words in the table and then ask students to complete the text.

Key	
	Search techniques are divided into three categories. The categories vary according to the [1] **intensity** of the search. There is no clear boundary between the categories and the extent of the investigation as each stage depends on the [2] **suspicion** aroused. Categories include:
	Initial check. The initial check is the first part of the searching process carried out on all vehicles and used to select vehicles for a more detailed [3] **examination**. This check is normally carried out without the occupants dismounting, although search personnel may ask the driver to open the trunk and hood. Search personnel at the entrance to barracks and other installations should know the [4] **threat** from large vehicle mounted bombs. Up to three personnel are required for the search, and the search normally takes about 3 minutes per vehicle.
	Primary search. The primary search is done on the vehicles [5] **selected** for a more detailed examination, due to either intelligence or suspicion [6] **aroused** during the initial check. During the

primary search, if any of the search unit becomes suspicious for any reason, a more detailed search may be conducted.

Secondary search. The secondary search is a [7] **thorough** search of highly suspect vehicles. It is recommended that search unit members work in pairs, examining the relevant section of the vehicle. For a more detailed search, have the occupants [8] **exit** the vehicle, and then search them.

Check any other unknown words or phrases afterwards. Choose at least one verb phrase, noun phrase and prepositional phrase from the text to explore with the students.

Task 6

This is a prediction task for Task 7. Elicit answers. They should be pretty obvious.

Task 7

Ask the students to read the text to see if they were correct.

Key	Patrol leader: remains off the road, uses radio to run a check of vehicle registration number, and selects vehicles to be searched.
	Stopper: stops vehicles, speaks to the occupants, and completes the appropriate form
	Searcher: targets areas of vehicle to search and searches the occupants.
	Cover man: covers the vehicle occupants, from a concealed position, and protects the searcher's equipment.

Check any other unknown words or phrases afterwards. Choose at least one verb phrase, noun phrase and prepositional phrase from the text to explore with the students. Choose at least one verb phrase, noun phrase and prepositional phrase from the text to explore with the students.

Task 8

Key	1. to control whole situations and trigger cut offs if necessary.
	2. So that it cannot be grabbed/used by the person being searched.
	3. So that he is not obvious.

Task 9

Use the pictures or slides to discuss which are the best places to hide things in different kinds of vehicles, and thus the most important places to search.

Extra Task: The photos P151.9 to P151.47 show vehicles of different kinds. Use these for vehicle description tasks. This will be useful practice before **Unit 152**. Use P151.7 and P151.8 for lexis to do with vehicles; these are also available in an **Extra Task Presentation**. You ask students to write descriptions of vehicles and then students could match photos and descriptions; or you could give each student, photos of two similar vehicles and ask them to compare them and so on.

You might want to make an extra lesson on this topic before **Unit 152**; it all depends on how familiar your students are with vehicle types. You might want to do this extra task before doing Task 9 in this unit.

Task 10

Role play vehicle searches – Use these instructions. [Also, see P151.6] this practice for the extended simulation in **Unit 152**.

Put four chairs together to make the seats in a car.

Four students should occupy these chairs.

The other students should work in threes and act as a stopper, searcher and cover man. Do an initial check, asking the driver to open the trunk and hood, then primary search, then ask the passengers sitting down to get out of the car, and then do a secondary search.

Don't forget: be respectful and polite but watchful.

The rest of the class watches and gives feedback after the search.

Task 11

Consolidation Tasks in Workbook.

Don't forget:

1. Spelling Challenge: World Cities to practice the NATO Alphabet.

2. Test the students on telling the time using the 24 hour clock, and using numbers, and DTG.

3. Test the students on the Key Tactical Verbs.

4. Grid references: test the students, or ask them to test each other, on grid references and terrain features, using a good map.

5. Test your students on a random medical problem. See who can answer the quickest.

6. Check the composition of a convoy and the role of key personnel.

7. Check the different kinds of IEDs and UXO, 5Cs, and 10-liner report.

Unit 152

About the Unit

This unit is an extended simulation, best done outside with real vehicles. The students have to demonstrate the set up and operation of a checkpoint, including person and vehicle searches.

You might want to check through the language of the Person And Vehicle Search Form first.

Give the students plenty of time to plan and rehearse before demonstrating their checkpoint.

As a teacher, give feedback on the language which they use. Let the other students give feedback on military skills.

Units 153 – 160 Patrols

This series of units is about the language of patrolling. The first two units are revision/extension units of language from **Unit 131**. The other units build up to units on patrol orders and a patrol briefing.

The model orders used here might be different from the orders which the soldiers are familiar with in their army e.g. in the sequencing of information. Patrol orders are considered to be different from OPORDs (Operational Orders) for the purposes of this book. This is not a problem as the soldiers should be aware of possible differences and welcome the opportunity to practice under different conditions. This will be discussed in **Unit 159**.

Unit 153

About the Unit

This unit reinforces the differences between reconnaissance and combat patrols.

Task 1

Ask the students to describe what they can see in the photos.

Task 2

This is a prediction task for the reading in Task 3. Elicit ideas.

Task 3

Students read the text to check their ideas from Task 2.

Key	1. For reconnaissance or combat.
	2. Reconnaissance patrols fight only when necessary or to defend themselves; combat patrols need to engage the enemy.
	3. Raid, contact, ambush and security.

Task 4

Key	1. Because of its small size and experience working together.
	2. To capture enemy documents, provide security, capture or destroy enemy equipment and installa-

> tions.
>
> 3. A raid is a complex mission and needs a lot of elements, so needs the number of soldiers a company provides.

Check any other unknown words or phrases afterwards. Choose at least one verb phrase, noun phrase and prepositional phrase from the text to explore with the students.

Task 5

Set the Text Analysis tasks in class or for homework.

Task 6 and Task 7

These two tasks are both self-check listening task about patrolling. Ask students to listen and make notes. Ask them to check with their partner, then ask them if they want to listen again. Listen again if necessary, then do a class check. If they have not got enough details listen again. Then ask them to check with the transcript. Ask them to rate their notes.

Task 8

Ask students to complete the phrases and then check by either listening again or checking with the transcript.

Task 9

Ask students to discuss and then tell you what equipment is normal for patrolling. Do not just ask for a list of items but ask them to explain why they take a particular item.

Task 10

Consolidation Tasks in Workbook.

Don't forget:

1. Spelling Challenge: World Cities to practice the NATO Alphabet.

2. Test the students on telling the time using the 24 hour clock, and using numbers, and DTG.

3. Test the students on the Key Tactical Verbs.

4. Grid references: test the students, or ask them to test each other, on grid references and terrain features, using a good map.

5. Test your students on a random medical problem. See who can answer the quickest.

6. Check the composition of a convoy and the role of key personnel.

7. Check the different kinds of IEDs and UXO, 5Cs, and 10-liner report.

8. Check the kinds of checkpoints and the language you can use when searching a person or vehicle.

About the Unit

This unit continues to revise and extend the language of types of patrols.

Task 1

Ask the students to describe what they can see in the photos. This is a prediction task for the reading in Task 3. Elicit ideas.

Task 3

Students read the text to check their ideas from Task 2.

Key	1. Advantages: range of possible terrain; difficult to detect; not dependent on weather. Disadvantages: slow; limited equipment and supplies; limited range.
	2. Advantages: faster, more range, more equipment and supplies. Disadvantages: restricted to certain types of terrain, avoid areas occupied by enemy infantry.
	3. Advantages: can cover waterways. Disadvantages: limited to waterways; bypass areas occupied by enemy.
	4. When terrain is not suitable for other types of patrol, or enemy activity makes them difficult.

Check any other unknown words or phrases afterwards. Choose at least one verb phrase, noun phrase and prepositional phrase from the text to explore with the students.

Task 4

Set the Text Analysis tasks in class or for homework.

Task 5 and **Task 6**

These two tasks are both self-check listening task about patrolling. Ask students to listen and make notes. Ask them to check with their partner, then ask them if they want to listen again. Listen again if necessary, then do a class check. If they have not got enough details listen again. Then ask them to check with the transcript. Ask them to rate their notes.

Task 7

Ask the students to explain the terms.

Task 8

Ask the students to complete the transcript extracts on the next page and then listen to check.

Task 9

Key	1. is not possible ⏐ becomes

2. known

3. should/must immediately destroy

4. is provided | should/must be arranged

5. is required | should/must be

Task 10

Consolidation Tasks in Workbook.

Unit 155

About the Unit

This unit is a vocabulary and listening unit on patrolling.

Teacher Briefing

Some armies use the term 'Rally Point' (RP) to designate a place to meet on a patrol etc.. For example, the Objective rally Point (ORP) is the last place of cover before the objective is reached. Here, the patrol does last minute checks and prepares for the actions on the objective. Another rally point will be designated for after the action, or after crossing a large open area. Other armies might use the term FRV – the final rendezvous instead of ORP, and designate other RVs.

Task 1

Ask the students to describe what they can see in the photos.

Task 2

Key	
	1. passage of lines: an operation to move through another friendly force's combat positions
	2. rally point: place to meet after an action
	3. frontlines: forward combat positions
	4. halt: stop
	5. objective area: target area
	6. friendly lines: own or allied combat positions
	7. passive security; measures like overwatch, setting sentries etc. to protect your force
	8. contact: meeting the enemy
	9. in pursuit: chasing
	10. reconnoiter: to patrol to find out intelligence about the activities, positions and resources of an

Task 3

This task is another self-check listening task about patrolling. Ask students to listen and make notes. Ask them to check with their partner, then ask them if they want to listen again. Listen again if necessary, then do a class check. If they have not got enough details listen again. Then ask them to check with the transcript. Ask them to rate their notes.

Task 4

Ask the students to complete the transcript extract on the next page with the words given and then listen to check.

Task 5

This task is a self-check listening task about patrolling. Ask students to listen and make notes. Ask them to check with their partner, then ask them if they want to listen again. Listen again if necessary, then do a class check. If they have not got enough details listen again. Then ask them to check with the transcript. Ask them to rate their notes.

Task 6

Ask the students to complete the collocations from the second listening text. Then listen to check.

Task 7

Ask the students to explain the terms. Do in pairs and then class check, or as a whole class. You might want to extend this to the collocations from T6.

Task 8

Consolidation Tasks in Workbook.

Don't forget:

1. Spelling Challenge: World Cities to practice the NATO Alphabet.

2. Test the students on telling the time using the 24 hour clock, and using numbers, and DTG.

3. Test the students on the Key Tactical Verbs.

4. Grid references: test the students, or ask them to test each other, on grid references and terrain features, using a good map.

5. Test your students on a random medical problem. See who can answer the quickest.

6. Check the composition of a convoy and the role of key personnel.

7. Check the different kinds of IEDs and UXO, 5Cs, and 10-liner report.

8. Check the kinds of checkpoints and the language you can use when searching a person or vehicle.

About the Unit

This is a short unit on movement formations.

Task 1

Ask the students to describe what they can see in the photos and discuss the questions.

Task 2

This is a prediction task for the short reading in Task 3.

Task 3

Students read to check their ideas from Task 2.

Task 4

Teach/check the words in the table. If appropriate, ask the students to agree on a translation of the terms.

Task 5

Ask students to match the formation name, diagram and description from the next page.

Task 6

Key		
Formation	**Diagram**	**Description**
Line	■■■■	All elements arranged in a row. Majority of observation and direct fires oriented forward; minimal to the flanks. Each subordinate unit on the line must clear its own path forward.
Column/file	■ ■ ■ ■	One lead element. Majority of observation and direct fires oriented to the flanks; minimal to the front. One route means unit only influenced by obstacles on that one route.
Vee	■ ■ ■ ■	Two lead elements. Trail elements move between the two lead elements. Used when contact to the front is expected.
Box	■ ■ ■ ■	Two lead elements. Trail elements follow lead elements. All round security.
Wedge	■ ■ ■ ■	One lead element. Trail elements paired off abreast of each other on the flanks. Used when the situation is uncertain
Diamond	■	Similar to the wedge formation. Fourth element follows the

		lead element.
Echelon (right)		Elements deployed diagonally left or right. Observation and fire to both the front and one flank. Each subordinate unit on the line clears its own path forward.

Task 7

This is a pre-listening discussion. Elicit ideas.

Task 8

This task is a self-check listening task about patrolling. Ask students to listen and make notes. Ask them to check with their partner, then ask them if they want to listen again. Listen again if necessary, then do a class check. If they have not got enough details listen again. Then ask them to check with the transcript. Ask them to rate their notes.

Don't forget:

1. Spelling Challenge: World Cities to practice the NATO Alphabet.

2. Test the students on telling the time using the 24 hour clock, and using numbers, and DTG.

3. Test the students on the Key Tactical Verbs.

4. Grid references: test the students, or ask them to test each other, on grid references and terrain features, using a good map.

5. Test your students on a random medical problem. See who can answer the quickest.

6. Check the composition of a convoy and the role of key personnel.

7. Check the different kinds of IEDs and UXO, 5Cs, and 10-liner report.

8. Check the kinds of checkpoints and the language you can use when searching a person or vehicle.

Unit 157

About the Unit

This unit focuses on the usage of the words 'camouflage', 'cover' and 'concealment'. It is quite a long unit so you may need to split it into two parts.

Task 1

Ask the students to describe what they can see in the photos.

Task 2

Ask the students to match the words with camouflage to make common collocations.

Key	camouflage clothing	artificial camouflage
	natural camouflage	camouflage material
	improvised camouflage	apply camouflage
	individual camouflage	camouflage face sticks

Task 3

This is a prediction task for the short reading in Task 4.

Task 4

Students read the text and discuss if they agree with it.

Check any other unknown words or phrases afterwards. Choose at least one verb phrase, noun phrase and prepositional phrase from the text to explore with the students.

Task 5

Key	1. concealed	7. concealment
	2. concealed	8. concealment
	3. concealed	9. concealment
	4. concealed	10. concealment
	5. concealed | concealment | concealed	11. concealment | concealment
	6. concealment	12. concealment

Task 6 and Task 7

Discuss the collocations and phrases with 'cover'. Do in pairs, then a class check.

Task 8

Ask the students to complete the text with the correct words.

Key	[1] **Camouflage** is the use of [2] **concealment** and disguise to minimize the possibility of detection and/or identification of troops, material, equipment, and installations. The purpose of [3] **camouflage** is to provide [4] **concealment** of military objects from enemy observation. [5] **Camouflage** is also used to [6] **conceal** an object by making it look like something else. A scout's mission usually requires
	Individual and equipment [7] **camouflage**. If natural [8] **camouflage** is not adequate, the position is [9] **camouflaged**. In using [10] **camouflage**, remember that objects are identified by their form (outline), shadow, texture, and color. The principal purpose of [11] **camouflage** in the field is to prevent direct observation and recognition.
	Individual [12] **Camouflage**: Successful individual [13] **camouflage** involves the ability to recog-

nize and take advantage of all forms of natural and artificial [14] **concealment** available (vegetation, soil, debris, etc.) and knowledge of the proper use of artificial [15] **camouflage** materials. Aids to Individual [16] **Camouflage**: A scout must recognize the terrain's dominant color and pattern and must change the appearance of clothing and equipment accordingly in order to blend and not contrast with the terrain. The helmet is [17] **camouflaged** by breaking up its shape, smooth surface, and shadow. Use of a helmet cover works best. In the absence of a helmet [18] **cover**, mud can be irregularly blotched on the helmet to disguise its form and dull the surface. A helmet [19] **cover** may be improvised from irregularly colored cloth or burlap to blend with the background. Foliage can be draped to prevent the visor of the helmet from casting a dark shadow across the face.

Any equipment that reflects light should be covered with a nonreflective material that aids in the [20] **concealment** of the weapon (for example, black electrical tape or mud). The straight line of the rifle or other infantry weapons may be very conspicuous to an enemy observer.

Task 9

Ask the students to describe what they can see in the photos in terms of terrain and cover, and explain opportunities for concealment. What kinds of equipment and camouflage would they need to operate in these terrains? You could also do this as a map exercise.

Don't forget:

1. Spelling Challenge: World Cities to practice the NATO Alphabet.

2. Test the students on telling the time using the 24 hour clock, and using numbers, and DTG.

3. Test the students on the Key Tactical Verbs.

4. Grid references: test the students, or ask them to test each other, on grid references and terrain features, using a good map.

5. Test your students on a random medical problem. See who can answer the quickest.

6. Check the composition of a convoy and the role of key personnel.

7. Check the different kinds of IEDs and UXO, 5Cs, and 10-liner report.

8. Check the kinds of checkpoints and the language you can use when searching a person or vehicle.

Unit 158

About the Unit

This is a briefing unit where students brief and show their military knowledge. Each slide shows one aspect of patrolling skills. The briefing on ambushes show 8 different kinds of ambushes.

Follow the instructions in the coursebook.

Be ready to give feedback on the language used in the briefings.

Unit 159

About the Unit

This unit introduces Route Cards and Patrol Briefing forms. There is a note explaining possible differences patrol orders. The main difference is that these patrol briefings discuss the Ground first and then move on to discuss the situation. **Task 1**

Ask the students to describe what they can see in the photo.

Task 2

This is a prediction task for Task 3. Elicit ideas (and the sequence) of information they would expect in a patrol briefing.

Task 3

Look through the Patrol Briefing Form on the next page.

Notes	Recce: reconnaissance	FRV: Final Rendezvous
	OP: Observation Post	I/C: In command
		2I/C: second in command

Task 4

This is a language awareness raising task.

Task 5

In this listening task the students have to complete a Route Card, mark the route on the map, and complete a Patrol Briefing Form. In real life they would <u>not</u> have to complete a Patrol Briefing Form – this is a learning task. You will need to judge how many times they need to listen to the briefing. Do a pair check, then a class check and then check with the transcript if necessary.

Don't forget:

1. Spelling Challenge: World Cities to practice the NATO Alphabet.

2. Test the students on telling the time using the 24 hour clock, and using numbers, and DTG.

3. Test the students on the Key Tactical Verbs.

4. Grid references: test the students, or ask them to test each other, on grid references and terrain features, using a good map.

5. Test your students on a random medical problem. See who can answer the quickest.

6. Check the composition of a convoy and the role of key personnel.

---

7. Check the different kinds of IEDs and UXO, 5Cs, and 10-liner report.

8. Check the kinds of checkpoints and the language you can use when searching a person or vehicle.

Unit 160

About the Unit

In this unit the students prepare briefings on a patrol. They should use maps and plan the route, completing a Route Card and Patrol Briefing Form. Then they should brief the class.

Note: You could ask them to use the Patrol Briefing Form from Unit 159 and deal with the Ground first, or let them brief in a different way if they are more comfortable with that.

At the end of the briefings the students check the information and make sure it is all correct.

Note on Task 3: This task asks the students to evaluate the briefings by using the **Patrol Order Delivery Evaluation Form** from the Workbook (page 205). You might want to assign a student to evaluate a particular briefing, or divide the sections of the evaluation up between a group of students. Think carefully about how best to do this with your particular students.

Give feedback on the language used.

Units 161 – 163 Attacks

This series of units is about attacks, and revises and extends some of the language dealt with in the patrolling units

Unit 161

About the Unit

This unit considers the difference between hasty (opportunistic) and deliberate (planned) attacks.

Task 1

Ask the students to describe what they can see in the photos.

Task 2

This is a prediction task for Task 3. Elicit ideas.

Task 3

Students read the text to check their ideas from Task 2.

Task 4

Students discuss the forms of attack in pairs and then check with the class as a whole.

Check any other unknown words or phrases afterwards. Choose at least one verb phrase, noun phrase and prepositional phrase from the text to explore with the students.

Task 5

This task is a self-check listening task about the different kinds of attack. Ask students to listen and make notes. Ask them to check with their partner, then ask them if they want to listen again. Listen again if necessary, then do a class check. If they have not got enough details listen again. Then ask them to check with the transcript. Ask them to rate their notes.

Task 6

Ask the students to complete the transcript extract on the next page with the words given and then listen to check, and then read the transcript if necessary.

Task 7

Consolidation Tasks in Workbook.

Don't forget:

1. Spelling Challenge: World Cities to practice the NATO Alphabet.

2. Test the students on telling the time using the 24 hour clock, and using numbers, and DTG.

3. Test the students on the Key Tactical Verbs.

4. Grid references: test the students, or ask them to test each other, on grid references and terrain features, using a good map.

5. Test your students on a random medical problem. See who can answer the quickest.

6. Check the composition of a convoy and the role of key personnel.

7. Check the different kinds of IEDs and UXO, 5Cs, and 10-liner report.

8. Check the kinds of checkpoints and the language you can use when searching a person or vehicle.

9. Test the students on the language of patrols.

Unit 162

About the Unit

This is a short unit which bridges between **Unit 161** and **163**.

Task 1

Ask the students to describe what they can see in the photos.

Task 2

This is a revision question about **Unit 161**.

Task 3

Key	
	1. **Penetration** is a form of maneuver in which an attacking element seeks to rupture enemy defenses on a narrow front to create both assailable flanks and access to the enemy's rear.
	2. **Infiltration** is a form of maneuver in which an attacking element conducts <u>undetected</u> movement through or into an area occupied by enemy forces to gain a position of advantage in the enemy rear.
	3. The **turning movement** is a form of maneuver in which the attacking element seeks to avoid the enemy's principal defensive positions by seizing objectives to the enemy's rear.
	4. **Envelopment** is a form of maneuver in which an attacking element seeks to avoid the principal enemy defenses by seizing objectives to the enemy flank or rear in order to destroy him in his current positions.
	5. **A frontal attack** is a form of maneuver in which an attacking element seeks to destroy a weaker enemy force or fix a larger enemy force along a broad front.

Task 4

Ask the students to study the diagrams in P162.3 – P162.7 and prepare to present the diagrams to each other in groups.

Task 5

Put the students in groups, or pairs and the students take turns explaining the diagrams from Task 4. Finally ask the students to explain the diagrams to you. The diagrams are also available in Standard and Widescreen Presentations for this unit.

Task 6

This is a preparation task for **Unit 163**. Elicit ideas from the students.

Unit 163

About the Unit

This unit follows on from the work done on attacks in **Units 161** and **162**.

Task 1

Ask the students to describe what they can see in the photos.

Task 2

This is a revision question about Task 6 in **Unit 162**.

Task 3

Students read the text so see if their ideas from Task 2 are in the text.

Task 4

Ask the students to reread the text to answer the questions.

<table>
<tr><td>Key</td><td>1. Preparation for the mission. Pre-combat checks and inspections, rehearsals and sustainment activities.

2. The point the unit crosses the line of departure.

3. Manoeuvrer is moving into position; movement is during an attack.

4. the assault position is the last concealed position before the objective is reached.

5. The position the assault starts from.

6. With direct and indirect fires on the objective.

7. Fire + movement; breach to establish a foothold; assault element moves through the breach to assault the objective.

8. Consolidation: to guard against counter-attacks; Reorganisation: to be ready for further operations</td></tr>
</table>

Check any other unknown words or phrases afterwards. Choose at least one verb phrase, noun phrase and prepositional phrase from the text to explore with the students.

Task 5

Set the Text Analysis tasks in class or for homework.

Task 6

Tell the students to listen to the text to decide which words they need to practice saying. This can be done as homework.

Task 7

Students test themselves on collocations from the text. They reread the text to check themselves.

Task 8

Consolidation Tasks in Workbook.

Optional Task: There are three maps: M163.1, M163.2 and M163.3, also available as Presentations: **Unit 163 Extra Task Standard/Widescreen**, which you could use for extra tasks.

You could ask the students to work in groups and to prepare disposition maps of defensive positions and attacks. You could set up six groups, for example. Three groups would prepare defensive dispositions based on M163.1, M163.2 and M163.3, while three groups could prepare offensive dispositions based on the same maps. They could brief about their positions. This would revise the disposition units (**Units 99 – 104**), **Units 125-6** and **Units 161 – 3**.

Note that these maps are extracted from old Soviet Union maps. You students might be unfamiliar with Russian and unable to use the names on the map to help the. This will force them to describe things and their position rather than name them.

Don't forget:

1. Spelling Challenge: World Cities to practice the NATO Alphabet.

2. Test the students on telling the time using the 24 hour clock, and using numbers, and DTG.

3. Test the students on the Key Tactical Verbs.

4. Grid references: test the students, or ask them to test each other, on grid references and terrain features, using a good map.

5. Test your students on a random medical problem. See who can answer the quickest.

6. Check the composition of a convoy and the role of key personnel.

7. Check the different kinds of IEDs and UXO, 5Cs, and 10-liner report.

8. Check the kinds of checkpoints and the language you can use when searching a person or vehicle.

9. Test the students on the language of patrols.

Study Page: Patrols: Revision and Extension

This study page is a revision self-check page for the students to test themselves about patrols. You could do it in class or set it as homework.

Task 1

Key	A patrol is a [1] **detachment** sent out by a [2] **larger** unit to conduct a [3] **specific** mission. Patrols operate [4] **semi-independently** and return to the [5] **main** body upon completion of their [6] **mission**.

Task 2

Key	[1] **gathering** information on the enemy, on the terrain, or on the populace.
	[2] **regaining** contact with the enemy or with adjacent friendly forces
	[3] **engaging** the enemy in combat to destroy him or inflict losses.
	[4] **reassuring** or gaining the trust of a local population.
	[5] **preventing** public disorder.
	[6] **deterring** and disrupting insurgent or criminal activity.
	[7] **providing** unit security.
	[8] **protecting** key infrastructure or bases.

Task 3

Students listen and make notes and check with the transcript.

Units 164 – 173 Orders

This series of units is about the language of orders. The units work through Warning orders to Operation Orders. These orders follow the 5 paragraph format common in the US military and elsewhere.

There are also three Study Pages of collocations with 'order'.

Teacher Briefing

The diagram on the next page shows the platoon order process, from the time the Platoon Leader (PL) receives the mission to the issuing of the OPORD. This does not include information about how the PL plans the mission.

Stage 1: The Company Commander issues a WARNO to Platoon Leaders.

Stage 2: The Platoon Leader receives the mission. [This could be through a Warning Order (WARNO/WARNORD), an Operation Order (OPORD) or Fragmentary Order (FRAGO). Here it is through a WARNO.]

Stage 3: The PL might need to do a Confirmation Brief to the Company Commander to show that he has understood the order.

Stage 4: The PL immediately issues his own WARNO to his section leaders or squad leaders, depending on how he has chosen to organise the platoon. This will include information about the mission, and where and when the full OPORD will be issued, who is participating in the mission, and a timeline, including tasks to be done before the OPORD is issued.

Stage 5: The section or squad leaders issue a WARNO down the chain of command so that everyone in the platoon is aware of the mission and what has to be done etc.

Stage 6: The section or squad leaders start carrying out tasks based on the WARNO.

Stage 7: Meanwhile the PL starts to develop his OPORD.

Stage 8: He might get a full OPORD from Company during this process if he did not get this at Stage 1.

Stage 9: He might have to backbrief Company on his OPORD.

Stage 10: Once his OPORD is ready, he issues his OPORD to his section leaders or squad leaders.

Stage 11: His section leaders or squad leaders issue the OPORD down the chain of command.

The Platoon Order Process

1. WARNO from CO

2. Platoon Leader receives mission

3. Confirmation briefing to Company Commanding Officer (CO) on WARNO

4. Platoon Leader issues WARNO to section/squad leaders

5. Section leaders issue WARNO to squad leaders or Squad leaders issue WARNO to Fire Teams

6. Section/Squad leaders start carrying out tasks based on the WARNO

7. Platoon Leader develops an OPORD plan

8. OPORD from CO

9. Backbrief on PL OPORD by PL to CO

10. Platoon Leader issues OPORD to section/squad leaders

11. Section leaders issue OPORD to squad leaders or Squad leaders issue OPORD to Fire Teams

Study Page: Collocations of Orders 1

This is first of three such pages of collocations with 'order'. Either do it in class or set as homework.

Key	give I await I review an order
	a/an appropriate I effective I specific I standing I oral Iverbal order
	a/an patrol I mission I operation order

Don't forget:

1. Spelling Challenge: World Cities to practice the NATO Alphabet.

2. Test the students on telling the time using the 24 hour clock, and using numbers, and DTG.

3. Test the students on the Key Tactical Verbs.

4. Grid references: test the students, or ask them to test each other, on grid references and terrain features, using a good map.

5. Test your students on a random medical problem. See who can answer the quickest.

6. Check the composition of a convoy and the role of key personnel.

7. Check the different kinds of IEDs and UXO, 5Cs, and 10-liner report.

8. Check the kinds of checkpoints and the language you can use when searching a person or vehicle.

9. Test the students on the language of patrols.

10. Test the students on the kinds of movement and attack.

Unit 164

About the Unit

This unit is about issuing orders, such as WARNO, OPORD etc.

Task 1

Ask the students to describe what they can see in the photos. What is happening?

Task 2

Teach/check the words in the table and then ask students to complete the text.

Key	Leaders receive their missions in several ways—ideally through a series of warning orders ([1] **WARNOs**), operation orders ([2] **OPORDs**), and briefings from their leader/commander. How-

ever, the [3] **tempo** of operations often precludes this ideal sequence, particularly at the lower levels. This means that leaders may often receive only a [4] **WARNO** or a fragmentary order ([5] **FRAGO**), but the process is the same.

After receiving an order, leaders are normally required to give a [6] **confirmation** briefing to their higher commander. This is done to [7] **clarify** their understanding of the commander's mission, intent, and concept of the operation, as well as their [8] **role** within the operation. The leader obtains clarification on any portions of the higher headquarters' plan as required.

Task 3

This is a prediction task for the reading in Task 4.

Task 4

The answer is clear from the text.

Task 5

Key	STEP 1. Receive the mission. STEP 2. Issue a warning order. STEP 3. Make a tentative plan. STEP 4. Start necessary movement. STEP 5. Reconnoiter. STEP 6. Complete the plan. STEP 7. Issue the complete order. STEP 8. Supervise.

Task 6

This is a prediction task for the reading in Task 7.

Task 7

Key	1. Assessment of situation, mission, larger operation, allocating time for planning and preparing. 2. METT-TC 3. A restated mission and timeline, leading to a WARNO.

Task 8

Teach/check the words in the table and then ask students to complete the text.

Key	Based on their knowledge, leaders [1] **estimate** the time available to plan and prepare for the mission. They issue a [2] **tentative** timeline that is as [3] **detailed** as possible. In the process they [4] **allocate** roughly one-third of available planning and preparation time to themselves,

allowing their [5] **subordinates** the remaining two-thirds. During [6] **fast-paced** operations, planning and preparation time might be [7] **extremely** limited. Knowing this in advance enables leaders to emplace [8] **SOPs** to assist them in these situations.

Task 9

Students complete the collocations from the text and then re-read to check.

Task 10

Students discuss the question in pairs and then discuss as a class.

Unit 165

About the Unit

This unit is the first of three units about WARNOs.

Task 1

This is a lead-in/prediction task for Task 2.

Task 2

Students match the paragraphs with the descriptions.

Key

Para 1: Situation:
Brief description of the enemy and friendly forces situations. Point out key locations on the ground, map or sketch. Attachments and detachments to the squad/platoon. (A)

Para 2: Mission:
Concise statement of the task and purpose (who, what, when, where, and why) If not all information is known, state which parts of the mission statement are tentative. (C)

Para 3: Execution:
Brief statement of the tentative concept of the operation. (B)
Time schedule: earliest time of move; Time and place of OPORD; probable execution time. Inspection times and items to be inspected different from SOP. Rehearsal time, location, and actions to be rehearsed. (G)
Tasks to subordinate key personnel: Platoon sergeant; squad leaders; RATELO; aidman; attachments. Tasks to soldiers helping prepare OPORD. Tasks as needed to others. (F)

Para 4: Service Support:
CSS tasks to be accomplished that are different from the TACSOP: Equipment and transportation. (D)

Para 5: Command and Signals:

Location of CP; succession of command (if not SOP). SOI in effect. Signals/code words. (E)

Notes 1	Para 4: Service Support might also be known as 'Sustainment' or 'Administration and Logistics'

Notes 2	CSS: Combat Service Support
	SOP: Standing Operating Procedures
	RATELO: Radio-telephone Operator
	TACSOP: Tactical Standing Operating Procedures
	SOI: Standard Operating Instructions
	CP: Command Post

Task 3

In this task, the students need to identify the examples of the paragraphs from Task 2.

Key	
This is a warning order. Hold your questions until I finish.	
1. Situation The scouts have identified a motorized rifle platoon with at least two BTRs defending Hill 876 vicinity GRID 123456. They are digging in and it looks like they plan to defend the road junction at GRID 126463. The rest of the enemy company is further to the west, around Hill 899.	Para: 1
Captain Williams just issued a warning order for the company to prepare for an attack at 11 0200Zulu July 19 to seize Hill 876 in order to provide suppressive fire for the Battalion's main attack on Hill 899. There are no attachments or detachments.	Para: 1
2. Mission It is the mission of Third Platoon to attack and seize Hill 876 GRID 123456 on 11 0200Zulu July 19 in order to provide fires on Hill 899 in support of the battalion's attack. We will be one of the two assault platoons along with Second Platoon. First Platoon will be the base of fire along with the company mortars and Javelins.	Para 2
3. Execution **[Note: in this order only the co-ordinating instructions are given; this could be criticized by the students]** **Coordinating Instructions** Timeline is as follows: I want a platoon rehearsal for squad and fire team leaders, the aidman,	Para 3

the Forward Observer, and, of course, Sergeant First Class Fowler here at our Command Post at 1330. Platoon rehearsals will be for action at the objective. Squads rehearse breaching and react to contact drills on your own. We have a company rehearsal for platoon and squad leaders at 1600 at the company Command Post. We will meet here at 1530 and move together. I will do a full platoon rehearsal at 2100 so we can do at least one go of it in the dark. Line of Departure time is 0200. The earliest we will have to move is 2330. After 2330 we have to be ready to move within 10 minutes of the order to do so. My final inspection will be here at the Command Post. My OPORD will be here at the platoon Command Post at 1030.

Sergeant First Class Fowler talk to me about resupply after this warning order. I want you to plan for casualty evacuation and to give paragraph 4 of the OPORD. Staff Sergeant Crawford, you and your squad will be the lead squad. Make sure you recon the route from here to the Line of Departure. Sergeant Brown, as Forward Observer, I need you to get the fireplan from the Fire Support Centre as soon as possible. Staff Sergeant Steele, send Sergeant White and his team up here in 20 minutes to begin making the terrain model of the objective. **Para 3**

4. Service Support   **Para: 4**
Each squad will carry four AT4s.

5. Command and Control   **Para: 5**
No changes to platoon organization. The platoon CP will stay here.
Standard Operating Instructions, we have are still in effect.

Time is now 0620. What are your questions?

| **Notes** | BTR: an eight-wheeled armoured personnel carrier |
| | AT4: an 84-mm unguided, portable, single-shot recoilless smooth bore anti-tank weapon |

Task 4

Key	1. GL 123456
	2. Hill 876
	3. 0200
	4. Hill 899
	5. To provide fires on Hill 899
	6. No.
	7. 1600.
	8. Platoon rehearsal.
	9. Full platoon rehearsal: action on the objective in the dark.
	10. Squads.
	11. SFC Fowler.
	12. So they know what the targets are.

Task 5

This is a final check of the language of the text.

Task 6

Ask the students to use their professional knowledge and evaluate the WARNO. Is it a good example of a WARNO? What would they change/add? What could be abbreviated? For example, could you say LD instead of Line of Departure?

Notes	Possible abbreviations:
	LD: Line of Departure
	FO: Forward Observer
	FIST: Fire Support Team
	ASAP: As soon as possible
	SOP: Standard Operating Procedure
	SOI: Standard Operating Instructions
	CP: Command post

Task 7

Tell the students to listen to the text to decide which words they need to practice saying. This can be done as homework.

Task 8

Consolidation Tasks in Workbook.

Don't forget:

1. Spelling Challenge: World Cities to practice the NATO Alphabet.

2. Test the students on telling the time using the 24 hour clock, and using numbers, and DTG.

3. Test the students on the Key Tactical Verbs.

4. Grid references: test the students, or ask them to test each other, on grid references and terrain features, using a good map.

5. Test your students on a random medical problem. See who can answer the quickest.

6. Check the composition of a convoy and the role of key personnel.

7. Check the different kinds of IEDs and UXO, 5Cs, and 10-liner report.

8. Check the kinds of checkpoints and the language you can use when searching a person or vehicle.

9. Test the students on the language of patrols.

10. Test the students on the kinds of movement and attack.

Unit 166

About the Unit

This unit is revision of all the language from **Unit 165**.

Task 1

This is a revision question from **Unit 165**.

Task 2

Students complete the gap fill, check with their partner, then check with the original text in **Unit 165**.

Task 3

In this listening task you should assign roles so they listen primarily for what their role should do, but also they should make notes on what everyone else is doing. The ten questions are there to guide them. Really they need to understand everything of the WARNO. Check as a class and see if they need to listen again. In real life they will hear the WARNO once but be able to ask questions at the end. This is basically the same as the WARNO in Task 2 but with different names and times. They can check with T166.1.

Key		
	1. Vicinity FN 786496	7. Squads
	2. Hill 956	8. Sergeant Kapenda
	3. 15 0100 Aug 16	9. Sergeant Angula
	4. Hill 934	10. No.
	5. No.	11. Sergeant Nampala.
	6. 1500	12. Sergeant Kapweya.

Unit 167

About the Unit

This unit practices WARNOs

Task 1

This is a revision question.

Task 2 -5

Students work in groups to prepare WARNOs. Follow the procedure and give feedback.

Study Page: Collocations of Orders 2

This is second of three such pages of collocations with 'order'. Start by seeing what collocations they remember from Collocations of Orders # 1. Either do it in class or set as homework.

Key	convey	wait for	issue an order
	a/an written	new	special	conflicting	initial order
	a/an deployment	unit	tasking	warning order

Unit 168

About the Unit

This unit is the first of five on OPORDs.

Task 1

This is a revision task.

Task 2

Ask the students to read through the paragraphs and identify which is Paragraph 1, 2, 3, 4, 5.

Key	Task Organisation: D (Given)
	Para 1: Situation: C
	Para 2: Mission: E
	Para 3: Execution: B
	Para 4: Service Support: F
	Para 5: Command and Signals: A

Check the language of OPORDS in detail, as the subsequent units will practice this.

Notes	PSG: Platoon Sergeant
	ADA: Air Defence Artillery
	CS: Combat Support
	ROE: Rules of Engagement
	HQ: Headquarters
	EPW: Enemy Prisoner of War
	SOP: Standard Operating Procedures

Task 3

Ask the students to use their professional knowledge and evaluate the OPORD instructions. What would they change/add?

Don't forget:

1. Spelling Challenge: World Cities to practice the NATO Alphabet.

2. Test the students on telling the time using the 24 hour clock, and using numbers, and DTG.

3. Test the students on the Key Tactical Verbs.

4. Grid references: test the students, or ask them to test each other, on grid references and terrain features, using a good map.

5. Test your students on a random medical problem. See who can answer the quickest.

6. Check the composition of a convoy and the role of key personnel.

7. Check the different kinds of IEDs and UXO, 5Cs, and 10-liner report.

8. Check the kinds of checkpoints and the language you can use when searching a person or vehicle.

9. Test the students on the language of patrols.

10. Test the students on the kinds of movement and attack.

Unit 169

About the Unit

This unit practices the language of OPORDs introduced in **Unit 168**.

Task 1

This is a revision question about **Unit 168**.

Task 2

In this task, the students need to identify the examples of the paragraphs of the OPORD.

TASK ORGANISATION	Task organization is First Squad with two of the platoon's machine guns, Third Squad, Second Squad with three Dragons. (K)
PARA 1 SITUATION	"Situation"
	Enemy forces: the scouts have confirmed a full strength motorized rifle platoon with Infantry Fighting Vehicles on our portion of the company objective. They are dug in and expected to fight hard to retain this terrain. Their approximate positions and orientation are as reflected on the terrain model. (J)

	Friendly forces: Charlie Company seizes OBJECTIVE FOX, vicinity of GRID 162827 to prevent enemy from concentrating combat power against the battalion main effort. Alpha Company on OBJECTIVE COW. The CO's intent is to isolate the northern portion of the OBJECTIVE preventing the enemy main effort from concentrating against our breach in the south. He wants to execute the main attack as quickly as possible. This will prevent the enemy from affecting the battalion attack. On our left First Platoon fix the enemy on OBJECTIVE FOX to allow Second Platoon to establish a breach. On our right, Second Platoon establish a breach, vicinity of GRID 163826 to allow main attack to clear OBJECTIVE FOX. To our rear, company mortars suppress enemy on OBJECTIVE FOX to screen breaching effort. Attachments and detachments: Second squad has three Dragons attached, which will remain under platoon control until seizure of OBJECTIVE CAT. (I)
PARA 2 MISSION	**"Mission"**
	3rd Platoon attacks 14 0200ZuluJun19 to seize western edge of Hill 652 OBJ CAT, vicinity of GRID 170834 to prevent disruption of battalion main attack. (A)
PARA 3 EXECUTION **Intent and concept of operation**	**"Execution"** Concept of the operation is to penetrate OBJECTIVE CAT from the northeast. First Squad will suppress the trench line allowing the main attack by Third Squad to maneuver and enter the trench. Once the foothold is established, Second Squad enters and clears the trench line from east to west. Key to this mission is speed in establishing the foothold (the decisive point) and providing suppressive fires to allow main attack access to the trench line. This should keep them busy and keep them from disrupting the battalion main attack. (H)
Maneuver	**"Maneuver"** First Squad suppresses trench line to allow Second Squad to enter the trench line. Second Squad, the main effort, clears the trench line preventing disruption of battalion attack. 3rd Squad establishes foothold in trench line allowing Second Squad to enter trench line. (L)
Fires	**"Fires"** Purpose of mortar fires is to screen observation of the breaching operation. First Squad has priority of 60 mm mortar fire. During consolidation, Third Squad will have priority of fires. Battalion will fire a three-minute preparatory fire on OBJECTIVE COW to disrupt enemy command and control. (B)
Tasks to maneuver units	**"Tasks to maneuver units"** First Squad, shift fires to contact point 1, allowing Second Squad a clear approach into the trench line. Second Squad, prepare satchel charges for

	bunkers. Third Squad, be prepared to assault IFVs. (G)
Tasks to combat support units	**"Tasks to combat support units"** Mortars will occupy firing positions, vicinity of GRID 167828 not later than 14 0425Zulu Jun 19. (F)
Co-ordinating instructions	**"Co-ordinating instructions"** Order of march for Company C is First Platoon, Command Post, Second Platoon, Mortars, Third Platoon. Order of march for the platoon is First Squad, HQ, Second Squad, Third Squad. Movement formation is platoon file, travelling overwatch. (C)
	Line of departure time 14 0300Zulu Jun 19. MOPP1 in effect. Platoon rehearsal for key leaders: 1300. Company rehearsal 1400. Consolidation is in accordance with terrain model. Timing: 1300 Platoon rehearsal; 1400 Company rehearsal; 1700 inspection; 1730 chow; 1830 rest; 2100 night rehearsals; 0045 stand-to; 0115 final inspection; 0200 Line of Departure time; 0515 Assault time. (M)
PARA 4 SERVICE SUPPORT	"Service support" Company trains will be located at this trail intersection, vicinity of GRID 161823 after seizure of OBJECTIVE FOX. (R)
Medical evacuation	Company casualty collection points are located here at GRID 162824 and GRID 165827. Platoon Casualty Collection Point after seizure of OBJECTIVE CAT will be directly behind this Infantry Fighting Vehicle position here at GRID 171835. (D)
Personnel	Company expects to receive some replacements late 15 June. We should receive two infantrymen. (N)
	Enemy Prisoner of War collection point will be behind First Squad objective. (Q)
PARA 5 COMMAND AND SIGNALS	Company Commander will follow us. He will set up Company Command Post in the vicinity of the trench line. I will follow First Squad during movement and will assault with Second Squad. Platoon Sergeant will follow Second Squad, then move to the support-by-fire position with First Squad. No changes to platoon organization. (P)
	Signals: Radio: Tactical frequency is 65 Khz; the TACEVAC frequency is 37 Khz. Challenge is: Arrow; Password is Maize; Running Password is Apache; the number combination password is seven (E)
	The time is now 1007. What are your questions? (0)

Notes	MOPP1: Mission Oriented Protective Posture 1: CBRN (Chemical, biological, radiological or nuclear) protective gear: Level 1: Protective suit worn; Protective mask carried; boots and gloves immediately available.

Possible abbreviations

CCP: Casualty Collection Point	IAW: In accordance with
NLT: Not Later Than	LD: Line of Departure
CO: Commanding Officer	CP: Command Post
MRP: Motorised Rifle Platoon	EPW: Enemy Prisoner of War

Task 3

Key	1. GL170834
	2. To seize the western edge of Hill 652 – Objective CAT.
	3. 0200/0515 (discuss)
	4. Objective COW
	5. Order of march for Company C is 1st Platoon, CP, 2nd Platoon, Mortars, 3rd Platoon. Order of march for the platoon is 1st Squad, HQ, 2nd Squad, 3rd Squad. Movement formation is platoon file, travelling overwatch.
	6. 1st Squad suppress trench line to allow 2nd Squad to enter the trench line. 2nd Squad, the main effort, clears the trench line preventing disruption of battalion attack. 3rd Squad establishes foothold in trench line allowing 2nd squad to enter trench line.
	7. Timing: 1300 Plt rehearsal; 1400 Co. rehearsal; 1700 inspection; 1730 chow; 1830 rest; 2100 night rehearsals; 0045 stand-to; 0115 final inspection; 0200 LD time; 0515 Assault time
	8. Company casualty collection points are located along the infiltration lane. Platoon CCP after seizure of OBJ CAT will be directly behind the BTR position.
	9. Commander will follow us. He will set up CP in the vicinity of the the trench line.
	10. Not specified apart from 'The number combination password is seven'.

Task 4

This is a final check of the language of the text.

Task 5

Ask the students to use their professional knowledge and evaluate the OPORD. Is it a good example of a OPORD? What would they change/add? What could be abbreviated?

Task 6

Tell the students to listen to the text to decide which words they need to practice saying. This can be done as homework.

Task 7

Consolidation Tasks in Workbook.

About the Unit

This is revision of all the language from **Units 168/9**.

Task 1

This is a revision question from **Units 168/9**.

Task 2

Students complete the gap fill, check with their partner, then check with the original text in **Unit 169**.

Task 3

Ask students to produce a sketch map based on the order. They can do this alone, in pairs, or in small groups. They should compare their maps – who has the best/clearest map?

Unit 171

About the Unit

In this unit the students will practice listening to an OPORD.

Task 1

This is the same revision question as in **Unit 170**.

Task 2

Assign the groups. They listen for what they have to do in the OPORD, and also to answer the other questions.

Key	1. GRID 226896 2. To seize northern edges of Hill 926 (OBJECTIVE LION) 3. 20 0415Zulu Aug 19 4. OBJECTIVE CROW 5. Order of march for Charlie Company is First Platoon, HQ, Second Platoon, Mortars, Third Platoon. Order of march for Third Platoon is First Squad, HQ, Second Squad, Third Squad. Movement formation is platoon file, travelling. Line of Departure time 20 0100Z Aug 19. 6. Answer depends on who 'you' are. 7. First Squad suppresses trench line to allow Second Squad to enter the trench line. Second Squad establishes foothold in the trench line allowing Third squad to enter the trench line. Third squad will move along and clear the trench line and take out the MBT. 8. 1300 Platoon rehearsal for squad and fire team leaders 1400 Company rehearsal 1700 Inspection 1730 Chow 1830 Rest 2100 Night Rehearsals 0045 Stand-To 0115 Final Inspection 0200 Line of Departure time 0415 Assault time. 9. Company casualty collection points are located along the infiltration line. Platoon casualty collection point after seizure of OBJECTIVE LION will be directly behind the tank position.

10. Company Commander will follow us. He will set up the Company Command Post in the vicinity of the trench line.

11. Radio: Tactical frequency is 62 Khz; the MEDEVAC frequency is 35 Khz. Challenge is: Bayonet; Password is Millet; Running Password is Geronimo; the number combination password is six.

Task 3

Ask students to complete the transcript on the next page, and then listen to check.

Options and Decisions: you might want to discuss if this is a good example of an OPORD with the students. Are there any improvements to be made?

Don't forget:

1. Spelling Challenge: World Cities to practice the NATO Alphabet.

2. Test the students on telling the time using the 24 hour clock, and using numbers, and DTG.

3. Test the students on the Key Tactical Verbs.

4. Grid references: test the students, or ask them to test each other, on grid references and terrain features, using a good map.

5. Test your students on a random medical problem. See who can answer the quickest.

6. Check the composition of a convoy and the role of key personnel.

7. Check the different kinds of IEDs and UXO, 5Cs, and 10-liner report.

8. Check the kinds of checkpoints and the language you can use when searching a person or vehicle.

9. Test the students on the language of patrols.

10. Test the students on the kinds of movement and attack.

Unit 172

About the Unit

In this unit the students practice giving an OPORD and do a self-check on how good their understanding was. Try to do an many OPORDs as you can with the number of students you have. They need as much practice of this as you can give them.

You will need good maps for this task.

Follow the instructions in the Coursebook, and be ready to give feedback on the language they used and their delivery.

Study Page: Collocations of Orders 2

This is third of three such pages of collocations with 'order'. Start by seeing what collocations they remember from # 1 and 2. Either do it in class or set as homework.

Key	obey	transmit	follow an order
	a/an clear	concise	lawful	illegal	legal	unambiguous	general order
	a/an duty	convoy order

Unit 173

About the Unit

This is the final practice of orders in the book. It is a large scale role play and simulates orders coming from Company level to squad level.

Follow the instructions in the Coursebook, and be ready to give feedback on the language the students used.

Unit 174

About the Unit

This unit is about debriefings after patrols, attacks etc.

Task 1

Students discuss the question and share their ideas with the class. Answers should include: for intelligence gathering, and for lessons learned.

Task 2

Elicit the students' ideas about these questions.

Task 3

Ask students to reorder the words in the sentences to make questions.

Key	1. Did the PL use the proper formation in crossing a danger area?
	2. Were reports made at checkpoints and on enemy contact?
	3. Did the PL select an adequate ORP?
	4. Did the PL (adequately) secure the site (adequately)?
	5. Did the PL maintain control of the patrol during the occupation of the ORP?

6. Did the PL maintain or ensure communications with the patrol?

7. If contact was made, did the PL take appropriate action?

8. Was security maintained during the leader's recon?

9. Did the PL issue a frag order for action at the objective?

10. Did the PL employ the terrain to the best advantage at the objective?

11. Did the PL make use of supporting arms at the objective?

12. Was the action at the objective successful?

13. Was the withdrawal from the objective accomplished quickly and orderly?

14. Did the patrol withdraw quickly and quietly from the ORP?

Task 4 and **Task 5** are linked tasks. The students plan a patrol, then agree what happened during the patrol, then are debriefed on the patrol.

Task 6

This is an extension task where the students make a radio calls based on their patrols and debriefings. There are three forms to use in the Workbook:

1. CASUALTY REPORT [CASREP]
2. INTELLIGENCE REPORT [INTREP]
3. PATROL REPORT [PATROLREP]

Unit 175

About the Unit

This is the last unit in Phase 2 and can be used as a progress test. The students should demonstration their ability to give briefings and to make notes during briefings. It is a speaking/listening/writing test.

The students should work in groups to prepare a briefing on one of four adventure Training Programmes. Follow the instructions in the Coursebook and note strengths and weaknesses of individual students. Give feedback at the end of the briefings as appropriate.

Part 4: Phase 3 Notes and Keys

As noted at the beginning of the book, Phase 3 of the course is about practising the language of tactical operations and adding peacekeeping English to the mix. There are five Tactical Problems to solve, then a series of units which focus on the differences between tactical and peacekeeping operations (mainly through listening tasks), and Peacekeeping Problem tasks to solve; the final two units are about deployment. Most of Phase 3 is either speaking or listening practice.

Unit 176 Prelude

About the Unit

This unit is a Prelude to Phase 3. It revises language taught in Phase 1 and 2 and brings the focus onto operations through a Case Study.

<u>Note</u>

The Case Study is modelled on a real incident in the Second Gulf War when a US Marine expeditionary corps fought their way through a town in their first major combat operation. Apparently, the main problem they had was with radio communication. There was an almost complete breakdown in radio communication discipline which mean that it was impossible for commanders to understand the situation on the ground or make the right tactical decisions. This led directly to a blue-on-blue friendly fire incident.

As a **Pre-Task 1** warmer you could elicit some of the things which can go wrong on operations and the reasons for them going wrong (e.g. poor planning, bad intelligence).

Task 1

Ask students to read through the case study text and look at the map. They should make notes on the key elements of the situation and check with their partner/group that they understand everything.

Task 2

This is a prediction task for the following listening task.

Task 3

Ask students to listen and make notes. After listening check if their predictions were correct, and then ask them to check their partner's notes. Do they agree on everything? The best way to do this listening is to listen to it in sections and check comprehension at each stage.

Task 4

Ask students to discuss the questions in pairs/groups before having a class discussion.

Units 177 – 181 Tactical Problems

This series of units presents tactical problems. The students should follow the detailed procedure outlined on page 327. It is important for you to remember that these are not real-world tasks. In such tactical situations the NCO or officer in command would evaluate the situation, decide on a course of action and issue their orders. Here, the students should discuss the situation and possible courses of action and decide on the best, and then present it. It is a language using task.

You might want to consider secretly appointing one member of each group to act as a 'devil's advocate' and to challenge the group throughout the task discussion to justify their decisions. They would ask questions throughout the discussion phase to ensure that there is a discussion and not just a quick consensus decision.

There are five tactical problems and you should decide if each group of students will do every problem (so you can compare solutions), or whether you will have five groups and do each problem only once. Will you do the problems one after the other in a block? As it is near the end of the course it might be a good idea to do all the problems and to give each group the chance to do each problem (to maximise their opportunities, if time allows), and to do them in a block rather than a thread. As the students work through the problems their use of English should improve.

You could do these tactical problems as speaking-discussion tasks, as they have been designed, but you could also adapt them to writing tasks (both collaborative or individual), or ask the students to create posters of their solutions; and you could also ask the students to write FRAGO orders for their solutions.

Units 182 – 189 Peacekeeping

This series of units look at peacekeeping and peacekeeping English. Each unit is based on a series of listening tasks, which mainly practice the language taught in Phase 2 but from a peacekeeping perspective.

Unit 182 looks at Peacekeeping Missions

Unit 183 Peacekeeping ROE

Unit 184 Peacekeeping Ops

Unit 185 Peacekeeping Patrols

Unit 186 Peacekeeping Checkpoints

Unit 187 Peacekeeping Convoys

Unit 188 Using Interpreters

Unit 189 Peacekeeping: Civil Disturbances

The students should use these units to find out how much they can understand about the topics. They should make notes and evaluate how good their notes are by comparing with their partners and checking with the transcripts. You could ask the students to rate themselves out of scale 1 – 5 (for example) after each listening.

As each unit follows a similar structure the unit notes below mainly focus on the keys (where the keys are not the transcripts). The units start with a discussion lead-in, introduce some key vocabulary, have a series of listening tasks, transcript and vocabulary tasks, and finish with a speaking task.

Unit 182

This unit is about peacekeeping missions and builds on the readings from Phase 1 Workbook.

Task 1

Ask students to discuss the questions and report to the class.

Task 2

Check and discuss the words in the table.

Task 3

Ask students to listen and make notes, then predict what the next part will be about.

Task 4

Ask students to listen and make notes, then predict what the next part will be about.

Task 5

Ask students to listen and make notes, then predict what the next part will be about.

Task 6

Ask students to listen and make notes, then predict what the next part will be about.

Task 7

Ask students to do the transcript tasks on the next page and then listen to check and/or check with the transcripts.

Task 8

Ask students to do the collocation task and then listen to check and/or check with the transcripts.

Task 9

Students should discuss and agree as per the instructions. This could be a whole class discussion, or they could work in pairs, then go into groups, and then discuss as a class.

All keys to be found in the transcripts.

Don't forget:

1. Spelling Challenge: World Cities to practice the NATO Alphabet.

2. Test the students on telling the time using the 24 hour clock, and using numbers, and DTG.

3. Test the students on the Key Tactical Verbs.

4. Grid references: test the students, or ask them to test each other, on grid references and terrain features, using a good map.

5. Test your students on a random medical problem. See who can answer the quickest.

6. Check the composition of a convoy and the role of key personnel.

7. Check the different kinds of IEDs and UXO, 5Cs, and 10-liner report.

8. Check the kinds of checkpoints and the language you can use when searching a person or vehicle.

9. Test the students on the language of patrols.

10. Test the students on the kinds of movement and attack.

Unit 183

This unit is about peacekeeping ROE.

Task 1

Ask students to discuss the questions and report to the class.

Task 2

Check and discuss the words in the table.

Task 3

Ask students to listen and make notes, then predict what the next part will be about.

Task 4

Ask students to listen and make notes, then predict what the next part will be about.

Task 5

Ask students to listen and make notes, then predict what the next part will be about.

Task 6

Ask students to listen and make notes, then predict what the next part will be about.

Task 7

Ask students to read the text and answer the questions.

Key	
	1. Yes.
	2. No.
	3. No.
	4. Only for security reasons or self-defense.
	5. Always.

Task 8

Ask students to complete the ROE with the words from the table.

Key　　**Commander's Guidance on Use of Force**

1. Mission

Your mission is to stabilize and [1] **consolidate** the peace in [X]

2. Self Defense

a. You have the right to use force (including authorized weapons as necessary) in self-defense.

b. Use only the [2] **minimum** force necessary to defend yourself.

3. General Rules

a. Use the [3] **minimum** force necessary to accomplish your mission.

b. Do not harm hostile forces/belligerents who want to [4] s**urrender.** Disarm them and turn them over to your superiors.

c. Treat everyone, including civilians and detained hostile forces/belligerents, [5] **humanely.**

d. Collect and care for the [6] **wounded,** whether friend or foe.

e. Respect private [7] **property**. Do not steal. Do not take "war trophies."

f. Prevent and report all suspected [8] **violations** of the Law of Armed Conflict to superiors.

4. Challenging and Warning Shots

a. If the situation permits, issue a [9] **challenge**:

(1) English: "IFOR! STOP OR I [10] **WILL** FIRE!"

(2) [In local language: with pronunciation guide]

b. If the person fails to halt, the on-scene commander may authorize standing orders to fire a **[11] warning** shot.

5. Opening Fire

a. You may open fire only if you, friendly forces, or persons or property under your protection is threatened with [12] **deadly** force. This means—

(1) You may open fire against an individual who fires or [13] **aims** his weapon at you, friendly forces, or persons with designated special status under your [14] **protection**.

(2) You may open fire against an individual who plants, throws, or prepares to throw an explosive or [15] **incendiary** device at you, friendly forces, or persons with designated special status or [16] **property** with designated special status under your protection.

(3) You may open fire against an individual who [17] **deliberately** drives a vehicle at you, friendly forces, and persons with a designated special status or property with designated special status under your protection.

b. You may also fire against an individual who attempts to take [18] **possession** of friendly force weapons, [19] **ammunition**, or property with designated special status, and there is no other way of avoiding this.

6. Minimum Force

a. If you have to [20] **open** fire, you must—

(1) Fire only [21] **aimed** shots

(2) Fire no more [22] **rounds** than necessary,

(3) Take all reasonable efforts not to unnecessarily destroy property, and - stop firing as [23] **soon** as the situation permits.

b. You may not [24] i**ntentionally** attack civilians or property that is exclusively civilian or religious in character, except if the property is being used for military purpose and your commander authorizes **[25] engagement.**

Task 9

Students should discuss and agree as per the instructions. This could be a whole class discussion, or they could work in pairs, then go into groups and then discuss as a class.

Don't forget:

1. Spelling Challenge: World Cities to practice the NATO Alphabet.
2. Test the students on telling the time using the 24 hour clock, and using numbers, and DTG.
3. Test the students on the Key Tactical Verbs.
4. Grid references: test the students, or ask them to test each other, on grid references and terrain features, using a good map.
5. Test your students on a random medical problem. See who can answer the quickest.
6. Check the composition of a convoy and the role of key personnel.
7. Check the different kinds of IEDs and UXO, 5Cs, and 10-liner report.
8. Check the kinds of checkpoints and the language you can use when searching a person or vehicle.
9. Test the students on the language of patrols.
10. Test the students on the kinds of movement and attack.

Unit 184

This unit is about peacekeeping observation posts.

Task 1

Ask students to discuss the questions and report to the class.

Task 2

Check and discuss the words in the table.

Task 3

Ask students to listen and make notes, then predict what the next part will be about.

Task 4

Ask students to listen and make notes, then predict what the next part will be about.

Task 5

Ask students to listen and make notes, then predict what the next part will be about.

Task 6

Ask students to do the transcript tasks on the next page and then listen to check and/or check with the transcripts.

Task 7

Students should discuss and agree as per the instructions. This could be a whole class discussion, or they could work in pairs, then go into groups and then discuss as a class.

Don't forget:

1. Spelling Challenge: World Cities to practice the NATO Alphabet.

2. Test the students on telling the time using the 24 hour clock, and using numbers, and DTG.

3. Test the students on the Key Tactical Verbs.

4. Grid references: test the students, or ask them to test each other, on grid references and terrain features, using a good map.

5. Test your students on a random medical problem. See who can answer the quickest.

6. Check the composition of a convoy and the role of key personnel.

7. Check the different kinds of IEDs and UXO, 5Cs, and 10-liner report.

8. Check the kinds of checkpoints and the language you can use when searching a person or vehicle.

9. Test the students on the language of patrols.

10. Test the students on the kinds of movement and attack.

Unit 185

This unit is about peacekeeping patrols.

Task 1

Tell students to describe the picture with their partner. Elicit a description.

Task 2

Ask students to discuss the questions and report to the class.

Task 3

Check and discuss the words in the table.

Task 4

Ask students to listen and make notes, then predict what the next part will be about.

Task 5

Ask students to listen and make notes, then predict what the next part will be about.

Task 6

Ask students to listen and make notes, then predict what the next part will be about.

Task 7

Ask students to do the transcript tasks on the next page and then listen to check and/or check with the transcripts.

Task 8

Students should discuss and agree as per the instructions. This could be a whole class discussion, or they could work in pairs, then go into groups and then discuss as a class.

Task 9

This task is similar to **Unit 160**, but with the addition of peacekeeping ROE. Give the students less time to prepare than you did in **Unit 160**.

Unit 186

This unit is about peacekeeping checkpoints.

Task 1

Tell students to describe the picture with their partner. Elicit a description.

Task 2

Ask students to discuss the questions and report to the class.

Task 3

Check and discuss the words in the table.

Task 4

Ask students to listen and make notes, then predict what the next part will be about.

Task 5

Ask students to listen and make notes, then predict what the next part will be about.

Task 6

Ask students to listen and make notes, then predict what the next part will be about.

Task 7

Ask students to do the transcript tasks on the next page and then listen to check and/or check with the transcripts.

Task 8

Students should discuss and agree as per the instructions. This could be a whole class discussion, or they could work in pairs, then go into groups and then discuss as a class.

Task 9

This task gives the students an opportunity to practise some of the language from the Checkpoint units from Phase 2.

Don't forget:

1.   Spelling Challenge: World Cities to practice the NATO Alphabet.

2.   Test the students on telling the time using the 24 hour clock, and using numbers, and DTG.

3.   Test the students on the Key Tactical Verbs.

4.   Grid references: test the students, or ask them to test each other, on grid references and terrain features, using a good map.

5.   Test your students on a random medical problem. See who can answer the quickest.

6.   Check the composition of a convoy and the role of key personnel.

7.   Check the different kinds of IEDs and UXO, 5Cs, and 10-liner report.

8.   Check the kinds of checkpoints and the language you can use when searching a person or vehicle.

9.   Test the students on the language of patrols.

10. Test the students on the kinds of movement and attack.

Unit 187

This unit is about peacekeeping convoys.

Task 1

Tell students to describe the picture with their partner. Elicit a description.

Task 2

Ask students to discuss the questions and report to the class.

Task 3

Check and discuss the words in the table.

Task 4

Ask students to listen and make notes, then predict what the next part will be about.

Task 5

Ask students to listen and make notes, then predict what the next part will be about.

Task 6

Ask students to listen and make notes, then predict what the next part will be about.

Task 7

Ask students to do the transcript tasks on the next page and then listen to check and/or check with the transcripts.

Task 8

Students should discuss and agree as per the instructions. This could be a whole class discussion, or they could work in pairs, then go into groups and then discuss as a class.

Task 9

This task gives the students an opportunity to practise some of the language from the Convoy units from Phase 2.

Unit 188

This unit is about using interpreters.

Task 1

Ask the students to discuss the questions and share their opinions and experiences.

Task 2

Teach/check the words in the table, and then speculate what they have to do with using interpreters.

Task 3

Ask the students to discuss the questions and share their opinions.

Task 4

Ask the students to read the text on the next page to check their ideas from T3.

Task 5

Key		
	1.	So that the audience pay attention to what is being said.
	2.	The interpreter will be loyal to his/her nation.
	3.	These affect how acceptable he/she is to the audience.
	4.	To make it easier to wok with them.
	5.	To split the work; to check each other; one can interpret and the other can watch the audience.

Check any other unknown words or phrases afterwards. Choose at least one verb phrase, noun phrase and prepositional phrase from the text to explore with the students.

Task 6

Ask the students to discuss the questions and share their opinions.

Task 7

Students listen to a talk on using interpreters and make notes. They should check their notes with their partner; then check with the class.

Task 8

Tell the students to do the transcript tasks on page 355 and then listen to check.

Task 9

Ask the students to work in pairs or small groups and decide on the five most important pieces of advice about selecting or using interpreters. Agree with the class.

Don't forget:

1. Spelling Challenge: World Cities to practice the NATO Alphabet.

2. Test the students on telling the time using the 24 hour clock, and using numbers, and DTG.

3. Test the students on the Key Tactical Verbs.

4. Grid references: test the students, or ask them to test each other, on grid references and terrain features, using a good map.

5. Test your students on a random medical problem. See who can answer the quickest.

6. Check the composition of a convoy and the role of key personnel.

7. Check the different kinds of IEDs and UXO, 5Cs, and 10-liner report.

8. Check the kinds of checkpoints and the language you can use when searching a person or vehicle.

9. Test the students on the language of patrols.

10. Test the students on the kinds of movement and attack.

This unit is about civil disturbances which might happen during peacekeeping missions.

Task 1

Ask students to discuss the questions and report to the class.

Task 2

Check and discuss the words in the table.

Task 3

Ask students to listen and make notes, then predict what the next part will be about.

Task 4 and 5

Ask students to do the transcript tasks and then listen to check and/or check with the transcript.

Task 6

Ask students to listen and make notes..

Task 7

Ask students to do the transcript task and then listen to check and/or check with the transcript.

Task 8

Students should discuss and agree as per the instructions. This could be a whole class discussion, or they could work in pairs, then go into groups and then discuss as a class.

Task 9

This simulation-challenge involves the students working in groups. Each group prepares a Situation Report (SITREP) for another group. That group can ask 10 questions to clarify. They then have to decide on a course of action and explain it to the original group. The original group evaluates the course of action.

Unit 190

About the Unit

This unit is the first of three on natural disasters.

Task 1

Ask the students to look at the photos and describe what they can see.

Task 2

Teach/check the words in the table.

Ask the students to decide on the order of seriousness, then go into a pair and agree on the order, then go into a group and agree on the order, then discuss as a class. At each stage they need to give reasons for their ranking.

Task 3

The students read the text and answer the questions.

Key		
	1.	No.
	2.	Typhoons – in the Pacific; Hurricanes: in the Atlantic.
	3.	Waterborne disease.
	4.	Disease and civil strife.
	5.	Because of the human decisions behind the breakdown in food productions and distribution.
	6.	Natural and man-made.
	7.	Earthquake and tsunami.

Task 4

Set the Text Analysis tasks in class or for homework.

Task 5

Tell the students to listen to the text to decide which words they need to practice saying. This can be done as homework.

Task 6

This is a similar ranking task to that in Task 2 but focussed on the response.

Task 7

The answer to this question will depend on local circumstances.

Don't forget:

1. Spelling Challenge: World Cities to practice the NATO Alphabet.

2. Test the students on telling the time using the 24 hour clock, and using numbers, and DTG.

3. Test the students on the Key Tactical Verbs.

4. Grid references: test the students, or ask them to test each other, on grid references and terrain features, using a good map.

5. Test your students on a random medical problem. See who can answer the quickest.

6. Check the composition of a convoy and the role of key personnel.

7. Check the different kinds of IEDs and UXO, 5Cs, and 10-liner report.

8. Check the kinds of checkpoints and the language you can use when searching a person or vehicle.

9. Test the students on the language of patrols.

10. Test the students on the kinds of movement and attack.

About the Unit

This unit looks at disaster response and builds on **Unit 190**.

Task 1

A revision task.

Task 2 - 4

These are note-taking exercises similar to the ones in the peacekeeping units.

Task 4 concludes with a discussion question based on the last listening. Ask students to give detailed reasons for their answers.

Unit 192

About the Unit

This unit has two briefings for the students to give. The first is about disasters and students should present one of the disasters to the group. The second is a set of slides about countries the students might be deployed to. This revises a lot of language from the course.

The students should make notes from the briefings. You should listen and also make notes in order to create questions to ask the students, like *'Which disaster had the highest death toll?'*. At the end of the briefings you should quiz the students to find out who has the best notes from the briefings.

Additional Task:

The quiz below is a series of questions on disasters you can use in this unit or during the rest of the course. Suggested answers are given as this information is not necessarily in this book.

Situation 1

You are in bed and an earthquake hits. What should you do?

Answer

If in bed, stay there and cover your head and neck with a pillow.

Situation 2

You are in a building and an earthquake hits. What should you do?

Answer

If inside, stay there until the shaking stops. DO NOT run outside.

Situation 3

You are in a vehicle and an earthquake hits. What should you do?

Answer

If in a vehicle, stop in a clear area that is away from buildings, trees, overpasses, underpasses, or utility wires.

Situation 4

You are in a high-rise building and an earthquake hits. What should you do?

Answer

If you are in a high-rise building, expect fire alarms and sprinklers to go off. Do not use elevators.

Situation 5

You are on a mountain slope and an earthquake hits. What should you do?

Answer

If near slopes, cliffs, or mountains, be alert for falling rocks and landslides.

Situation 6

An earthquake hits and the building you are in is damaged. What should you do?

Answer

If in a damaged building, go outside and quickly move away from the building.

Situation 7

You are holidaying at a seaside beach resort and an earthquake hits. What should you do?

Answer

If you are in an area that may experience tsunamis, go inland or to higher ground immediately after the shaking stops.

Situation 8

You are at home and a hurricane hits. What should you do?

Suggested Answer

Go to a small, interior, windowless room or hallway on the lowest floor that is not subject to flooding.

Situation 9

A hurricane hits and you are trapped in your building by rising flood waters. What should you do?

Suggested Answer

If trapped in a building by flooding, go to the highest level of the building. Do not climb into a closed attic. You may become trapped by rising flood water.

Situation 10

A hurricane hits and your town is flooded. How can you escape the floodwater?

Suggested Answer

Wait for rescue by boat or helicopter. Do not walk, swim, or drive through flood waters. Turn Around. Don't Drown! Just six inches of fast-moving water can knock you down, and one foot of moving water can sweep your vehicle away.

Situation 11

There is a tornado warning. What should you do?

Suggested Answer

If you are under a tornado warning, find safe shelter right away. If you can safely get to a sturdy building, then do so immediately. Go to a safe room, basement, or storm cellar.

Situation 12

There is a tornado warning but the building you are in does not have a basement. What should you do?

Suggested Answer

If you are in a building with no basement, then get to a small interior room on the lowest level.

Situation 13

There is a tornado outside. Should you go and have a look at it passing your house?

Suggested Answer: Stay away from windows, doors, and outside walls.

Situation 14

There is a tornado coming. You are in the open. You see a bridge. Should you shelter under it?

Suggested Answer: Do not get under an overpass or bridge. You're safer in a low, flat location.

Situation 15

You are trapped in a building in a flood situation. What should you do?

Suggested Answer

If trapped in a building, then go to its highest level. Do not climb into a closed attic. You may become trapped by rising floodwater. Go on the roof only if necessary. Once there, signal for help.

Situation 16

You are in a flood situation. The bridge over the flooded river looks ok. Should you try to cross the bridge to safety?

Suggested Answer

Stay off bridges over fast-moving water. Fast-moving water can wash bridges away without warning.

Situation 17

You are driving in a flood situation. You car is surrounded by fast running water. What should you do?

Suggested Answer

If your vehicle is trapped in rapidly moving water, then stay inside. If water is rising inside the vehicle, then seek refuge on the roof.

Situation 18

There is an an alert about the volcano 10 kms away from your house. Should you evacuate or wait to see what happens?

Suggested Answer: Follow evacuation orders from local authorities. Evacuate early.

Situation 19

The volcano near your house starts erupting. You decide to evacuate. Which way do you go? Upwind or downwind?

Suggested Answer

Avoid areas downwind, and river valleys downstream, of the volcano. Rubble and ash will be carried by wind and gravity.

Situation 20

You are at home when the volcano near your house starts erupting. The air is full of ash. You have supplies at home but you fear a bigger eruption. What should you do?

Suggested Answer

Take temporary shelter from volcanic ash where you are if you have enough supplies. Cover ventilation openings and seal doors and windows.

Avoid driving in heavy ash fall.

Situation 21

You are fishing on a boat when a thunderstorm rolls in. What should you do?

Suggested Answer

If boating or swimming, get to land and find a sturdy, grounded shelter or vehicle immediately.

Situation 22

You are outside in your garden watering the plants when a thunderstorm rolls in. What should you do?

Suggested Answer

When thunder roars, go indoors. A sturdy building is the safest place to be during a thunderstorm.

Situation 23

You have just come inside because there is a thunderstorm. What should you do?

Suggested Answer

If indoors, avoid running water or using landline phones. Electricity can travel through plumbing and phone lines.

Protect your property. Unplug appliances and other electric devices. Secure outside furniture.

Situation 24

You are in the open field when a thunderstorm rolls in. There is a forest 500 m away but an isolated tree 50 m away. What should you do?

Suggested Answer

Crouch down as low as possible and stay down. Do not go to the isolated tree. The forest is too far away to make it safely.

Situation 25

You are in a boat and there has been an earthquake and now the sea is rushing out away from the land. What should you do?

Suggested Answer

If you are in a boat, then face the direction of the waves and head out to sea. If you are in a harbor, then go inland.

Don't forget:

1. Spelling Challenge: World Cities to practice the NATO Alphabet.
2. Test the students on telling the time using the 24 hour clock, and using numbers, and DTG.
3. Test the students on the Key Tactical Verbs.
4. Grid references: test the students, or ask them to test each other, on grid references and terrain features, using a good map.
5. Test your students on a random medical problem. See who can answer the quickest.
6. Check the composition of a convoy and the role of key personnel.
7. Check the different kinds of IEDs and UXO, 5Cs, and 10-liner report.
8. Check the kinds of checkpoints and the language you can use when searching a person or vehicle.
9. Test the students on the language of patrols.
10. Test the students on the kinds of movement and attack.

Unit 193

About the Unit

This unit is about dealing with the media, which most soldiers will not have to do.

Task 1

Ask the students to look at the photos and describe what they can see.

Task 2

Ask the students to discuss and then report on the three questions.

Task 3

Teach/check the words in the table and discuss the question.

Task 4 and 5

Ask the students to listen to the talks and make notes.

Task 6

Ask the students to do the transcript tasks and listen to check.

Task 7

This role play is based on the advice given in the talks. Set up the role play as explained in the unit. The single soldier has to walk through the media without answering questions e.g. by say 'No comment'. Encourage the 'media' to crowd around the soldier aggressively asking questions.

Task 8

This role play is a more formal and civilised situation than that in Task 7. The five role cards give you five different situations so there can be five different press conferences. Choose the most able students to be the media relations officers and give them time and support to prepare. Make sure everyone else is fully prepared with questions to ask, and ready to ask more questions based on what is said by the media relations officers. You could repeat this task with different students taking the role of media relations officer.

Units 194 – 198 Peacekeeping Problems

This series of units presents peacekeeping problems. The students should follow the detailed procedure outlined on page 327.

Like the Tactical Problems earlier in this Phase, it is important for you to remember that these are not real-world tasks. In such situations the NCO or officer in command would evaluate the situation, decide on a course of action and issue their orders.

Here, the students should discuss the situation and possible courses of action and decide on the best, and then present it. It is a language using task.

As before you might want to consider secretly appointing one member of each group to act as a 'devil's advocate' and to challenge the group throughout the task discussion to justify their decisions. They would ask questions throughout the discussion phase to ensure that there is a discussion and not just a quick consensus decision.

There are five peacekeeping problems and you should decide if each group of students will do every problem (so you can compare solutions), or whether you will have five groups and do each problem only once. Will you do the problems one after the other in a block? As it is near the end of the course it might be a good idea to do all the problems and to give each group the chance to do each problem (to maximise their opportunities, if time allows), and to do them in a block rather than a thread. As the students work through the problems their use of English should improve.

Like the tactical problems, you could do these peacekeeping problems as speaking-discussion tasks, as they have been designed, but you could adapt them to writing tasks (both collaborative or individual), or ask the students to create posters of their solutions; or you could ask the students to write FRAGO orders for their solutions.

Unit 199

About the Unit

This unit is about travelling, and air travel in particular. Some of your students might never have been to an airport or on a plane.

Task 1

Ask the students to discuss and then report on the three questions.

Task 2 and 3

Check the vocabulary with the help of the photos.

Task 4

Ask the students to order the events in the most logical order. Suggested order:

Key	Book a flight
	Check-in on-line
	Print boarding card
	Take a taxi to the airport
	Go to Check-in/baggage drop
	Go through security
	Go through passport control
	Buy something in the duty free shops
	Wait in the departure lounge
	Go to the Gate
	Show boarding card
	Board the plane
	Put your hand luggage under your seat or in the overhead bins
	Fasten your seat belt
	Listen to the safety instructions
	Take off
	Reach cruising speed and altitude

Prepare for landing
Land
Disembark from the plane
Go through passport control
Collect luggage/baggage from Baggage Reclaim
Go through Customs
Leave the airport

Task 5

Ask the student to identify who would say what in the table, and then check the words and phrases in bold.

Key	
I don't like making my own **travel arrangements** on the Internet, I go to a **travel agent** and get them to do all the work.	Traveller
I have to go on a **business trip** to Paris next week.	Traveller
Have a **safe journey!**	Airport/airline employee
It was a really **tiring journey**. I had to wait **for ages** for a bus to come.	Traveller
It's an **international flight** so the **check-in time** is two hours before the **departure time**.	Traveller
The **check-in desk** is over there – number 18 – with the big queue. Once we get our **boarding cards** then we can go through **passport control** and do some shopping!	Traveller
Did you pack all your **baggage/luggage** yourself?	Airport/airline employee
I have two bags to **check-in** and one bag as **hand-luggage**.	Traveller
I have checked you in on your **connecting flight**.	Airport/airline employee
Would you like a **window seat** or an **aisle seat**?	Airport/airline employee
Boarding time is usually half an hour before the plane leaves – check your **boarding card.**	Airport/airline employee
We've done our shopping, let's go to the **departure lounge** and sit and wait for the flight.	Traveller
The **in-flight entertainment** will be a selection of recent film releases.	Airport/airline employee
They will be waiting for us in **arrivals** at the airport.	Traveller

Task 6

Ask the students to read the text an answer the questions.

Key	
	1. On a business trip.
	2. At 4 am.
	3. Riga – Frankfurt – London.
	4. 5 hours for the first one and 2 hours in Frankfurt.

Task 7

Ask the students to listen and answer the questions.

Key	
	1. From Riga to Montenegro (and back).
	2. 0330
	3. To the airport
	4. Riga to Frankfurt.
	5. Two hours + 1.5 hours delay = 3.5 hours.
	6. Frankfurt to Belgrade
	7. A man and his wife.
	8. They were trying to fly from Switzerland to Albania (Switzerland to Frankfurt to Vienna to Tirana; but Frankfurt to Vienna was cancelled, so they were flying Frankfurt to Belgrade and then to Tirana, but when they got to Belgrade they had to fly to Vienna and then to Tirana].
	9. 19.30.
	10. 21.00
	11. Very long.
	12. From Podgorica to Istanbul.
	13. In a hotel in Istanbul.
	14. 25 hours [2 pm to 3 pm the next day]
	15. His bag was lost and arrived the next day.

Task 8

Ask the students to discuss the question in pairs and then report.

Unit 200

About the Unit

This unit is the test unit for Phase 3 of the course.

There are two parts.

1. **Test 1**: Deployment Briefing: Group Test

2. **Test 2**: A Two Minute Mini-Presentation on a Military Topic: Individual Test

Test 1: Deployment Briefing: Group Test

In this test the students have to work in groups and then brief the class on a deployment.

Follow the instructions in the Coursebook.

The students should make notes from the briefings. You should listen and also make notes in order to create questions to ask the students, like *'Which deployment starts at 0800 on Tuesday*?'. At the end of the briefings, in **Task 4**, you should quiz the students to find out who has the best notes from the briefings.

Test 2: A Two Minute Mini-Presentation on a Military Topic: Individual Test

This is an individual test based on a task they might be asked to do during the oral interview part of the **NATO STANAG 6001** Test of English.

Give the students a topic each to present on. They have one minute to prepare their presentation. Then they talk for two minutes about the topic. There is a **Mini Presentation Frame** in the coursebook to help them prepare.

Part 5: Workbook Keys

1. Functional Grammar Keys

1. Functional Grammar: Facts

Task 1

1. I speak French. Present Fact
2. I am a soldier. Present Fact
3. I visited Namibia last year. Past Fact
4. She is 25 years old. Present Fact
5. The train leaves in ten minutes. Future Fact
6. The meeting is at 2 pm on Wednesday. Future Fact
7. I love you. Present Fact
8. I lived in Rome for two years. Past Fact
9. I went to the USA for training in 2010. Past Fact
10. I like playing football. Present Fact

Task 3

Complete the sentences with the correct form of the verb given.

1. I went to school in Nairobi. Past Fact
2. She joined the army when she left school. Past Fact
3. I saw David Bowie in concert in 1983. Past Fact
4. I love fishing. Past Fact
5. I live in a small flat. Past Fact
6. When I was younger I was very unfit. Past Fact
7. We leave in ten minutes – be ready. Future Fact
8. I met John yesterday. Past Fact
9. He exercises every day. Past Fact
10. She takes photographs wherever she goes. Past Fact

2. Functional Grammar: The Condition Of Something

Task 1

1. It is hot.   *'hot'* is about *'it'*
2. I am tired. 'tired' is about I
3. The film is boring. 'boring' is about the film
4. The spy was shot. 'shot' is about the spy
5. The weather is very bad. 'very bad' is about the weather
6. The road is closed. 'closed' is about the road
7. I am a soldier. 'soldier' is about I

8. They are angry. 'angry' is about they
9. She is bored. 'bored' is about she
10. He has been arrested. Arrested is about he

Task 3

1. It is very late.
2. The car is being repaired.
3. We are under observation.
4. I have been thinking.
5. She is angry.
6. The base is under attack.
7. We are being ambushed.
8. The outpost has been overrun.
9. Our defences are being probed.
10. He is being court-martialled.

3. Functional Grammar: Education and Qualifications: No Key

4. Functional Grammar: Active or Passive?

Task 4

1. I **live** in Nairobi.
2. He **was wounded** by a sniper.
3. They **are closing** the road.
4. The road **is closed/ is being closed**.
5. The bombing **killed** a lot of civilians.
6. A lot of civilians **were killed** by the bombing.
7. We **are leaving** at 1200.
8. The convoy **was delayed** by bad weather.
9. Make sure you **take** enough ammunition.
10. He **was promoted** to sergeant last year.

5. Functional Grammar: Ongoing Processes

Task 1

1. He is practising on the firing range. Ongoing
2. I am thinking of going to the cinema on Friday. Ongoing
3. I am a soldier. Fact
4. We are being attacked. Ongoing
5. She is serving in the 1st Armoured Division. Ongoing
6. I am working. Please don't disturb me. Ongoing

7. I'm feeling sad for some reason. Ongoing
8. The Brigade is being reorganised. Ongoing
9. I was patrolling the base perimeter yesterday when I saw some suspicious activity beyond the wire. Ongoing in past + Past Fact

Task 3

1. It is raining heavily.
2. She is looking for a new job.
3. The platoon is running the assault course this morning.
4. I 'm thinking of retiring.
5. The army is being restructured to make it more effective.
6. They are having a good time.
7. I have an old car.
8. I'm having trouble answering this question.
9. I 'm leaving in ten minutes.
10. The company was patrolling by the river when they were ambushed.

6 and 7. Functional Grammar: Noun Phrases 1 and 2: No Key

8. Functional Grammar: Prepositions of Time

Task 2

1. The operation starts in ten minutes.
2. The tank was invented in World War 1.
3. I'm going fishing at/on the weekend.
4. The briefing starts at 0700.
5. He works during the night and sleeps during the day.
6. The deadline is 1700 – we have to get it finished by then.
7. It snows a lot here in February.
8. There is a conference call on Monday at 0900.
9. You can't leave until 1700. We work 9 to 5.
10. We could meet this evening. I'm free at/from/after six.

9. Functional Grammar: Looking Forwards From Now

Task 1

1. I have to leave soon. Now + future
2. I went to Ghana in the summer. Past fact
3. I live here. Present fact
4. She dies last year. Past fact.
5. I need you to take that hill. Now + future.
6. I have to get my hair cut. Now + future.
7. I am a soldier. Present fact.

8. She needs to see the commanding officer. Now + future.

9. I want to retire soon. Now + future.

10. The truck needs to be repaired. Now + future.

Task 3

1. I need to go to the doctor.
2. She wants to have children.
3. He is married.
4. She wants to get married.
5. I expect to finish soon.
6. I hoped to be promoted but I wasn't.
7. He wants to join the special forces.
8. He attempted to climb the wall but failed.
9. I tried to persuade him but I couldn't.
10. I would like to help you but I can't.

10. Functional Grammar: Looking Backwards 1

Task 1

1. I was born in Abuja. Past Fact
2. I live in Kampala. Present Fact
3. I have been to the USA twice. Before Now
4. I have never been to Brazil. Before Now
5. He is a soldier in the Ugandan army. Present Fact
6. He served with the Multinational Force in Lebanon (MNF) for six months. Past Fact
7. I joined the army in 2007. Past Fact
8. I am based in Nairobi. Present Fact

Task 3

1. I went to school in Nairobi.
2. I have been with the regiment for six months.
3. I have served in the infantry and air cavalry but now I'm studying at the School of Armoured Warfare.
4. He has been serving in the army since 2010.
5. We send out patrols every day.
6. She has been to see the doctor.
7. He has gone out.
8. We have conducted patrols of the area for the last three months.

11. Functional Grammar: Looking Backwards 2

Task 4

1. He had just finished the report when the CO came in.
2. He hadn't had did not have time to get everything ready for the inspection.

3. The expedition will have explored this whole river by the end.

4. By the time we get there we will have walked 10 kms.

5. We will not have managed to do everything before we leave.

12. Functional Grammar: Expressing Certainty

Task 1

1. He's dead. Fact

2. I'm sure he's dead. Personal Certainty about a fact

3. He will be dead soon. Personal Certainty about a fact

4. It will rain soon. Personal Certainty about a fact

5. I'll do it for you. Personal Certainty about a fact

6. The sun rises in the east. Fact

7. Sunrise is at 0450. Fact

8. The sun will rise at 0450. Personal Certainty about a fact

9. I'm certain that's right. Personal Certainty about a fact

10. That won't work. Personal Certainty about a fact

Task 3

1. That's enough. That will do.

2. What will you do if you get leave?

3. I might/will be in my office all afternoon. Both.

4. I might/will be seeing the doctor later today. Both but *will* more likely.

5. He might/will be retiring from the army soon. Both.

6. When might/will you be ready?

7. We might/will be leaving at 0800. Both but *will* more likely.

8. I might/will decide about that tomorrow. Both but *will* more likely.

9. Next month I will have been in the army for 10 years.

10. A: Someone called you last night
    B: Yes? That will been John. He said he'd call.

13. Functional Grammar: Expressing Distant Certainty

Task 2 and 3

1 I will do it. Personal real certainty: I promise

   I would do it if I could. Conditional/unreal certainty

2 Will you help me please? Request: direct

   Would you help me please? More polite/formal request

3 If I go to Brazil, I'll lie on a beach all day. Possible future.

If I went to Brazil, I would lie on a beach. Unlikely, though still possible future.

4   He will be 50 this year. Real certainty (if he lives)

     He would be 50 this year if he hadn't died. Unreal certainty condition.

5   He will keep asking silly questions. Certainty of real repeated actions.

     He would keep asking silly questions but then the CO told him to stop. Past certainty.

14. Functional Grammar: Expressing Potential

Task 1

1. I speak French. Fact.
2. I can speak French. Potential.
3. It rains a lot here in May. Fact.
4. It can rain a lot here in May. Potential.
5. Pigs can't fly. Negative Potential.
6. You can expect to be promoted soon. Potential.
7. You can see the road very well from the OP. Potential.
8. I can't see very clearly from here. Negative Potential.
9. Can I help you? Potential.
10. That's impossible. That can't happen. Fact + Negative Potential.

Task 3

1. It could/can rain later.
2. You can't be serious.
3. We could be in for a big fight.
4. He could be the killer.
5. I can/could do it.
6. I could do it if I had time.
7. I could drive when I was sixteen.
8. It can get very cold here at night.
9. You could be wrong.
10. If I could help you I would but I can't.

15. Functional Grammar: Should

Task 1 and 2

(a) You should get a haircut. Your hair is too long. Should = desirable.
(b) Should that happen we're going to be in trouble. Should = if.
(c) You should clean and oil your rifle. Should = desirable.
(d) Should it rain, we'll get wet. Should = if.

(e) You should work harder for the test. It's going to be difficult. Should = desirable.

(f) All recruits should have X, Y and Z. (list from website) Should = desirable.

(g) Squeeze the trigger gently. You should be surprised when the gun fires. Should = desirable.

(h) If you should find yourself in this situation, stop. Don't panic. Should = if.

Task 3

1. After firing your weapon you should clean it.
2. You shouldn't point your weapon at anyone unless you are willing to shoot.
3. All soldiers should salute superiors.
4. Taking this objective shouldn't be too difficult.
5. Should we meet resistance, we'll punch through.

16. Functional Grammar: Expressing Probability

Task 1

1. That should work. Probable.
2. That won't work. Negative certainty.
3. That can't be true. No potential = impossible.
4. There's a 56% chance of that working. Probable.
5. He should be ok now. Probable.
6. He should have arrived by now. Probable.
7. Really? That shouldn't happen. Probable – negative.
8. She should be there. Probable.
9. He should manage to pass the exam. Probable.
10. That should be enough. Probable.

Task 3

1. The leader should never try to be the navigator. Desirable.
2. At the end of the course the soldiers should be ready to be a leader. Probable.
3. You should wear ear defenders on the range. Desirable.
4. Should the worst come to the worst, we'll retreat. Probable.
5. He should live. Probable.
6. Routes through cities should be direct and easy to follow. Desirable.
7. That shouldn't have happened but it did. Improbable.
8. The soldiers should travel in small groups. Desirable.
9. All soldiers should receive this training. Desirable.
10. Should that happen, we'll be in trouble. Probable.

17. Functional Grammar: Expressing Desirability

Task 1

1. Get you hair cut. Order.

2. You should get your hair cut. Desirable.

3. Clean your rifle. Order.

4. You should take care of your rifle. Desirable.

5. You should go to the party. Desirable.

6. Should I go to the party? Is this desirable?

7. You should apologise. Desirable.

8. I shouldn't eat so much. Desirable.

9. You shouldn't have done that. Desirable.

10. You should have a holiday. Desirable.

Task 3

1. All maps should be considered as documents that require special handling.

2. A map should be carried in a waterproof case.

3. Any map overlay should contain the latest possible information.

4. Soldiers should be familiar with the compass and its uses.

5. Compasses should be cared for carefully.

6. Soldiers should take physical fitness very seriously.

7. Training exercises should be as realistic as possible.

8. All soldiers should be in bed after lights out.

9. A navigator should not be given any other duties.

10. You should take special care of the optical sights.

18. Functional Grammar: Evaluating Actions in the Past

Task 2

1. You should have checked your equipment before you went on patrol.

2. You should have posted sentries during the rest stop

3. The FAC should have checked/known where the friendly forces were before giving permission for an air strike.

4. They should have counted their paces.

Task 5 Example answers:

They should have taken a spare radio.

They should have taken/carried sleeping bags.

They should have taken/carried tents.

They should have headed south.

They should have followed the ERV procedure.

19. Functional Grammar: Prepositions of Place 1

Task 2

1. He's very sick – he's in hospital.

2. I'm sorry but she's in a meeting.

3. I can't find my phone. I know it's in this room somewhere.

4. Have you looked under the table?

5. Submarines can remain under the surface of the water for a long time.

6. The drone is flying over/above the battlefield.

7. She had two files under/in her arm.

8. He's at lunch now.

9. I'm on my way but I'm stuck in a traffic jam.

10. They're at a football match this afternoon.

11. The bunker was built under the ground.

12. The mountain peaks are above the clouds.

13. He was very scared and hid under the bed.

14. He's left school and now he is studying at university.

15. He has got a lot of tattoos on his arms.

16. He keeps his guns in his gun safe.

17. I saw her standing at a bus stop.

18. He was wearing four thick layers of clothes under his coat.

19. The POW was made to wear a blindfold over his eyes.

20. She's gone to meet him at the airport.

21. This is my first time on the battlefield.

22. I will meet you at the entrance.

23. The building is on fire. Call the fire brigade.

24. It was a lovely day and he went out to sit under a tree.

25. It's a great life in the army.

26. I'll meet you at the library.

27. He spent 5 hours studying in the library.

28. Before you leave home you should look in the mirror.

29. You can't make that decision – it's above your pay grade.

30. Get on the roof and give me some overwatch. Now!

20. Functional Grammar: Expressing Possibility

Task 1

1. He's dead. Facts.

2. He might be dead. Possibility.

3. You may be right. Possibility.

4. He might have got lost.

5. That's true. Facts.

6. That might be true. Possibility.

7. You might have to go to hospital. Possibility.

8. He might be working late. Possibility.

9. May I help you? Possibility.

10. Might I help you? Possibility.

Task 3

1. It **might/may** rain later.
2. He **may/might** have been delayed in traffic.
3. They **may/might** be late.
4. He **might/may** have to have an operation on his leg.
5. The brigade **is** being posted to Germany.
6. I **may/might** be seeing him later.
7. He **may/might** have killed her.
8. **May/might** I be of assistance?
9. She **may/might** not be able to do it.
10. He m**ight/may** be able to help you.

21. Functional Grammar: Talking About Obligation

Task 1

1. You must get your haircut before the sergeant sees you. Obligation.
2. You should get your hair cut – you're looking scruffy. Desirable.
3. You have to get your haircut to regulation length. Obligation.
4. You have to drive on the left in Britain, Namibia and Japan. Obligation.
5. That was rude son. You really must apologise. Obligation.
6. A field sketch must show the north arrow and scale. Obligation.
7. A first aid kit must be available at the start and finish. Obligation.
8. The regulations tell you what you have to do. Obligation.

Task 3

1. You have to/must/should make sure that your locker is all squared away.
2. You shouldn't have done that. It wasn't a good idea.
3. Crew-served weapons have to/must/should be loaded and manned at all times.
4. If you have to open fire, you should fire only aimed shots.
5. If reports must be handwritten you should/must write in capital letters.
6. In a survival situation you will have to use what is available.
7. If rafting ashore is not possible and you have to swim, wear your shoes and at least one thickness of clothing.
8. You also have to/must/should make an effort to learn about leading through study and reflection
9. I think we should find out what went wrong.
10. You could buy her a present if you wanted to. You should, you know.

22. Functional Grammar: Prepositions of Place 2

Task 2

1. The base is in the middle of the desert.
2. The post office is opposite the cinema, on the other side of the street.

3. There are three people in the picture. The general is in the middle between the colonel on the left and the major on the right.

4. The colonel is standing next to the general.

5. It's five minutes walk to the beach. It's very near.

6. The bank is not far from the hotel: about 10 minutes walk.

7. The hotel is a long way from the city centre – about a 30 minute drive.

8. You can just see him, standing behind that wall.

9. It's very easy to see – right in front of you on the desk.

10. There are two zebras in that herd of wildebeest.

23. Functional Grammar: Prepositions of Movement

Task 2

1. Move your men **across/over** the river and patrol on the other side.

2. We have to climb **up** to the ridge.

3. We're moving slowly **towards** the objective.

4. Take your men as **far as** that tall tree and stop there.

5. Patrol **along** this road to the next village.

6. We're going to have to go **over** this mountain. There's no way **around**.

7. We'll have to swim **under** water to avoid being seen.

8. The detour will take too long. We'll have to go **through** the swamp.

9. Move **to** the drop off point at 0530.

10. You should plan an alternate route **to** and from the objective.

24. Functional Grammar: Zero Conditionals

Task 2

1. If people eat too much, they get fat.

2. If you touch a hot stove, you get burnt.

3. People die if they don't drink.

4. Snakes attack if they get scared.

5. If it rains, the grass gets wet.

6. Plants die if they don't get enough water.

7. If John calls, tell him I will be late.

8. Meet at the RV if we get separated.

9. Ask Paul if you are not sure about anything.

10. If you want to come to the party, let me know.

25. Functional Grammar: First Conditionals

Task 1

Will is about certainty; *might* is about possibility.

Task 2

1. If it rains, we'll get wet.
2. If he is late again, I will get angry.
3. If I have time, I will finish the report today.
4. If you do not leave, I will call the police.
5. If you fall asleep on duty, you will be punished.
6. If you open fire from here, I will attack on the right flank.
7. If you are late for parade, you will be put on a charge.
8. If you go AWOL, the MPs will catch you.
9. If you break the law, you will be sent to jail.
10. If you attack now I can support you.

26. Functional Grammar: Second Conditionals

Task 2

1. If I got promoted, I would buy a new car. Unlikely but real.
2. If I got a weekend pass, I would go to see my parents. Unlikely but real.
3. If I were you, I'd take more care of your equipment. Unreal conditional.
4. If private Jones was a general, we'd be in trouble. Unreal conditional.
5. If we could go anywhere on holiday, where would you like to go? Unreal conditional.

Task 3

1. If you went to bed earlier, you wouldn't be so tired. Real.
2. If you really loved me, you would buy me a diamond ring. Real.
3. If I knew where she worked, I would go and see her. Unreal.
4. If I were taller, I would buy that suit. Unreal.
5. If I were an animal, I would be a leopard. Unreal.
6. If I were you, I'd give up smoking. Unreal.
7. If we attacked now, we could win. Real.
8. If we were attacked now, we wouldn't stand a chance. Real.
9. If the general inspected us today, we would be in trouble. Real.

27. Functional Grammar: Third Conditionals

Task 2

1. If I had known you were coming, I would have tidied up.
   Did I know you were coming? No. Did I tidy up? No.
2. If I had known you were in hospital, I would have visited you.
   Did I know you were in hospital? No. Did I visit you? No.
3. I would have brought you a present if I had known it was your birthday.
   Did I know it was your birthday? No. Did I bring you a present? No.

Task 3

1. If you had invited me, I would have gone to the party.
   Did you invite me to the party? no. Did I go? No.
2. If we had attacked together, we would have won.
   Did we attack together? No. Did we win? No.
3. If we hadn't had sentries out, we would have been surprised.
   Did we have sentries out? Yes. Were we surprised?No.
4. I wouldn't have lost if you hadn't cheated.
   Did I lose? Yes. Did you cheat? Yes.
5. We would have been ambushed if we hadn't had scouts out.

   Were we ambushed? No. Did we have scouts out? Yes.

28. Functional Grammar: Mixed Conditionals

Task 2

1. If he had caught that plane, he would be dead now.
   Did he catch that plane? No. Is he dead? No.
2. I would be a millionaire by now if I had invested in Google.
   Am I a millionaire? No. Did I invest in Google? No.
3. If I had not hit the sergeant, I wouldn't be being court-martialled.
   Did I hit the sergeant? Yes. Am I being court-martialled? Yes.
4. If I had learned to ski when I was a boy, I could go skiing now.
   Did I learn to ski as a boy? No. Can I ski now? No.
5. If we had had sentries out, we wouldn't be prisoners now.
   Did we have sentries out? No. Are we prisoners now? Yes.

Task 3

1. If we hadn't met at that party, we wouldn't be married now.
   Did we meet at that party? Yes. Are we married now? Yes.
2. If I hadn't joined the army, I would be unemployed.
   Did I join the army? Yes. Am I unemployed? No.
3. If I had trained hard, I would be in the lead in the competition.
   Did I train hard? No. Am I in the lead in the competition? No.
4. If I had applied for a promotion, I would be a corporal.
   Did I apply for a promotion? No. Am I a corporal? No.

29. Functional Grammar: If, Unless and In Case

Task 2

1. If he is late, he will be in trouble.
2. You should always take extra water with you in case you run out.

3. Cover the flank in case the enemy attack us there.

4. In case of attack radio for reinforcements.

5. In case I forget later, here are the keys to the car. Don't crash it.

6. If the weather improves we'll have some air support.

7. Unless we are reinforced soon, we're going to be in trouble.

8. Unless you have a better idea. I suggest we attack now.

Task 3

1. [Example] *Unless we are reinforced soon, we're going to be in trouble*

2. In case of attack, call for help.

3. If things don't improve, we will have to retreat.

4. Let's take some warmer clothing and winter boots in case it snows.

30. Functional Grammar: Punctuation

Task 2

1. The team consisted of Colonel Ngongo, from South Africa; Captain Smith, from the UK; and Captain Bauer, from Germany.

2. London is the capital of England and the United Kingdom.

3. He likes watching football; his wife likes watching rugby.

4. What shall I call you?

5. If you'd like me to, I'll help you .

6. That white Hilux is Henry's.

7. It's going to rain, isn't it?

8. He asked, 'Can I help you?'

9. The patrol, which was lost, dug in for the night.

10. Dr. Jones will be here in a minute; he'll be able to see you then.

2. Peacekeeping Fact File Keys

Peacekeeping Fact File 1 Key

1. Republic of Liberia
2. In west Africa.
3. About 4,700,000.
4. Mostly flat coastal plains with mangroves and swamps. Hilly plateau and low mountains in the north-east. Tropical rainforests, elephant grass and semi-deciduous forests. Equatorial climate which is hot year-round with heavy rainfall from May to October.
5. Support for the implementation of the Peace Process
6. 19th September 2003
7. Current year – 2003 = ?
8. 47.7%
9. More local civilians.
10. 199

Peacekeeping Fact File 2 Key

1. Western Sahara
2. North Africa.
3. Just over 500,000.
4. Low, flat desert; small mountains. 43–45 °C in summer
5. To monitor settlement plan; working towards a referendum.
6. 29 April 1991
7. Current year – 1991 = ?
8. 52%
9. This is not clear.
10. 16

Peacekeeping Fact File 3 Key

1. Ivory Coast/Côte d'Ivoire
2. West Africa.
3. Over 23 million.
4. Not given.
5. Protecting civilians and supporting the Government in DDR and security sector reform.
6. 27 February 2004
7. Current year – 2004 = ?
8. 7.9%
9. More local civilians.
10. 144

Peacekeeping Fact File 4 Key

1. South Sudan
2. In East-Central Africa
3. 12 million.
4. Tropical forest, swamps, and grassland; White Nile and Bahr al Jabal swamp.
5. Protecting civilians, monitoring human rights and supporting implementation of cessation of hostilities agreement
6. July 2011
7. Current year – 2011 = ?
8. 84%
9. More local civilians.
10. 48

Peacekeeping Fact File 5 Key

1. Abyei Area in Sudan
2. In North Africa.
3. Not given.
4. A large rift basin.
5. Demilitarizing and monitoring peace in the disputed Abyei Area
6. 2011
7. Current year – 2011 = ?
8. 95%
9. More international civilians.
10. 21

Peacekeeping Fact File 6 Key

1. Lebanon
2. In the eastern Mediterranean
3. About 6 million
4. The coastal plain, the Lebanon mountain range, the Beqaa valley and the Anti-Lebanon mountains; a moderate Mediterranean climate.
5. Monitoring cessation of hostilities and helping ensure humanitarian access to civilian population
6. 1978
7. Current year – 1978 = ?
8. 93%
9. More local civilians.
10. 312

Peacekeeping Fact File 7 Key

1. Cyprus
2. In the Eastern Mediterranean
3. 1,170,125
4. Two main mountain ranges and a central plain; subtropical, Mediterranean and semi-arid climate zones
5. Contributing to a political settlement in Cyprus
6. 1964
7. Current year – 1964 = ?
8. 86%
9. More local civilians.
10. 183

Peacekeeping Fact File 8 Key

1. Darfur
2. In western Sudan.
3. Over 9 million.
4. An arid plateau with low sandy hills; volcanic peaks (with a temperate climate and permanent water). Most of Darfur has a warm desert climate or a warm semi-arid climate with very low annual rainfall.
5. Protecting civilians, facilitating humanitarian aid and helping political process in Darfur.
6. In 2007.
7. Current year – 2007 = ?
8. 85%
9. More local civilians.
10. 244

Peacekeeping Fact File 9 Key

1. Democratic Republic of the Congo
2. In Central Africa
3. Over 78 million
4. Congo river basin; northern grasslands; southern savannah highlands; eastern mountains. The climate is hot and humid in the Congo river basin, cool and dry in the southern highlands, and cold and wet in the Rwenzori Mountains.
5. Protecting civilians and consolidating peace in the Democratic Republic of the Congo
6. July 2010.
7. Current year – 2010 = ?
8. 83.6%
9. More local civilians.
10. 107.

Peacekeeping Fact File 10 Key

1. Haiti
2. On the island of Hispaniola in the Caribbean Sea.
3. 10.8 million
4. Mountain ranges with small coastal plains and river valleys; a hot and humid tropical climate
5. Restoring a secure and stable environment
6. June 2004.
7. Current year − 2004 = ?
8. 80%
9. More local civilians.
10. 186.

Peacekeeping Fact File 11 Key

1. Republic of Mali
2. In west Africa.
3. 18 million.
4. Mostly in the southern Sahara Desert; extremely hot, dusty savanna.
5. Supporting political process and helping stabilize Mali
6. April 2013
7. Current year − 2013 = ?
8. 89%
9. More local civilians.
10. 114

Peacekeeping Fact File 12 Key

1. Central African Republic
2. Central Africa
3. Around 4.6 million
4. Flat or rolling savannah; a semi-desert zone in the north; desert in the north-east, and a rain forest zone in the south; generally tropical climate
5. To protect civilians and support transition processes in the Central African Republic
6. April 2014
7. Current year − 2014 = ?
8. 91%
9. More international civilians.
10. 32

3. Report Writing Keys

1. Report Writing Task 1

Firstly, we should consider soldier fitness. A high number of soldiers are unfit for duty because they are overweight. This means that the units are combat ineffective. Because of this we need to urgently consider increasing physical exercise requirements for each soldier: every soldier should do physical training every day.

Secondly, adventure training has been cut back this year. There has been no adventure training for the last six months. This means that soldiers' skills such as land navigation and survival skills have deteriorated. As a result, the soldiers would find it difficult in extreme operational conditions. More soldiers would die.

Task 2

An infantry fighting vehicle (IFV) is a type of armoured fighting vehicle used to carry infantry into battle and provide direct fire support with its weapons of 20 – 40 mm auto-canon, coaxial machine guns and sometimes anti-tank guided missiles (ATGMs). They are distinct from armoured personnel carriers (APCs), which are transport vehicles armed only for self-defence. IFVs basically possess heavier armament (and armour) than an APC, and can take a more active part in the engagement. IFVs are usually tracked, but there are some wheeled IFVs as well, like the Ratel. They are much less heavily armed and armoured than main battle tanks (MBTs), but when equipped with a 40 mm auto-canon or ATGMs they can engage all but the heaviest MBTs.

Task 4

The main battle tank (MBT) is a Cold War era development of World War 2 tanks. Their powerful engines, good suspension systems and lightweight composite armour give the MBT tank the firepower of a super--heavy tank, the armour protection of a heavy tank, and the mobility of a light tank, all at the weight of a medium tank. As they are armour-protected and manoeuvrable and can provide direct fire, they are considered a key component of modern armies. They are usually used in armoured formations with the support of mechanised infantry (travelling in Infantry Fighting Vehicles) and supported by close air support (CAS). Despite air power and man-launched anti-tank missiles, the best defence against a tank is still another tank.

2. Sample Report Task 1

1. Introduction
2. The UK
3. The British Armed Forces
4. The Current Army
5. The Army in 2020
6. Vehicles
7. Conclusion

Part 6 Extras

There are a number of extra resources available – presentations and photographs for example, and these will be added to over time. Extra photos are number as PX – Photo Extra + unit number etc. For example PX1.1 would be the first extra photo for **Unit 1**.

These resources will be made available from the course website page: www.englishideas.org/MilitaryEnglish

Please register your use of the course from the website and we will be in touch about new resources etc.

If you have any suggestions for extra resources, please let us know.

Sources and Acknowledgements

Sources

Many of the texts included in this book are from, or adapted from US Army Field Manuals, which are in the public domain, as they are published by the United States Government and its agencies. These sources are indicated under the texts. Some forms are kindly provided courtesy of the Montenegrin Armed Forces.

The patrol orders and route cards were sourced from https://www.arrse.co.uk/wiki/E-nirex, under the GNU Free Documentation License 1.2 cited on the site [https://www.gnu.org/copyleft/fdl.html]. Other texts use public domain information and are specially written for this book. The downloadable photographs and presentations include photographs sourced the US Department of Defense (and so are in the public domain), and the Ministry Of Defence (subject to Crown Copyright), and from Wikipedia, used according to the various Creative Common's licenses cited on Wikipedia. All the other photographs are my own, except for one, which is courtesy of Hamish McIlwraith. The whole set of photographs and presentations are therefore published under the same Creative Common's licenses and can be shared and used freely, as per the original license noted on the Wikipedia images. Maps are sourced from The US Geological Survey, or the Soviet Union.

Acknowledgements

Trialling in Latvia: Thanks to Aigars Saulīte, Inese Kinēna, Karīna Suruda, Andris Vasiļjevs, Ainārs Goldmanis and Jānis Tomašūns.

Trialling in Namibia: Many thanks to Beuhla Beukes of the British Council in Windhoek, and the University of Namibia, and the Namibian Armed Forces for organizing the trialling. Many thanks to Wing Commander Luther Kaunda Moongo, Lt. Col. Erick Nakanyala Toivo, Lt. Col. Laimi Pauvaneko Hawala, Col. Natanael Nangolo Ngolo, Capt. (N) Wilbard A Kapweya, Maj. Epafras Shaanika, Capt. Albin Kashuku, Maj. Titus H Iipinge, Maj. Emilia Nakambunda, Capt. Porisee Emsy Katjivena, Lt. Col. Wakaa Tjiveze, Maj. Martin David, Chief Curator Nikanor Chisengo, Lt. Col. Dawid Ashipala, Maj Rauna Shikongo, Capt. Martin Awala, Maj. Vaino M Kamelo, Capt. Elia Iileka, Capt. Vean Shigneg, Lt. Col. Martha Namufohamba, Capt. Onesmus S Aiyambo, Sqn. Ldr. Sebedeus N. Kanunga, Lt. Col. Simeon Nahole. and Senior Private Secretary Lea LK Pohamba for taking part in the trialling.

Military Advice: Particular thanks are due to SFC Ilgars Ciprus (Latvian Army), Mcpl/Cplc Aaron Hawthorn (Canadian Armed Forces), Lt. Naphtali Rivkin (U.S. Army, Retired), Lt. Col. Ugis Roamnvos (Latvian Army, Retired) for some advice on military matters. All remaining errors are mine.

Audio Recordings: Featuring the **Voice Talents** of (in alphabetical order) Alister McCarty, Cezars Torres, Christine Maxwell, Craig Rose, Dan Valahu, Daniel Puzzo, David Harris, Donald Maxwell, Graham Jones, Ilgars Ciprus, James Egerton, Michael Hudson, Michael Orr, Penny Roux, Phil Edwards, Robert Buckmaster, Ruth Waters, Tom Linton, and Vik Singh. Thanks guys.

And finally: Special thanks are due to my co-trainer in Namibia, Nick Fletcher, especially for the idea of using weapon specifications for speaking tasks. And also Hamish McIlwraith and Claire Whittaker, my colleagues at McIlwraith Education, a great team to work with. And of course, my long suffering family – thank you for your support and patience.

Made in United States
Troutdale, OR
04/25/2024

19433504R10177